THE DO-IT-YOURSELF
Business Promotions Kit

JACK GRIFFIN

PRENTICE HALL
Englewood Cliffs, New Jersey 07632

Prentice-Hall International, Inc., *London*
Prentice-Hall of Australia Pty., Ltd., *Sydney*
Prentice-Hall Canada, Inc., *Toronto*
Prentice-Hall Hispanoamericana, S.A., *Mexico*
Prentice-Hall of India Private Ltd., *New Delhi*
Prentice-Hall of Japan, Inc., *Tokyo*
Prentice-Hall of Southeast Asia Pte., Ltd., *Singapore*
Editora Prentice-Hall do Brasil, Ltda., *Rio de Janeiro*

© 1995 by
Prentice Hall

Library of Congress Cataloging-in-Publication Data

Griffin, Jack.
The do-it-yourself business promotions kit / by Jack Griffin.
    p.   cm.
Includes index.
   ISBN 0–13–106014–7. — ISBN 0–13–106006–6 (pbk.)
   1. Advertising.   2. Advertising media planning.   3. Communication
in marketing.   4. Small business—Management.   I. Title.
HF5823.G72   1995
658.8'2—dc20

94–39938
CIP

ISBN 0-13-106006-6 (P)
ISBN 0-13-106014-7 (C)

PRENTICE HALL
Career and Personal Development
Englewood Cliffs, NJ 07632

Simon & Schuster, A Paramount Communications Company

PRINTED IN THE UNITED STATES OF AMERICA

Why This Book Is for You

The Do-It-Yourself Business Promotions Kit gives the small business owner and operator everything needed to put together a program of promotion that is both effective and cost-effective. The book was written from three simple assumptions:

1. Small businesses have limited budgets for advertising.

2. Small business owners and operators envy the promotional budgets of bigger businesses.

3. All small businesses have a special power that big businesses do not possess and, for all their capital, cannot buy.

Assumption #1 needs no explanation—although this book will show you how to make the most of your resources, no matter how limited, and it will help you determine just what your promotional budget should be. It will also demonstrate to you that you can buy a lot more advertising than you think.

Assumption #2 is also self-explanatory.

Now, assumption #3—that gets more interesting. I won't make you read on to find out what your secret power is. I'll tell you right here: it's being small.

I know, being small gives you all kinds of grief with staffing problems and with cash flow problems and with financing capital costs. But it's also an extraordinarily valuable asset. Being small allows you to relate to your clients and customers on an intimate, direct, and human level that no big business can duplicate. No matter how big and powerful, no big business can buy what it means to be small. This book shows you how to promote the *small* in *small* business.

Now that we've discussed the assumptions that underlie this book, let's turn briefly to a definition.

What is *promotion?*

The fact is, this book is really about advertising. So why didn't I call it *Advertising Your Small Business?*

Because I'd like you to think about advertising in a broader context than what the word traditionally implies. Think of "advertising," and you think of newspapers, magazines, radio, and TV. They're all here—but not until Parts III and IV of this book. Parts I and II, the biggest sections of *The Do-It-Yourself Business Promotions Kit,* tell you how to use the mail, electronic equivalents of the mail (chiefly fax and E-mail), and the telephone to advertise. Familiar (and not so familiar) direct mail methods are covered, but I extend the definition of advertising even further. For any business—but especially and emphatically for the *small* business—every customer contact you make is an advertisement. This means that every letter, every fax, every phone call is an advertisement, whether you want it to be or not. This includes how you handle a customer's request for information and even how you handle an irate customer's complaint. Parts I and II of *The Do-It-Yourself Business Promotion Kit* show you how to turn communications of all kinds—letters, faxes, E-mail, phone calls—into positive, effective, and cost-effective advertisements. Parts III and IV explore the potential of small-business advertising in the more familiar sense of the term: in the print media and in the broadcast media.

Finally, readers looking for theories of advertising won't find them here. This is a *kit,* after all, not a textbook. It consists of two types of "tools":

1. "How-to" guidance for creating small-business advertising of all kinds

2. Actual models of small-business advertising of all kinds

Wherever possible, I have created these models generically (complete with blanks to fill in), so that they are as ready to use—"right out of the box"—as I can make them. To put it more accurately, I've tried to present models that you can quickly modify and customize for your own use. In cases where generic models would not have much useful meaning, I have supplied advertising examples intended to inspire and guide your own unique creations.

CONTENTS

v

Part IV: On the Air

PART I

In the Mail

Postage Envy—And How to Overcome It

Junk mail: it's depressing. And not just because what you were waiting for is that check to arrive, or that special letter from your "significant other," or good news from a big client. To the owner or manager of a small business, what's really depressing about junk mail is how effective, efficient, and polished it seems. All those thick, multipart, full-color contest applications, subscription forms, legume-of-the-month catalogs, and seven-year-locust insurance offers! All that slick paper, all those forms, all that photography, four-color reproduction, and dearly bought address lists strategically targeted by zip code! You've got to be big to put out mailings like that, large-scale, impressive mailings so professional that they seem the work of some minor deity. Overwhelmed by the conspicuous display of production values and the very bulk of the custom-printed, computer-addressed, clear-windowed envelope, you shake your head in dismay as you toss the mailing (unread) into the circular file.

Now Who Should Be Depressed?

It's lavish, expensive, undoubtedly impressive, but it's still called junk, and more often than not, it's treated as such. Why? Precisely because it is perceived as a product of big business, mass produced, one-size-fits-all, and, despite the computer-generated merge letter that mentions you by name several times, about as personal as a paper cup. I'm not saying that elaborately produced mass mailings are worthless. But I am suggesting that, far from envying the kind of work the big boys can buy, you should celebrate your smallness, exploit it, and give thanks for it.

You are riding the crest of the wave of the future: downsizing. In the faltering economy of the 1980s and the uncertain economy of the early 1990s, one segment of the business universe actually multiplied in number: the small firm. Whereas *small* used to be synonymous with *small time*, it's now coming to mean smart—smart for you and smart for your clients—even as some of the bluest of the blue-chip behemoths are discovering that the word *big* often gets followed by *dumb*. This is not a passing fad, and it may not even be very new. After all, how large a cheering section did David's adversary Goliath ever command? Play to your strengths. Play up your smallness.

Begin by realizing that, impressive as state-of-the-art direct mailing packages can be, they face a hurdle formidable as a brick wall. Most folks actually resent being on the receiving end of a mass mailing. Your impulse is to throw away junk mail just as you hang up every time you get one of those robot-dialed recorded telephone messages. No one enjoys being treated like a target, a mark. Worse, receiving mail is supposed to give you the pleasurable sensation of feeling like an individual, someone unique and special. Getting junk mail, of course, has just the opposite effect. It makes you feel like nothing more than a number in a zip code directory, a three-cent name on somebody's well-thumbed mailing list, and you resent it. Finally, there is the very real negative environmental impact created by the megatons of junk mail churned out each year: a lot of felled trees and a lot of new landfill. It is the cynical and out-of-touch manager who fails to recognize the public's acute and growing sensitivity to environmental issues. Nobody appreciates more garbage, especially when it is deposited at your door.

You're small, so you can neither reap the benefits nor suffer the scourges of mass-produced, state-of-the-art sales letters. Regardless of the nature of your business, you are selling one thing for certain, and you probably have to sell it before you can sell anything else.

You are selling yourself.

There was a time in American business when people spoke about a big corporation selling its all-but-priceless name. You didn't buy a car, you bought a Ford. You didn't buy a computer, you bought an IBM. Small-business owners or managers do not sell a mere name, they sell themselves, responsible human beings from whom clients can expect direct and personal service and to whom customers can turn if something goes wrong. No numbered forms to fill out. No endless automated voice-mail loops. But a person with whom the proverbial buck stops once and for all.

Most of your customers most of the time would much rather deal with a person than with a company. Service is the most sought-after product of the 1990s, and the personal service of a human being with a name and a phone number is the most desirable form of this product. Lucky for you, this is one product you can offer in abundance. How do you sell it? With good letters, for one thing. Not slick bulk mail, but direct sales communications written from one human being to another.

And you will find much more. Junk mail is by definition "cold solicitation," an attempt to prospect for customers. Nothing wrong with that, as far as it goes. The trouble is, it doesn't go nearly far enough. Part I, "In the Mail," takes you from the prospecting stage, through the art of the follow-up before, during, and after the sale, and into the ongoing process of customer-relations maintenance. This section defines the "sales letter" not as a one-pot-shot-in-the-dark missive written in the fond hope of bagging a customer, but as a series of special letters meant to create and foster a relationship over time. The professionally written letters here will not only help you sell better and sell more, they will help you find, cultivate, maintain, and develop your customer base through every stage of the sales cycle. These are letters for your whole business.

CHAPTER 1

Coming in from the Cold: Writing Effective "Cold" Letters

How to Do It

Direct mail copy writers have traditionally enshrouded their profession in mystery. Writing sales letters, they say, not only requires a divine gift, it involves knowledge of certain secrets and occult phrases keyed to very specific readers. Those uninitiated into the copy writers' guild have no knowledge of this magic and (so the implication runs) had better steer clear of writing sales letters lest they invite disaster.

Strangely enough, there is some truth to these claims. Writing a sales letter can be mysterious and complex insofar as it involves thorough knowledge of what your customer is looking for and what he is willing to spend in order to get it. However, the basic anatomy of all good sales letters is actually quite simple:

1. Get your reader's attention.

2. Identify a need the reader has.

3. Show how you can satisfy that need.

4. Persuade the reader to let you satisfy that need.

5. Induce the reader to act—now.

Before we explore this simple anatomy further, let's address the more mysterious and complex issue I mentioned. Why do I call it "mysterious and complex"? Because I don't understand it.

But you do.

Before you sit down to write a cold solicitation sales letter, summon up all that you know about the product or service you sell. Think about who will buy your wares. If you are selling advanced accounting software, don't bother writing to the guy who owns the pizza joint down the street, but do make it your business to obtain lists of accounting firms—not just from the telephone book, but from the appropriate professional organizations, newsletters, and so on. Don't, however, stop with accounting firms. Write to corporations you have reason to believe require the kind of software you sell. Before you write, take the time and steps necessary to identify just who in the company you should address your letter to—the head of accounting, for example, not the CEO or head of advertising. The point is to do everything you can to find the hottest leads possible for the cold solicitation. This does not require your hiring a consultant or a direct mail specialist, but it does require thought and some research.

One "universe"—that is, the pool of likely prospects to whom you address your correspondence—you should not overlook consists of businesses and individuals new to your area. These folks are always looking to establish contacts, including reliable suppliers. It is also a good idea to keep your ear to the ground and become aware of new hirings and promotions. When Sprowl Sprockets hires a new director of accounting, why not send her a letter of congratulations that also invites her to call on you for her software needs—or, better yet, a letter that sets up a sales call? Such letters serve three purposes.

1. They make the recipient feel good and important.

2. They let the recipient know that you are alive and alert—an insider.

3. They give the recipient a chance to hit the ground running with knowledge of a reliable supplier of goods and services.

Of course, it is not always possible to focus all your solicitation letters so sharply. There are times when it is desirable or necessary to write cold letters in the classic sense: hopeful epistles broadcast in an effort to get business. Even these, however, can be focused by such factors as geographical area (perhaps you should restrict your letters to your metropolitan area, or to surrounding neighborhoods) or even by the very fact that the recipient has never done business with you before. A letter written to folks and businesses in the neighborhood might begin with "Hi, Neighbor!" or "Introducing Our Good Neighbor Policy," or "We're so close"—anything that establishes a community of interest between you and the potential client. A letter written to someone who has never done business with you before should begin by exploiting that very fact: "Where have you been all my life?" is one excellent way to begin.

Whether through knowledge of your territory, research, or common sense, start your sales communication by establishing a community of interest. The message is not *gimme,* but *I have something that you want.* Done right, this approach will always command attention.

Now that you have your reader's attention, the next step—one would think—is to tell her just what you have to offer. Well, that's not quite the next step. It is far more effective to tell the reader not what you have to *offer,* but what he *needs* (even if you don't know for sure). "I am well aware that the sprocket business makes special demands on accounting software—that the one-size-fits-all approach just won't work—and I would welcome the opportunity to listen to you tell me just what your special needs are."

Build next on the community of interest and the identification of need by persuading your reader that you are capable of satisfying that need. Again, at this stage, you do not have to possess precise knowledge of what your reader actually does require. "I'm one of the world's great listeners, and the only thing I do better than listening to problems is working with my clients to solve them."

The great enemy of life is also the great enemy of sales: inertia, the universal tendency toward inaction and maintaining the status quo. End your letter with an inducement to action or, better yet, an offer to act *for the reader.* "I've set aside June 12 through July 8 to meet with directors of accounting for various firms in our area. I hope to set up an appointment with you, and I will call within the next day or two."

As you examine the model letters that follow, bear in mind the keywords common to virtually all successful sales processes: focus, community, need, satisfy, act.

— WORDS TO USE —

act	establish	serve
advise	extra	service
answer	help	smart
assist	immediate	solution
available	listen	special
commitment	more	successful
confident	need	supply
create	personal	unique
direct	problem	value
discerning	require	welcome
do	resolve	
especially	savvy	

— PHRASES TO USE —

always available	special offer
ask our advice	special value
best effort	start-to-finish
best price	tell us what you need
committed to you	unique opportunity
deal direct	we listen
expect extra effort	we care
expect more	we won't leave you
here to serve you	we can help
let us help	we're here to help
listen to you	what do you need?
personal service	you can talk to us
prompt attention	

Welcome to the Area

Dear *(Name)*:

I've chosen a very special sheet of paper to welcome you to our community—Savoy Deluxe Extra Creamy Watermarked, one of our family of distinguished and affordable custom stationery sheets.

As you know, a new location presents the opportunity and the challenge of making a first impression that will go a long way in building your customer list. You know quality when it comes to making *(correspondent's product)*. We know quality when it comes to supplying a stationery sheet of which you can be proud. Please let us show you how to convey your commitment to quality with every letter you write. I've set aside *(date)* through *(date)* to show some of our key accounts our new fall line of fine stationery. It seems to me that this would be a good time for us to get acquainted, to discuss your stationery needs, and for me to welcome you to the area by sharing with you some of my knowledge of this business community.

I'll call you in a day or two to set something up.

Sincerely yours,

Congratulations on a Promotion

Dear *(Name)*:

Good news travels fast. My highly placed sources tell me that you've been promoted to systems manager. You're working for a very savvy firm. My congratulations to you *and* your company.

I'd like to help you hit the ground running by inviting myself over to listen to *you* tell *me* about the special software needs of your company. Our unique modular systems combine the tailor-made features of custom programming with the instant turnaround time, reliability, and economy of off-the-shelf software.

No systems manager wants to plow somebody else's field. So let's talk about some fresh programs you can put into action without incurring any down time. Besides, I'd like the opportunity to congratulate you in person. I'll call next week for an appointment.

I look forward to seeing you.

Sincerely yours,

You've Never Done Business with Us

Dear *(Name)*:

Where have you been?

What have you seen?

What have you been doing?

And how come you never call on us?

We're Flash, the fastest messenger service in the *(Name of community)* metro area. Maybe you have seen us. We're well-dressed blurs: every messenger neatly uniformed and beeper dispatched. Maybe you've seen us, but you haven't talked to us—yet.

We'd like to sit down for a minute (catch our breath) and listen to you tell us what you need in a messenger service. We've got the rates, we've got the people, we've got the look, and we've got the system. Tell us how we can put these to work for you.

My name is *(Name)*. I own the place, so you know I'm committed to doing the best job for you. Because if I don't, there's no one else to blame. I'll call next week for an appointment. Hope to meet you soon!

Sincerely yours,

Are You Satisfied with Your Income?

Dear *(Name)*:

Here's why I like writing letters: I can ask you a question, and you don't have to answer me or anyone else—except yourself.

Here goes.

Are you satisfied with your income? Happy with the money you make?

You'll find my phone number at the top of this letter. But don't pick up the phone to answer me yet.

Answer *yourself* first.

Do you have all the money you need to do everything you want? To get your kids a great education? To take a vacation when you want and where you want? To drive a car you'd be proud of? To indulge yourself—while providing everything your family needs? To build a secure future for your family?

Or simply to pay the mountain of bills all of us face?

Now, please, ask yourself one more: Are you getting paid what you deserve for the job you do? And, while you're asking this one, why not think about this: Do you have the *job* you deserve? Or can you do better?

Maybe you are among those fortunate few—and they *are* few— who are perfectly happy with what they have and what they do.

But if your answers to the questions I've asked tell you that you could—or even *must*—do better and get more, believe me, my company and I can help.

The name of my company, Opportunities Unlimited, is the best introduction to what we do. We equip you with the keys you need to unlock your potential and work productively toward everything you deserve. Our program guides you through three of the biggest, most rewarding, and most exciting steps you've ever taken or will ever take:

First: We guide you through our unique Career Analyzer, a series of diagnostic evaluations you do yourself and in the privacy of your home. As revealing as they are fascinating, these tests will help you and our staff of experts determine just where your next career move should take you.

Second: We guide you through our special Reality Checker, a do-it-yourself kit that will enable you to determine just how much money you need *now* and to attain your *future goals*.

Finally: We work with you to plan your campaign strategy to get you what you need, what you want, and what you deserve.

Now ask yourself one last question: Interested?

If you've answered *yes* to this one, take a few moments to read the enclosed brochure, and then give Opportunities Unlimited a call at 555-555-0000.

Now that you've answered my questions, I'm ready to answer yours.

Sincerely,

Congratulations on a New Enterprise

Dear *(Name)*:

I just read in *Personal Shopper News* that you are expanding your concierge and personal shopping service into the south-central region.

Of course, you've studied the market carefully and know that this region is ripe for what you have to offer, so you don't really need my congratulations—but please accept them nevertheless. I am confident that you will enjoy great success here.

Now, so you won't have to take your congratulations from a stranger, let me tell you who I am.

I am marketing director of the largest importer of fine stationery and specialty papers in the *(region)*, and, to be perfectly honest with you, I'd like to be a part of your success. Please take a few moments to look through the catalog I have enclosed. You will find in it a vast array of very special gift-quality papers that, I know from experience, cannot fail to delight the discriminating giver and recipient alike. And that, of course, is just what your business is all about.

Speaking of *delighted,* that's what you'll be when you examine the enclosed discount schedule, which applies even to relatively small quantities. And me? I'd be delighted to send you any samples you might care to see. Call me on my direct line, 555-555-0000, or send a fax to 555-444-0000.

Once again, congratulations on what I'm sure you'll find is a great move!

Sincerely,

Debt Problems?

Dear *(Name)*:

I didn't send this letter to you in a green polka-dotted envelope *just* to get your attention. I also wanted you to know: THIS IS NOT ANOTHER BILL!

We all get plenty of those—too many. And, for most of us, at least sometimes, they get to be not only too many, but too much.

If you're finding that debt is a problem for you, we can help.

No, we're not here to lend you money, but we *are* here to make things better.

Wouldn't it be great if your creditors would work *with* you rather than *against* you? It would be great for *you*—and for the folks you owe money to as well. General Credit Counseling Service knows that, when you really give the matter some thought, you and your creditors actually want the same thing: to get *you* out of debt. We work with you and with your creditors so that you *all* can work toward that goal.

We start by counseling you to create a budget you can live with. Then we approach each of your creditors to find a creative solution to the problem both sides want to solve. Finally, we help you plan your financial future to make it possible to move in the right direction and to avoid repeating the wrong turns of the past.

No, this is NOT ANOTHER BILL. But it may just be your ticket to a life with less worry, strife, and stress. Our fees are based on your ability to pay. We won't call you, so why not dial 555-555-0000 for details? Of course, our conversation will be held in strictest confidence.

Sincerely,

Pay Too Much for Car Insurance?

Dear *(Name)*:

I don't have to tell you that your car costs you plenty—to buy, to run, and to service. Are you making a costly situation even more costly by paying too much for automobile insurance?

If you call us at 555-0000, we would be happy to help you answer that question. And if you're like the overwhelming majority of folks who call us, the answer will be *yes, you are paying too much for auto-mobile insurance.*

Fortunately, we can help you cut your insurance costs *now.*

The *(Name)* Agency is an independent full-service automobile insurance agency dedicated not only to finding you the lowest-priced auto insurance, but to providing just the coverage that you need—no more and no less.

(Name) Agency has served the greater *(Name of community)* region for *(number)* years. We get satisfaction from helping our customers save more of their hard-earned money.

Why not let us help you? Use the enclosed reply card or give us a call at 555-0000 today.

We'll answer your questions for free. The insurance? Well, that will cost you—but probably a good deal less than you're paying now.

Sincerely yours,

Need Cash?

Dear *(Name)*:

Does your bank have a sense of humor?

I bet you won't answer yes.

Then why does your bank like to play games when you come to them for a loan? You know, it was Mark Twain who said that a bank will loan you money as long as you can prove that you don't need it. Mark Twain was a funny man. But, sad to say, he spoke the truth.

That is precisely the game your bank likes to play.

Where, then, do you go if you really need cash?

There are plenty of private lending institutions that will tell you they have money to give you. But you'd better choose carefully. If you needed a doctor, you wouldn't wander into the first medical office you happened to find. Want a lawyer? Would you knock on the door of any old law office?

Doctors, lawyers—you put your life in their hands—so you think carefully before you choose one.

Why treat your loan needs any differently? A good loan, when you really need it, can change your life. Unfortunately, a bad loan can change your life even more dramatically.

If you're tired of playing games with your bank, don't just run out to the first private lender you find.

At *(Name)* Finance, we offer a generous array of loan services, each tailored to your special needs. We begin by assuming that, if you had the money you needed, you wouldn't be coming to us. Then our loan counselors will talk *with* you—and listen *to* you— before they go to work *for* you to put together a financing package that's tailored to your personal needs. Seriously. No kidding. No games.

Whether you want a home equity loan, an auto loan, enterprise capital, or a line of credit, give us a call at 555-0000 to set up an appointment. You owe it to yourself.

Sincerely,

Say Goodbye to Your Landlord

Dear Mr. and Mrs. *(Name)*:

You work hard. You work hard for your present and for your future. Now, how would you feel if all that hard work was wasted and came to nothing?

I don't think the word *angry* would be sufficient to describe how you would feel.

Well, ask yourself how much of your paycheck goes to your land-lord. Then ask yourself what becomes of that money. After a year of paying rent, what do you have to show for all that money? After ten years? Thirty years?

Unless you like to paper your walls with rent receipts, the answer is ABSOLUTELY NOTHING.

In contrast, after one year of paying off a mortgage, a home owner is one year closer to owning a home. After ten years, a decade closer. After thirty, that home belongs to the family—if, of course, they haven't sold it years earlier at a healthy profit. And all that time, Uncle Sam gives you a nice fat tax break to help you pay for your home.

There is no break for renters.

Now, my purpose is not just to make you angry. After all, if you're like most families, you are not renting by choice, but because you believe that you cannot afford to own your own home.

Conventional sales wisdom says the customer's always right. This time, maybe, just maybe, you are wrong.

Mr. and Mrs. *(Name)*, if you are paying *($ amount)* each month in rent, you *can* afford to own your home. And I don't mean a plywood box in some forgotten corner of the world, but a genuine *(Name)* Deluxe Home in a prestigious neighborhood with great schools, convenient shopping, and terrific neighbors.

Please, stop working for nothing better than ugly wallpaper. Sit down, relax, and take a look through the enclosed brochure. Then call me direct at 555-555-0000 for the whole story on how you can say goodbye to your landlord and step into your own *(Name)* Deluxe Home.

I look forward to talking with you.

Sincerely,

Let Us Help

Dear *(Name)*:

Effective managers never confuse stasis with stability. They recognize that staff must expand and contract with the changing demands of business. They also realize that finding good temporary staff can be a full-time job, leaving precious little time to do what you must do and what you do best: run your company.

We at *(Name)* Temps agree. Finding good temporary staff *is* a full-time job, and finding *great* temporary staff takes even longer. In fact, it takes much more time than you've got.

But at *(Name)* Temps, that's all we do. Our business is finding and furnishing great temporary employees for your business.

Why not let us help you with your temporary staffing needs? We have highly motivated, professional self-starters available in the following areas:

(list)

Give me a call at 555-0000 to discuss your special needs.

Sincerely yours,

Indulge Yourself

Dear *(Name)*:

You don't need to spend $850 on a new CD player. You can buy one for $150. Okay, so it won't deliver the kind of sound quality you really want. So spend $400 or $500. You can get a very fine CD player for that kind of money.

So why would you *want* to spend $850?

Well, the Jekyll-Karton JK98U includes the following features that make it, quite simply, the definition of the state of digital audio art:

(list features)

But, then, do you really need the state of the art?

(Name), you do if you're the kind of person who refuses to be happy with anything less than the very best. The truth is that at $850, the JK98U is an expensive CD player. But at $850, the chance to own and enjoy the very best—of anything—is a terrific bargain. What's the sticker price on the car of your dreams? How much would your dream house cost? Want to buy a private island paradise? What's the price tag on *that* piece of real estate?

Here is your opportunity to purchase the very best, to indulge yourself without, after all, breaking the bank. Why don't you tempt yourself? Come on in to the shop at *(address)* in *(Name of town)*, and let me show you the JK98U as well as the other state-of-the-art indulgences I have to offer.

Give it some thought.

Sincerely yours,

Reward Yourself

Dear *(Name)*:

You work hard year 'round.' You *earn* your vacation—which should be time off from work, carefree and relaxing. If it ends up being just another chore—rifling through brochure after brochure, making phone call after phone call, juggling reservations, calculating prices, fighting crowds, and scheduling months in advance—well, it may be a change of scene, but it's definitely NOT a vacation.

Taking a well-deserved break shouldn't be harder work than the job you do the rest of the year. Getting there shouldn't be as tough as your morning commute. And elbowing through a mob of fellow vacationers once you're there isn't a whole lot different from fighting the competition on the job.

You work hard. You deserve a vacation that's easy, always available to you, relaxing, and so private that *it's all yours and yours alone.*

Stop teasing yourself with vacations that don't live up to everything the word should mean. Stop teasing yourself, and start rewarding yourself.

Imagine owning beautiful lakeside or other wooded property only a few hours away from home but a whole world away from the daily grind.

Something only the rich and famous can afford?

It may just be something you cannot afford—to pass up.

For *(number)* years now, Vacation Properties Unlimited has been selling affordable properties—ranging from as little as one-half acre to 20 acres, in the woods, on the lake, and near the beach—to hard-working folks like you who want relaxation and recreation that really is relaxing and fun.

We offer a selection of properties that are ready for building as well as others that already include beautiful cottages. Some of our properties are even suitable for year-round living, if you choose.

There is no better investment than vacation property. It's putting money into your own health and happiness. And it is putting money into great real estate with proven *resale* and high *rental* value.

What other vacation *pays* you back—in cash income?

We have enclosed a full-color brochure highlighting some of the vacation property opportunities waiting for you. We invite you to sit back, relax, and look through the brochure. Then give us a call, toll-free, at 1-800-555-0000. It may just be the last time you'll find yourself on the phone trying to make vacation plans.

Sincerely,

Put Yourself in Professional Hands

Dear *(Name)*:

Congratulations on selling your house! One of the many big steps you'll be taking next is selecting a moving company to transport treasured furniture, keepsakes, and other valuable—even irreplaceable—items to your new home.

Moving is a high-stakes operation, and we urge you to put yourself in the hands of professionals.

(Name) Van Lines has been moving families like yours for the past 75 years. That's three quarters of a century of handling furniture and artworks with the utmost professionalism. Even more, that's three quarters of a century of treating your valued possessions not as mere goods, but as your memories, dreams, and hopes.

Make a professional move. Call us at 555-0000 today. We'll be happy to come to your home to give you a free estimate.

Best wishes for a great move,

Give Yourself an Edge

Dear *(Name)*:

Do you have any competition?

Stupid question, huh?

With all your competition breathing down your neck, your top priority is survival, right?

Maybe it's time you gave new thought your top priority.

At *(Name)* Software, we don't believe in survival. We believe in growth, in achieving greater and greater success, and a bottom line that just keeps getting better. Survival is just a place to begin.

You work just as hard as your competition. Maybe harder. Your product is just as good as theirs. Maybe better. You price your goods and services just as aggressively as they do. Maybe you even cut your customers a better deal.

So what more can you do? What's the secret?

In a word, *contact*.

Intelligently managed customer contact is your edge on the competition. Each moment you spend with a customer is an infinitely valuable opportunity to learn something new about that customer's needs and how you can serve them. You should nurture customer contacts as carefully as you care for any of your company's other assets.

Let *(Name)* Software show you how.

Let *(Name)* Software show you how to keep track of contacts and how to manage them to give you an edge on your competition and increase profits. It's a lot easier than you think.

And the first step?

That's easiest of all. One of our representatives will telephone you within the next week. When he calls, here's all you do: pick up the phone, say hello, listen, and ask questions. We'll take it from there and set you up with the customized *(Name)* Software package that's right for you.

Don't want to wait? We can't blame you. Why not give *us* a call at 800-555-0000?

We're here for you now.

Sincerely,

Give Your Children an Edge

Dear *(Name)*:

Parental paranoia. You know what it is: that nagging, guilty, worrisome feeling that you—somehow—aren't doing absolutely all you can to help your child excel in school and emerge from this all-important learning experience a winner.

Well, the last thing we want to do is add to your parental paranoia. No, we don't want to drive you crazy.

But . . .

We do want to disturb you just a little bit—just a little bit that can mean a great deal to your child.

What is your home library like? Maybe you're pretty proud of it. You've got many of the classics. A good dictionary. A fine set of encyclopedias.

Maybe you think your home library could be better.

But how do you know you've got the best? How do you know what you need to give your child the edge he or she needs in today's increasingly competitive classroom?

We can help.

We're Educational Advice Associates, an organization of top-level educators and seasoned teachers who have given a lifetime of thought to just what children need to read at each grade level to give them the competitive edge.

Now that's an ever-changing requirement, and no single book can hope to give you all the answers.

Instead, we offer a subscription to our monthly *Educational Advisor,* which includes:

❑ Suggested and "must have" additions to your family library

❑ Updates on television shows of value to your child

❑ Building an educational video and software library

❑ What's new at your local library

❑ Ongoing research tips

❑ Hot issues in education that will have impact on you and your child

❑ And much more

Subscribe now, and we will include *The Basic Home Library,* the one book that will help you build the foundation of a home library that will grow with your child and give him or her that vital edge.

The enclosed brochure tells you more about us, about *The Educational Advisor, The Basic Home Library,* and how to subscribe.

Give yourself the satisfaction and peace of mind that come with the knowledge that you are giving your child the learning equipment he or she needs for today—for tomorrow—and for all the school days to come.

Sincerely yours,

We Give You Credit

Dear *(Name)*:

Need cash?

Too bad.

At least, that's how a lot of banks seem to see it. As Mark Twain said, a bank will lend you money—as long as you can prove you don't need it.

Well, here at *(Name)* Finance, we think that's a pretty dumb way to do business—if you can even call that doing business.

At *(Name)* Finance, we understand what should be obvious to any lending institution: you wouldn't be coming to us if you didn't need the money!

At *(Name)* Finance, we give you credit

❏   For your borrowing record

❏   For your willingness to work for your family

❏   For all your bright ideas

❏   For all your worthwhile dreams and ambitions

At *(Name)* Finance, we regard our clients as partners, not as debtors. We work with you, not against you. Unlike traditional bankers, who begin by "screening" you—looking for reasons to deny you credit—we start out determined to lend you what you need.

We believe you'll find our approach refreshing. We know you'll find it helpful.

It costs nothing to discuss your borrowing needs with us and to find out if you qualify. Why not call us today at 1-800-555-0000.

Sincerely yours,

Take Advantage of Us

Dear *(Name)*:

We're stuck.

We've just taken over a huge consignment of children's clothing from a major retailer going out of business. Here's our problem: we're about to lose our lease on our current warehouse space, and we would much rather sell our huge stock of merchandise than move it.

Are we asking you to help us out?

No. We're asking you to take advantage of our dilemma. Exploit our situation. Kick us while we're down.

We have no choice but to offer you savings of 50 to 75 percent on items like

(list)

and brands that include

(list)

The catch? Just one: you're not the only shopper we've written to. So we suggest you come to our warehouse outlet at *(address)*, today! We're open from 9:30 to 6 Monday through Saturday.

Sincerely yours,

Is Your Family Safe?

Dear *(Name)*:

We'll lay our cards on the table.

We sell security: home alarm systems, security lighting systems, and closed-circuit television systems. Now, just like you, we hate scare advertising tactics, and like you, we would be suspicious of many of our competitors who use it—

Lines like: 2 OUT OF 10 *(NAME)* COUNTY HOMES ROBBED LAST YEAR

Or: ELDERLY COUPLE SLAIN BY BURGLAR

Or: FORCED ENTRIES RISE SHARPLY IN *(NAME OF CITY)*

Yes, our competitors use lines like these to scare you into buying a home security system.

We don't *want* to scare you. But the truth is, the scare tactics our competitors use come straight out of the newspaper. The truth is, they're for real.

Burglary and violent crime *are* on the rise here. Crime in our community is still the tragedy it has always been, but it is no longer an unusual occurrence.

Now here's another truth. *(Name)* Systems can help protect you, and we can do it more effectively, more efficiently, more quickly, and for less money than our leading competitors.

How safe is your family?

Let us come out to your home and perform a free security check and then make our security recommendations. After we do that, we suggest that you do NOT place an order with us.

That's right.

Call any of our competitors, invite them out to your house, get their best price on a comparable system. We guarantee you that we'll beat it.

How safe is your family?

Why not call us today—now—at 555-0000 and find out?

Sincerely,

Give Yourself the Best

Dear *(Name)*:

Here's a depressing thought: None of us lives forever.

And if that's not enough, here's another: You can't afford a thirty-room oceanside mansion. You can't afford a completely new designer wardrobe each and every fall. You can't afford to vacation in Monte Carlo with the rich and the famous.

But—and here's the good news—you can still afford the very best when it comes to providing wholesale meat for your family.

(Name) Beef is purveyor of the finest cuts of steak, lamb, and pork to such restaurants as *(list)*, restaurants where thousands of satisfied customers are pleased to pay top dollar for what they know is the greatest dining experience money can buy.

Now we at *(Name)* Beef are pleased to announce that the same fine meat we supply to the city's best restaurants is available directly to you in small wholesale quantities at great prices.

Yes. Now. At last. You can afford the best.

Compare our prices to what you pay for ordinary supermarket meat:

(comparison listing)

Don't ask yourself if you can afford the best. Ask yourself how you can afford *not* to buy the best—now that the best will cost you less than the ordinary.

Start living with the best. After all, you owe it to yourself and to your family. Give us a call today at 555-0000. To make it even easier, we also lease and deliver a full line of home freezers.

Sincerely yours,

Save Money

Dear *(Name)*:

I am writing you what people in the letter-writing business call a "cold letter." A "cold letter" is one that's sent on the chance that you just *might* be interested in what it has to offer. Usually, two or three out of every *hundred* cold letters get a response.

Usually, it's a shot in the dark.

Usually.

But I'm sure that *this* "cold letter" will warm you up. Because, while I know plenty of people who don't like spending money, I don't know anybody who is *not* interested in saving money.

Yes, I *am* selling something. But what I'm selling is savings.

The average family spends *($ amount)* on automobile repair and maintenance each and every year. If you currently spend even *half* that amount, I will save you money. Guaranteed.

How? I invite you to read the enclosed brochure explaining how a *(Name)* Garage exclusive maintenance contract will save you 60 to 75 percent off what you currently spend on automobile maintenance and repair.

Take a look at the brochure, then call me at 555-0000. And why don't you do it before you spend another penny on car repair at some ordinary, high-priced garage?

Sincerely yours,

You Can Do Better

Dear *(Name)*:

If you're like most folks, you dread taking your car in for service.

There's the cost, of course. Often that turns out to be a very unpleasant surprise.

And there's the inconvenience and the waiting. Maybe you sit in the waiting room for an hour or two or more. Maybe you grab a cab home or, if you're lucky, inconvenience your spouse or a friend by asking for a ride.

Then you make wagers with yourself on whether the car really will be ready by the end of the day. Or the next day. Or the next.

Your car is important to you, and what you need is a full-service garage that understands that—a garage that will serve your automobile *and* you.

You can do better. You can do better than worry, and wait, and be inconvenienced.

At *(Name)* Garage

❒   we provide accurate estimates

❒   we offer a spacious, clean, and comfortable waiting room, complete with telephone to help you stay in touch

❒   we offer you a free ride to commuting facilities or back home

❒   we provide a guarantee of on-time delivery as promised—or you deduct 15 percent from the repair bill

❒   and, finally, we do top-quality work, we do it right the first time, and we do it for less than our major competitors

Because we value your business, we're offering you a special value. Bring the enclosed coupon into *(Name)* Garage, and you will receive a 20 percent discount on any of the following repair or routine maintenance work:

(list)

We're easy to reach. *(Provide directions)*. To ensure prompt service, we suggest that you call ahead at 555-0000.

Sincerely,

Stop Wasting Money

Dear *(Name)*:

I'm a complete stranger to you, but at the risk of sounding impolite, I'm offering you some blunt advice:

Stop wasting your money!

You are one of a select group of people whose success and sense of responsibility have been rewarded by an excellent credit record and an impressive array of credit cards.

Congratulations!

But have you given thought to just how much your good credit is costing you?

Debt consolidation is not just for people who feel overburdened by bills. It's for people like you who want to manage their money more effectively and are tired of paying a lot of high-interest credit cards.

Debt consolidation is for people who want to stop wasting money.

Let *(Name)* Financial Consultants show you how to join the ranks of successful, prudent individuals who have decided to take charge of their finances in the fullest possible way. We have a variety of debt consolidation plans that we can tailor exclusively to your special needs.

The sooner you call us at 555-0000, the sooner we can help you stop wasting your money.

Sincerely,

Stop Killing Yourself

Dear *(Name)*:

Hot enough for you?

Here in the middle of August, it's sure hard to remember what this past winter was like. Let me refresh your recollection: record low temperatures averaging 16 degrees from December through February and a cumulative snowfall of 40 inches.

Beginning to remember now?

On January 12-13, our area was socked with 18 inches of the white stuff. And it was bitterly cold, too—frozen solid.

Did you enjoy digging out of that one?

I didn't think so.

Hot as it is now, winter is sure to come around again. Maybe it won't be as cold. Maybe it will be colder. Maybe we won't get as much snow. Maybe we'll get more. But then there's next year, and the next . . .

Isn't it time you stopped killing yourself with that old snow shovel?

I want to tell you about a better way to dig out. The Snow Dynamo Removal System is a revolutionary hand-held rotary plow/blower that will let you face winter—this winter and all those to come—with a smile on your face. And, as if that were not good news enough, let me tell you that the Dog Days of summer is the best time to purchase a Snow Dynamo.

Why?

First, because we have plenty in stock—*right now.*

Second, because we'll sell you any Snow Dynamo model at a 25 percent discount through the end of the month.

Now, with that in mind, I ask you to read the enclosed brochure data sheet on the Snow Dynamo Removal System. Then come in and see us at *(Name)* Equipment. We'll give you a 25 percent discount—and free delivery within a twenty-five mile radius.

Don't kill yourself this winter.

Sincerely yours,

I Sell Peace of Mind

Dear *(Name)*:

I am writing to introduce myself and my company. My name is *(Name)*, and I have been a master locksmith for twenty-two years. My father was a locksmith before me, and so was his father.

I know locks. I know what they will do to protect you and your family.

And I know what they will not do.

Well, for the first time in more than two decades, I've found a lock that will do just about everything, everything to protect you, your property, and your family. Now I'm pleased and proud to offer that lock—the Guardian Iron Man Model RVT—to homeowners and business owners in your area.

Here's what you need to know about how the Model RVT can protect you, your valuables, and the people you love:

(present comparative test data on the product)

Expensive?

I can answer that in one word: no.

Let me explain: Fully installed, the Model RVT does cost an average of 15 to 20 percent more than ordinary locks. That means that if you ask me to install four locks in your house, you'll pay $35 more than if you had installed ordinary locks.

What do you get for your $35? I could tell you that you get the finest, strongest, more efficient, and most trouble-free security lock in the business. And that would be true enough.

But you are getting something more. I sell locks, yes, but what I really sell is peace of mind. And how much is *that* worth to you?

You can spend thousands of dollars on elaborate security systems. But, as any law officer will tell you, your best security investment is the very best lock you can buy—installed by an expert.

You owe it to your peace of mind to give me a call today. My service is fast and fully guaranteed.

Sincerely yours,

Accept This Free Offer

(Name)
Hospitality Coordinator
Association of Artists' Agents, Inc.
(address)

Dear *(Name)*:

If you're like me, when somebody approaches you with a so-called "free offer," you run the other way.

And—usually—that's about the best thing you *can* do. As the saying goes, there is no such thing as a free lunch.

Except that's exactly what I'm offering you.

A free lunch.

Really.

A big part of your job is entertaining clients and others important to your organization. You take them to lunch. I'd very much like for you to take them to lunch here, at my restaurant, *(Name of restaurant)*.

I could spend another paragraph or two telling you how great my place is. I love talking about it: the marvelous food and beverage, the prompt and courteous service, the quiet, friendly atmosphere so conducive to truly a great business lunch. Everything about *(Name of restaurant)* tells your important guests just how important you consider them to be.

But don't get me started talking about my restaurant. I'll never stop.

Instead, I invite you to come in and have a full lunch, with beverage, on the house. The dining experience at *(Name of restaurant)* is my best advertisement. Why not give me a call at 555-0000 to make a reservation?

I look forward to seeing you.

Sincerely yours,

You Owe It to Yourself

Dear *(Name)*:

At first glance, this might strike you as a stupid question:

Do you need an answering service?

The answer, of course, is:

Of course, I don't.

I've got an answering machine, voice mail, a secretary.

Of course.

Of course?

Today's technology is great. And maybe you don't miss any important calls—at least the calls from folks who aren't put off by a recorded voice.

But how many hangups do you get?

Okay, so you've got a secretary—with a human voice—to answer your calls. But what about folks who call after hours or on weekends?

If you're like a lot of busy executives, you don't take chances on missing important calls. When you're out of the office, you have your calls automatically forwarded to your home or your car—or your vacation home, or your boat, or the bleachers when your kid's playing the big game.

Do you really want to be interrupted whenever *anybody* thinks they've got something important to say?

Yes, technology is great. But you owe it to yourself to look into something even better.

At *(Name of company)* we have that better something. We call it an IAS—Intelligent Answering System. And IAS puts you in control.

❐ IAS is an answering service run by intelligent human beings who, in effect, act as additional staff for you.

❐ You tell IAS when to answer.

❐ You tell IAS when to call you.

❐ You tell IAS who to put through to you immediately and who to schedule for callbacks.

❐ You tell IAS what to say, depending on who is calling.

❐ At your option, IAS will record all incoming calls.

❐ You may issue instructions to IAS as often as you wish: weekly, daily, hourly—it's up to you.

You owe it to yourself to look into a great new business communications idea that combines old-fashioned, time-tested service techniques with the latest in high technology to give you and your business a competitive edge.

The menu of services we offer is entirely customizable, and therefore, pricing is variable. It costs you nothing to discuss your needs with us and let us come up with a cost-effective start-up plan. Give us a call at 555-0000. We guarantee that you won't get an answering machine.

Sincerely yours,

How Can You Afford to Miss?

Dear *(Name)*:

Have you ever dreamed of owning a fine Oriental carpet? A carpet fashioned by the hands of the world's greatest craftsmen? A carpet made of the finest and most luxurious materials? A one-of-a-kind work of art? A carpet that will endure for generations as a cherished heirloom?

Yes, we all dream of such things. But who can afford the luxury of a fine Oriental masterpiece? Sadly, the usual answer is—only the very few and the very wealthy.

But, on rare occasions, an opportunity arises.

(Name) Orientals, which has been established in your area for *(number)* years, is closing its doors. And they are selling their entire stock of masterwork carpets at savings of 50, 75, even 85 percent!

The catch? This is a very limited opportunity. The sale will be conducted from *(date)* through *(date)*, after which *(Name)* Orientals will close its doors forever.

As far as fine Oriental carpets are concerned, the usual question is, *How can you afford one?*

Now, between *(date)* and *(date)*, the question will be: *How can you afford to miss an opportunity to own the Oriental carpet of your dreams?*

(Name) Orientals is located at: *(address)*.

Sale hours are *(list hours)*.

I look forward to seeing you there.

Sincerely,

Need More Self-confidence?

Dear *(Name)*:

Are you happy with your job? Are you satisfied with your salary? Have your reached the top of your profession? Have you gone about as far as you can go?

If your answer to all these questions is *Yes,* congratulations—and you might as well stop reading. Throw the letter away with the rest of the afternoon's junk mail.

But . . . but if you aren't so sure . . . or if your answers are *no, no,* and *no,* I invite you to read on. This letter might just change your life.

Let's ask a few more questions: Do you need more skills? Do you need more education? Do you need more experience?

I'll answer these for you: maybe yes, maybe no.

But there is one more question I can answer with an emphatic *yes.*

Do you need more self-confidence?

Yes. Yes, tests have demonstrated that, regardless of background, level of education, and level of experience, a high degree of self-confidence is the key to professional advancement, personal satisfaction, and a substantial salary.

Great. Wonderful. But isn't self-confidence one of those things you're born with? Either you've got it or you don't?

No. Self-confidence is a combination of attitude and personal skill that, like any attitude or skill, can be learned.

Now, you can take a chance and hope that you will learn the fundamentals of self-confidence on your own—someday. And let's be honest: many people *do* learn those fundamentals—bye and bye. Sooner or later.

But why not sooner instead of later? Why wait when you can take charge—take charge of your life *now* and of your advancement in the *future?*

From *(date)* to *(date)*, *(Name)* Professional Seminars will offer our highly acclaimed series *Ten Steps Toward Self-confidence,* an interactive and aggressively dynamic short course in building the attitudes, feelings, and interpersonal skills you need not only to be *your* best, but to turn *your* best into *the* best, period.

Here's what other successful professionals have said about *Ten Steps Toward Self-confidence:*

(quote testimonials)

You would expect to pay top dollar—corporate rates—for a seminar series as valuable as *Ten Steps Toward Self-confidence.* But *(Name)* Seminars is committed to individuals, not organizations, and we know how hard you work for your money. That's why we've priced *Ten Steps Toward Self-confidence* at a very special *($ amount)* for the entire ten-hour course. And at *(Name)* Seminars we also know that your work and family schedules leave little time for much else, so we've scheduled the series to suit you:

(list schedule)

For very good reasons, *Ten Steps Toward Self-confidence* is our most popular seminar series, and, we're sorry, but enrollment is strictly limited. To take advantage of this opportunity, we urge you to register today by calling 1-800-555-0000.

It could be the most important phone call you'll ever make.

Sincerely,

Take a Vacation

(addressed to place of business)

Dear *(Name)*:

You're busy. You have a million pieces of paper on your desk. It's nine in the morning, and already the phone has been ringing off the hook.

Why am I bothering you with the kind of "junk mail" you usually receive at home?

Because I really want you to take a vacation.

And that has everything to do with business, *your* business, and making *your* business better.

Professional Travel Consultants is not an ordinary travel agency. We specialize in stress-relief vacations specially designed to provide that "down time" all high-powered, successful business people know they need but usually put off indefinitely.

For the successful business professional, vacation time should not be an interruption of "serious work," or a chance to play hooky, or an unproductive period of goofing off. A good vacation is an integral part of your professional life. A good vacation is a productive period of simultaneous unwinding and retooling, of relaxing your focus so that you can sharpen it. It is a time to take the edge off so that you can keep your edge when you really need it. For the business professional, a vacation is not an excuse. It is a necessity.

Professional Travel Consultants specializes in designing vacation packages for the business professional. Such people are our only clients. Here's what we do:

❐ We make all the arrangements, and we make sure that everything about your trip goes smoothly. A vacation should not be more stressful than a business trip.

❐ We secure special "business pleasure class" accommodations at the world's finest hotels.

❏ We provide just the degree of isolation you want. If you want to disappear for a week or more, we'll see to it. If you want to maintain daily contact with your office, we'll see to that.

Finally, no travel agency offers the array of truly special vacation specials we offer. Please take a few moments out of your day—here and now—to look at the enclosed brochure of vacation ideas for the business professional. Then give us a call at 800-555-0000. We'll do the rest.

Sincerely,

Refinance Now

Dear Mr. and Mrs. *(Name)*:

With fixed-rate mortgages at their lowest levels in more than a decade, it is all too easy to overlook an even better value in mortgages. For many people like you, the Adjustable Rate Mortgage represents the best mortgage value available today. Now, it's not for everybody, but an Adjustable Rate Mortgage will certainly slash your current payments and is an especially savvy financial move if you are planning to sell your house within the next several years.

Let's look at some numbers.

(Name) Mortgage, Inc., offers Adjustable Rate Programs starting as low as *(% amount)* percent with an APR of *(% amount)* percent.

What does this mean to you?

❏ On a *($ amount 1)* mortgage, you pay *($ amount 2)* per month

❏ On a *($ amount 3)* mortgage, you pay *($ amount 4)* per month

❏ On a *($ amount 5)*, you pay *($ amount 6)* per month

Spectacular, yes? But what's the downside?

The bad news is that these are adjustable rates and are geared to the prevailing Prime Rate. The good news is that our loan programs have both yearly and lifetime caps, and they adjust only once per year. There are no surprises.

(Name) Mortgage will tailor a program to suit you, and we have a wide variety of no-income/no-asset-verification programs. For more information on these and other money-saving, savvy ways of managing your money, call one of our loan representatives toll free today at 1-800-555-0000. We offer a free, no obligation income and equity analysis.

Sincerely yours,

Exclusive Private Sale I

Dear *(Name)*:

You should know about an EXCLUSIVE PRIVATE SALE for *(Name of store)* preferred customers only. For just 12 hours on Thursday, September 22 and 12 hours on Friday, September 23 (10 A.M. to 10 P.M. both days), *(Name of store)* is offering an incredible selection of cloth and fur coats at specially reduced prices.

How much will you save?

We have reduced *everything we sell* from 15 to 50 percent. And, for this exclusive sale only, we have made it especially easy for you to take advantage of these extraordinary savings. Put down 30 percent on any purchase, and you make no further payments and pay no interest for one full year.

Prices like these and a deal like this do not come along every day, *(Name)*.

You'll save on our new line of fall coats, including everything we stock from *(Brand 1)* and *(Brand 2)*. You'll save on exquisite furs from *(Brand 3)* and *(Brand 4)*.

The sale will be held at our *(Location)* store at the junction of *(Road 1)* and *(Road 2)*. But please note that this exclusive private sale will not be advertised to the general public, and you must present this letter to receive these limited-time-only prices and payment terms.

Save on every item in the store. Save on every cloth coat. Save on every fur.

If you're planning your fall and winter outerwear wardrobe now, you owe it to yourself to attend this special private sale. Why not mark your calendar now:

Thursday, September 22—10 to 10
Friday, September 23—10 to 10

Isn't the way you look and feel . . . *worth it?*

Very truly yours,

Exclusive Private Sale II

Dear *(Name of store)* Customer:

Now that the fall season is upon us, our stores are overflowing with exciting new fashions—for you and for your entire family. And, as one of our valued credit card customers, you are invited to a very special PRIVATE SALE just for you.

For three days and three days only—September 15, 16, and 17— you will receive an extra 15 percent off any and all fashion items you purchase. There's even more: this special discount INCLUDES items already sale priced. That's right:

Every winter coat and jacket is on sale at significant savings. Present this letter and get an additional 15 percent off!

Every wool sweater from *(Brand 1)* and *(Brand 2)* is on sale for 35 percent off list. Present this letter, and these wonderful sweaters are yours for 50 percent off.

Men's fall suits are going at two for $350, which represents a savings of 20 to 30 percent off list. With this letter, your savings jump to 35 and even 45 percent!

And this is just the beginning.

I invite you to mark your calendar now: September 15, 16, 17 at our store in *(Location)* *(Road 1)* and *(Road 2)*, open 10:30 to 10 all three sale days.

Sincerely yours,

Sell Your House

Dear Homeowner:

If you love your house and wouldn't dream of leaving it, don't bother reading this letter. Because the offer we at Corporate Relocations Unlimited are prepared to make will tempt you.

It would tempt anyone . . . especially in today's stagnant home resale market.

We're in the business of finding homes for executives relocating to new communities, communities like yours. Some of America's top corporations call on us to locate—and locate fast—homes in a variety of price ranges. We arrange the purchase, and the homeowner pockets the profit.

Here's the deal. You call us at our special toll-free number, 1-800-555-0000, and we send a representative to evaluate the potential of your home as a Corporate Relocations Unlimited property. If your home qualifies, we will pay you a fee (based on the assessed value of your home) for the right to list your home exclusively with us for a set period—usually three months. In addition to making money on this part of the deal, we can guarantee that your home will be offered to the kind of high-profile clients who will pay top dollar for it and who will move quickly to conclude the purchase.

That's why we told you NOT to read this letter if you don't plan to move.

Tempted?

We warned you.

Why not give Corporate Relocations Unlimited a call, now, at 1-800-555-0000?

Sincerely yours,

Protect Your Investment

(Name)
General Manager
(Name of company)
(address)

Dear *(Name)*:

Savvy and prudent managers like you routinely protect their firm's investment in office equipment—copiers, fax machines, and computers—with on-site service contracts. But *busy* managers like you don't always have the time available to get the very best deal on such contracts. And that's a shame. Because, as with any other insurance product, guaranteed on-site service comes in a bewildering variety of levels and prices, and it's not always easy to get the best deal.

Until now.

And let's cut to the chase, shall we?

Minuteperson Specialists offers you

❐ The best, factory-trained, factory-authorized service for virtually all your office equipment, including copiers by *(list brand names)*, fax machines by *(list brand names)*, and computers by *(list brand names)*

❐ The greatest flexibility of coverage programs, including guaranteed 3-hour response, guaranteed next-day response, and guaranteed 48-hour service, and programs that range from emergency repair, to installation, to regularly scheduled maintenance programs

❐ The lowest prices, period

Now, let's talk about that last item just a bit. We know from experience that the overwhelming majority of service suppliers charge the equivalent of *(% amount)* to *(% amount)* percent of the original purchase price of your equipment for each annual contract. That's a sweet deal—for them. But it is a stiff price for you.

And you can do much better with us.

Figured as a percentage of the original purchase price of your equipment, our fees typically range from *(lesser % amount)* to *(lesser % amount)* percent.

Look, you're right to protect your investment. But why throw money away to do it? Let one of our service representatives put together a service plan custom made for you and designed to grow with you.

Call us at 555-0000 today.

Sincerely yours,

CHAPTER 2

Inviting Yourself to Call: Setting Up Sales Calls

How to Do It

No matter what media gurus and direct mail specialists may tell you, the sales call—close-up and personal—is the most effective method of selling. The goal of a letter setting up a sales call is to convince a busy person to see you, to get an appointment with a person who may know little or nothing about you or your company.

Where, then, to begin?

The obvious answer is to begin with you and your company. But, in this case, the obvious answer is not the best answer. Better to begin with what is guaranteed to interest your correspondent most: *herself* and *her* company.

Experts on job hunting will tell you that the best way to handle yourself in an employment interview is to demonstrate to the interviewer a knowledge and understanding of her company and her needs. The same holds true in a letter setting up a sales call. Before you write, learn as much as you can about the company or individual to whom you are writing. Ask yourself questions:

What is the company's status within the industry?

What does the company (or department, or individual) need?

What is the company (or department, or individual) looking for?

What problems does the company (department, individual) face?

Then frame your letter as a set of answers to such questions. The object is to convince your correspondent that what you offer is tailor-made to what your correspondent needs.

A caveat: Don't *limit* your appeal to your perception of the potential customer's needs. Even if you've done your homework diligently, you could guess wrong, and, besides, even if you are right on target, it is unlikely that you've covered every conceivable need of this particular customer. Begin your letter by focusing on the customer's anticipated needs, then broaden out to the full range of your products and services.

Two additional elements will help to clinch an appointment. Be sure to include a review of past or current satisfied customers—perhaps even a testimonial remark or two or more—and close with any special offers you may be prepared to make: discounts, coupons, free estimates, free appraisals, and so on.

Finally, it is a mistake to limit this type of letter to new customers. Securing an invitation to make a sales call is a highly effective tool not only for maintaining contact with current customers, but for reviving inactive accounts as well, including those who have taken their business elsewhere because of dissatisfaction with your products or services. The personal sales call, if you can arrange one, is a great way to make amends, to assure a customer that you will try harder, that you are eager to make up for anything that may have gone wrong in the past.

— WORDS TO USE —

alternatives	complete	expectations
answers	comprehensive	features
appreciate	confident	free
arrange	congratulations	friends
assessment	cost-effective	genuine
bargain	delighted	give
best	demonstrating	hear
boost	discuss	help
campaign	effective	hope
choice	excited	impressed
choices	exciting	improve
choose	exclusive	inclusive

increase	potential	strategies
interest	privacy	strategy
invest	projections	study
listen	promote	terrific
listening	promoting	transform
offer	proving	update
opportunity	questions	upside
optimistic	reasonable	urge
option	reduce	urged
package	respected	valuable
pleased	savings	value
pleasure	service	willing
pluses	special	

— PHRASES TO USE —

acquaint you with	hands-on demonstration
answer your questions	has to be seen to be appreciated
appreciate a bargain	hope to hear from you
at your convenience	how we can help you
be among the first	I am confident
busy person like you	I can help
commitment to quality	I look forward
cost effectively	I will listen
custom design	I'll give you
discuss strategies	increase your productivity dramatically
discuss with you	invite you to ask
don't want to waste your time	judge for yourself
double (triple, etc.) your business (volume)	key staff
enjoyed talking with you	let me show you
exclusive showing	meet or beat your best price
free assessment	no obligation
free of charge	number on
friends and associates	outline a set of strategies
greatly appreciate	personal demonstration

personal productivity	terrific service
pleasure of demonstrating	test it for yourself
reasonable price	total quality
recognize value	valuable time
revenue increases	very earliest convenience
review these services (or products)	very latest
special terms	ways in which we can help you
state of the art	willing to invest
substantial savings	

Selling Yourself as the New Kid on the Block

(Name)
(Name) Flood Control, Inc.
(address)

Dear *(Name)*:

I've heard some very good things about you and your company.

I've heard that you are the most respected flood control engineer in the state. *(Name 1)*, one of your clients, credits you with saving his property during the floods last year. A number of your accounts have told me how well your bids stack up against those of others.

I heard something else, too. *(Name 2)* said that he thought you were one of "best kept secrets" in the area.

Wow!

A vote of confidence. But do you really want to be kept a secret?

Now, maybe you're wondering why I've been asking so many questions about you. Well, for *(number)* years I have specialized in promoting small service companies like yours. I have been based in *(Name of city)*, and my clients include:

(list)

And many others.

I have just opened up a branch office in *(Name of city)*, and, I'll be upfront with you: I am hungry for business. When you're hungry, you ask questions. You find out who does what in the area, who does it best, and who needs what you've got to offer.

(Name), it is clear to me that you do what you do best, and it is equally clear that you need what I've got to offer.

I want to create a promotional campaign for *(Name)* Flood Control. I want to custom design it for you and for your customers. I want to triple your business within six months. And I want to do it for you at a very special price.

I'm not crazy, and I'm not a good Samaritan. I want to promote you, so that I can promote myself and establish Professional Promotions here in *(Name of city)*.

Now, a generalized sales pitch in a letter or brochure is waste of your time and a waste of mine. What I'd like to do is call on you at your office. I won't do a lot of talking—not right away, at least. But I will do a lot of listening. I will listen to you tell me what you're business is all about, who you want to reach, and just how much business you *(want)* to do. That's the start—for both of us.

I'll call you no later than *(date)* to arrange my visit. If you want to get started sooner, just call me at 555-0000.

Sincerely yours,

––––––––––

Dear *(Name)*:

Maybe you've seen my truck—the bright green pickup with the roses on the doors. I've been driving around *(Name of community 1)* quite a bit, looking at property.

Oh, I'm not in the market for a house.

I'm in the market for customers.

I offer a full range of lawn maintenance and landscape services—everything from spring clean-up, to weekly maintenance, to major planning and planting.

I've been doing this work for *(number)* years in the *(Name of community 2)* area, and now I've set up on my own out here.

They say people in this community are set in their ways and don't like to try new things. Well, I'm not sure about that. But I do know that folks out here, like everyone else, appreciate a bargain. Now, a bargain doesn't just mean services at a reasonable price. It means genuine value: a reasonable price for terrific service, service you'd be happy to pay even more for.

Being new in an area is great motivation for offering that kind of value. And I'd like to prove that to you, if you'll let me. Call 555-0000 for a free assessment of your lawn and landscaping needs and a free estimate. Just for asking me to visit, I'll mow your property for free. That's a *($ amount)* value. There's no obligation. It's just my way of getting in the door.

I hope to hear from you at 555-0000.

Sincerely,

Consulting Service

Dear *(Name)*:

If you're like *(% amount)* percent of personal computer users, you aren't getting what you should out of your PC dollar. In fact, a study in *(Name of publication)* recently showed that the vast majority of PC users take advantage of only about *(% amount)* percent of their machine's power and capability. That means that for every $1,000 you've spent on PCs and PC peripherals, you are realizing only *($ amount)* of actual value.

Can you afford to lose *($ amount)* each year?

If you answered *no,* I can help.

The trouble with most computer consultants is that you need to tell them what to do. There are a lot of us around who can tell you how to implement this or that database system, or a particular network system, or set up an accounting system. I've done all these things, and I'm very good at it. Just ask some of my customers, who include:

(list)

But, strange as it may seem, I know of only one consultant who can come into your office, look at what you do, look at the equipment you do it on, and tell you how to do what you do more effectively than you now do it—without buying a single new piece of equipment and, at most, spending *($ amount)* on new software.

I am that consultant.

If you are willing to invest fifteen minutes with me, I can outline a set of strategies for enhancing your PC usage and making your entire business more cost-effective.

I'll call you next week.

Sincerely yours,

Offer to Demonstrate Product

Dear *(Name 1)*:

I recently had the pleasure of demonstrating *(product)* for your colleague, *(Name 2)*. He was so impressed that he not only purchased *(product)*, but urged me to contact some of his friends and associates about it. You were among the individuals *(Name 2)* wanted me to call on.

Why?

(Name 2) knows that, like him, you need a *(product)* that can do all the following—and do them quickly and cost effectively:

(list of functions)

Now, I could have stuffed this envelope with a lot of Madison Avenue talk about *(product)*. But I don't want to waste your time.

I want to *use* your time in the most effective way. And that means coming to your home or office and treating you to a full, hands-on demonstration of *(product)*. The demonstration can take as little as fifteen minutes—but I find that most of my customers want to take their time. Usually, we spend at least a half an hour putting *(product)* through its paces.

I will call no later than *(date)* to set up an appointment. I look forward to sharing the many features of *(product)* with you.

Sincerely,

Offering Demonstration

Dear *(Name)*:

The *(product)*, the latest entry in our fine family of *(type of product)*, will be introduced during *(month)*. I would like to give you an opportunity to get a jump on this release date and receive a free demonstration of *(product)* in the privacy of your office.

You need only invest a half-hour for a full demonstration.

(Product) is designed to be operated by the people who work for you right now. Our Installation Support Program gets you up and running without hidden charges and without your having to call in costly outside consultants.

By *(Month)*, a great many managers like you will discover the difference our *(product)* can make. Why not get the jump on them? Call me at 555-0000, and I'll set up a free demonstration for you. As soon as tomorrow, if you wish.

Sincerely,

Anticipating Resistance

Dear *(Name)*:

If you're like me, you spend a sizable portion of your workday dodging salespeople. Tell you the truth, it's a survival skill. But there's a downside to it, especially when it becomes a kind of reflex. After all, some things are worth investing in, especially items that can help you accomplish

❏ More

❑ Faster

❑ Cheaper

Our line of *(products/services)* will help you accomplish

❑ More

❑ Faster

❑ Cheaper

Therefore, I ask that, when I telephone next week, you take my call. Give *me* five minutes. I'll give *you* as much time as you want.

Sincerely,

To Someone Who Has Been Avoiding You

Dear *(Name)*:

I try never to let anyone sell me anything. Maybe you're that way, too. Certainly, I've had a difficult time reaching you by telephone. Well, I understand. As I say, I try never to let anyone sell me anything.

But *give* me something? *That* I'll take the time for.

And what I'd like to give to you is the opportunity to increase your productivity by *(% amount)* percent. That's right, *(% amount)* percent. Maybe even more.

I represent *(Name of company)*, designer, manufacturer, and distributor of *(product)*, an entire productivity system, which is guaranteed to increase your personal productivity by *(% amount)* percent in the following areas:

(list)

The system has to be seen to be appreciated, and I would like to invite you to our offices for a free, no-obligation demonstration. You set the time—just give me a call at 555-0000—and I'll arrange for your personal demonstration.

I will *not* bother you with another phone call, so it's entirely up to you. But, if you do decide to come in for a forty-five-minute demonstration, I will provide limousine service door to door.

I hope to hear from you.

Sincerely,

———————

Dear *(Name)*:

The last thing a busy person like you needs is another telephone call. That's why I've stopped trying to reach you over the wire.

Here's my message: Seeing me for twenty minutes is likely to add *($ amount)* to your bottom line.

Twenty minutes is all the time I need to introduce you to our new line of *(products/services)*, which have already meant substantial savings and sharp revenue increases for such firms as:

(list)

But I will not pester you with a call. If you choose to invest twenty minutes, just give *me* a call at 555-0000, and I'll come out to your office.

Cordially,

Setting Up a Call with a New Contact in a Company

Dear *(Name 1)*:

Congratulations on your appointment as *(job title)*! I've been doing business with *(Name 2)* for *(number)* years, and I know that, excited as she was about her new job, she was sorry to leave *(Name of company 1)*. However, she was pleased to be leaving her position in such good hands.

As I mentioned, *(Name 2)* and I have worked together for a long time, so I thought I would take this opportunity to introduce myself to you and to acquaint you with the full line of *(products or services)* my company, *(Name of company 2)*, has to offer. *(Name 2)* called on us for:

(list services or products)

I would like to review these services *(or products)* with you and discuss other ways in which we can help you in your new position.

I'm sure you've got your hands full at the moment, but that's all the more reason to get together soon. I'll call next week.

Sincerely yours,

————————

Dear *(Name 1)*:

Your predecessor, *(Name 2)*, used to take me to lunch at *(Name of restaurant)* at least once a month. Now, I tell you this not to cadge an invitation from you, but to let you know that I would like to get acquainted with you and talk over what you see as your department's needs in the following areas:

(list)

So, why not accept *my* invitation to *(Name of restaurant)*? We can relax, get to know one another, and discuss strategies that can help you get your department running the way *you* want it to.

I'll call you soon to set up a date.

Sincerely,

Invitation to a Plant Tour

Dear *(Name)*:

Let's have lunch—not at *(Name or restaurant 1)* or *(Name of restaurant 2)*, but in my office at our plant.

I want you to see our factory. Once you do, I am confident that you'll gain a new appreciation of the phrase *state of the art*. And that—quite frankly—is bound to translate into business for us.

I'll call you next week to set up a lunch and a plant tour.

Sincerely,

Rescheduling

Dear *(Name)*:

After writing to set up a meeting with you to show our new line of *(products)*, I find myself in the position of writing to persuade you to delay that meeting by one week.

No, It's not that I'm out of my mind or—even less—that "something's come up." It's just that *(number)* of our latest *(products)*—*(list)*—which were not scheduled to ship until *(date)* are shipping early. Samples will be in my hands exactly one week after our scheduled appointment.

I want to show you our very latest, and I certainly don't want to take up twice as much of your valuable time as is absolutely necessary.

So, if we can reschedule for *(date)*—same time, same place—you'll be treated to more than either of us bargained for.

I'll call next week to confirm the new date.

Sincerely,

Old Product, New Uses

Dear *(Name)*:

My salesman father used to tell me, "Once you've made the sale, it's time to shut up."

Well, the sale I made to you was last year, and here I am about to open my mouth. Why? The fact is that a whole new range of uses has opened up for the *(product)* you bought last year. That's because of a great new accessory package *(Name of company)* has developed. With it, you can transform your *(product)* into:

(list)

But don't just take my word for it. Let me show you—in your home and using your *(product)*.

Why not give me a call at 555-0000 so that I can set up a demonstration?

I look forward to hearing from you.

Sincerely,

New Product, Established Customer

Dear *(Name)*:

The new *(product)* line we've been waiting for since *(Month)* will be delivered by *(date)*. I know that you want to be among the first of our customers to see it and to be given an opportunity to place quantity orders.

This stuff promises to be hot, and, I must tell you, I think our production people erred on the conservative side in determining runs. So it *is* important that I show the line to you at your very earliest convenience. I don't want you to be shut out or disappointed in quantities available.

Please take a look at your appointment calendar for *(date)* and *(date)*. I can come out at either time. Just give me a call at 555-0000.

I look forward to seeing you.

Sincerely,

New Business, Old Customer

Dear *(Name)*:

You know us as a fine *(type of business)*, and we've had a lot of good years together. That's why I am excited to tell you that we have expanded into *(another type of business)*. We offer a comprehensive line of great *(types of product)*, including:

(list)

And we can private label any of these items in virtually any quantity.

Because this is a new business for us, we are very eager to get established in it quickly. What I'm saying is: we're ready to deal. But, first, let me show you the merchandise. I know you'll be impressed, and I can guarantee that we'll meet or beat your best price.

I'll call next week to set up an appointment.

Best regards,

————

Dear *(Name)*:

My name's the same, but the letterhead is brand new. After *(number)* years working for others, I've started my own *(type of company)*. It's a new company, but it's built on my *(number)* years' experience as a *(job title)*—many of those years spent working with you.

I'd like to continue working with you, *(Name)*, doing pretty much what we've always done together—only doing it even faster and even more cost effectively.

I know what you expect and demand. We both know how well we work together. And I'm hungry enough to make bringing me your business especially worth your while. If I walked that extra mile for you in the past, I'm prepared to *run* that distance now.

I'll be calling you next week. I'd like to take you to lunch and fill you in on what I am sure will be a bright future for us both.

Sincerely,

Reviving an Inactive Customer

Dear *(Name 1)*:

It's been a while since we last worked together, and I thought you'd appreciate an update on our most recent customers and activities.

For *(Name of company 1)*, we developed a brand-new *(product/service)*, which has exceeded even our optimistic expectations in the following areas:

(list)

(Name of company 2) commissioned us to create *(product/service)*, which helped to take them into the number one position in their region.

(Name 2), at *(Name of company 3)*, asked us to come up with *(product/service)*. What we delivered was *(number)* alternatives, and *(Name of company 3)* opted to purchase them all!

So, *(Name)*, as you can see, it has been a banner year for us. I would love to get together with you and review some of these new *(product/services)* with you. I am confident that you would find the time well spent. I'll call in a few days to set something up.

Sincerely,

Reviving an Inactive, Dissatisfied Customer

Dear *(Name)*:

You've been too easy on us. Let's not put too fine a point on the matter: We failed to live up to your expectations. Sure, we patched things up, and you, who had every right to be furious and disappointed, were gracious and understanding.

But then you bowed out of the picture.

You let us off too easily.

You see, while I appreciate your graciousness, what I really want is your business. What I want is the opportunity not merely to live up to your expectations, which I know are high, but to exceed them. And I want to do this at a very special price and on very special terms.

I will call you no later than *(date)* to set up an appointment. I want to show you—personally—what we're capable of doing for you. I would greatly appreciate the opportunity.

Cordially,

Follow-up to a Phone Call

Dear *(Name)*:

I enjoyed talking with you on the phone this morning, and I am delighted by your interest in *(product/service)*. As you suggested, I will call you after *(date)* to set up a tour of our plant and arrange for you to meet with our key staff.

We are all looking forward to your visit.

Sincerely,

———————

Dear *(Name)*:

Many thanks for your time on the telephone yesterday. I always enjoy talking about the *(type of business)* business, especially with a market leader like yourself.

As I mentioned, *(Name of company)* offers a full line of *(type of products/services)*, including:

(list)

Just about any of the *(products/services)* in our *(Name of product/service line)* should be of interest to you, and I've enclosed a brochure on these. I'll call you next week—after you've had time to review the literature—to set up a meeting.

It was a pleasure talking with you.

Sincerely,

Contact!
Following Up After the Sales Call

How to Do It

After you have set up and made a sales call, there are eight possible courses the balance of the sales process may take:

1. You make the sale as a result of the call. No additional communication is strictly necessary—but see Chapter Six on postsale follow-up letters.

2. The sale is not immediately concluded. You write a letter thanking the customer for seeing you, and you ask her if she has any questions or if there is more information she requires to make a decision.

3. You need to supply additional information as a result of the sales call. Until you supply that information—answer those questions, address those doubts, overcome that resistance—the sale will not be closed.

4. You need to confirm details, requirements, specifications, and preferences relating to the transaction.

5. The sales call does not result in an immediate sale. You sit passively waiting for the customer to call you.

6. The sales call does not result in an immediate sale. The customer does not contact you. You write a letter to push the process along.

7. The sales call results in the customer choosing not to purchase your product or service. You drown your sorrow in a bottle of very cheap wine.

8. The sales call results in the customer choosing not to purchase your product or service. You write a letter to accomplish some or all of the following:

    a. Thank the correspondent for her time, courtesy, and attention.

    b. Attempt to determine why the correspondent declined to buy. What would make it possible for her to say yes? *Revive the sale now.*

    c. Attempt to determine why the correspondent declined to buy. What would make it possible for her to say yes—*next time?*

Follow-up letters after the initial contact can nurture a budding relationship, develop a sale, collect and/or furnish information, rescue a sale, and retain a customer—even if the present sale is unsuccessful.

Why write rather than call? Sometimes it *is* better to call or fax (and all the letters in this chapter can be sent via fax, if you wish). A phone call is best if, when you made the sales call, you were lacking an item or two of information necessary to close the sale. A quick call is the usually the best way to provide such information. A phone call is also fine if you need quickly to advise the customer of a shipping date or other straightforward item of information.

On the other hand, good letters:

1. Both formalize and personalize the business relationship.

2. Are evidence that you are investing *real* time in this customer by producing a *tangible* communication—not just making a quick phone call.

3. Spell out, for the record, terms, specifications, and so on relating to the sale.

4. Are less intrusive and, therefore, less likely to provoke a knee-jerk rejection.

In cases where the sales call has failed to produce a sale, a friendly letter is a means of maintaining—or reopening—contact with the customer on the customer's terms. He is not trapped by a phone call, but can read and respond to the letter at his or her leisure. A letter is a form of communication that, in and of itself, empowers the recipient, whereas a phone call, by its nature, to some degree backs the recipient of the call into a corner.

— WORDS TO USE —

absolutely	decision	kindness
accommodate	defer	know-how
accurate	delighted	necessary
address	easier	no-nonsense
advantage	enjoy	offer
alternatives	evaluate	options
answers	evaluation	performance
appreciate	experience	please
associate	facilitate	pleasure
assurance	favorable	possible
astute	favored	prequalified
attractive	future	present
availability	generous	presentation
available	guarantee	pride
benefit	handshake	priority
benefits	hear	productivity
brief	help	proud
briefly	helpful	prudent
caution	hospitality	questions
certain	important	range
choice	impressed	reservations
choose	improvement	review
clear	included	savings
clearly	includes	savvy
confirm	invest	schedule
consideration	investment	serve
conversation	issues	service
convinced	key	serving

significant	successful	valuable
sophisticated	support	visit
special	sure	vital
standard	terms	warranty
straightforward	thanks	wise
study	understand	
substantial	understanding	

— Phrases to Use —

absolutely guaranteed	I appreciate
absolutely certain	I can assure you
accurate information	I understand
address any additional issues	important features
all inclusive	important new features
allowing me to meet with you	impressed by your plant *(office, etc.)*
as much information as possible	improve your bottom line
attractive features	in the driver's seat
best for you	includes everything
big step	increase productivity
caution and care	key purchase
complete package	let me be of further assistance
cover all the bases	make it possible
custom tailored to your specifications	my direct line
decision-making process	no extra cost
defer initial payment	nothing more to buy
don't hesitate to call	opportunity to talk with you about
easy to live with	pay for itself
enjoy talking with you	plan for your
favored customer	please give me a call if
fully covered	pleasure to see you
good news	range of terms
greater performance	range of products (services)
hear from you soon	review the brochures
help you to	run-on discount

save time	to your advantage
seriously considering	top priority
significant improvement	unanswered questions
sought-after features	very helpful
special option	visiting with you
special program	wide range
spread your payments	you are certainly correct
technical support	your bottom line
thank you for your time and attention	work together

Thanks for Seeing Me

Dear *(Name)*:

It was a great pleasure seeing you on *(day)*. I was highly impressed by your plant *(or offices)* and by your entire operation. I am convinced that our *(product/service)* can make you even more successful by facilitating such tasks as:

(list)

If you have any questions that I did not answer on *(day)*, please don't hesitate to give me a call at 555-0000.

Sincerely,

———————

Dear *(Name)*:

Many thanks for your hospitality on *(day)*. I always enjoy talking about our *(product/service)*, but it's a lot more fun in comfortable surroundings and over a great cup of coffee.

If I can be of further help as you review what we have to offer your company, please don't hesitate to call me on my direct line, 555-0000.

Sincerely,

Dear *(Name)*:

Just wanted to thank you for your time and attention on *(day)*. I am confident you'll find that it was time very well spent. *Invested* is the better word for it—because our range of *(products/services)* will repay you manyfold in time saved and productivity increased.

If there is any way I can help you as you review the brochures I left with you, please call me at 555-0000.

Cordially,

Did I Mention?

Dear *(Name)*:

I had such a good time visiting with you yesterday that I simply can't recall whether I mentioned that our *(product)* includes all these accessories:

(list)

The brochure I left with you lists all these, but they're worth a special mention, since we're the only manufacturer who doesn't charge you extra for these essential accessories.

Please give me a call at 555-0000 if there is any other information I can help you with.

Sincerely,

———

Dear *(Name)*:

Thanks for seeing me on *(day)*. I'm writing because I'm not sure that I reviewed our special financing options, which, I believe, are very important features of our *(product/service)*. There are *(number)* options:

(list)

As you can see, we're in the business of making it possible to *do* business with us.

Please give me a call if I can answer any additional questions. I'm at 555-0000.

Cordially,

Forgot to Mention

Dear *(Name)*:

I so much enjoyed talking with you yesterday about *(product/service)* that I believe I got a little carried away and neglected to mention one very important set of features:

(list)

The folks in our design *(or other)* department would have my head if they found out that I forgot to bring these features to your attention. So, please . . . don't tell them!

If you have any questions as a result of our talk, please give me a call at 555-0000.

Cordially,

———————

Dear *(Name)*:

I'm such a superslick salesperson that I slipped right over a very important piece of information about our *(product/service)*, namely, *(supply information)*.

The omission is more than slightly embarrassing—since these are some of the most attractive features of our *(product/service)*. If there is anything else you need to know as you evaluate the material I left with you, please call me at 555-0000.

I Misspoke

Dear *(Name)*:

Thanks for letting me see you on *(day)*. You know, I'm very proud of our prices, and the figure I quoted—*($ amount)*—for *(product/service/quantity)* is a figure to be proud of.

Trouble is, it's the wrong figure.

The *right* price is even lower: *($ amount)* for *(product/service/quantity)*!

I made a mistake—used an expired price book. I apologize, but I am also pleased to be able to offer you our fine *(product/service)* at an even better price.

Cordially,

———————

Dear *(Name)*:

I was just reviewing the notes from our discussion on *(day)*, and I've discovered that I misquoted prices for the following:

(list)

The prices I quoted were for these items without *(feature)*. I see from my notes that you want to include *(feature)*. Here are the revised prices:

(list)

I am very sorry for my error—though, as you can see, the inclusion of *(feature)* adds very little to the bottom line.

I hope my mistake has not caused you any inconvenience, and I thank you for your understanding. If you have any questions, please call me at 555-0000.

Sincerely yours,

Dear *(Name)*:

I greatly enjoyed meeting with you on *(day)* to discuss our line of *(products)*.

When I got back to my office, I did what I always do after a meeting—I reviewed my notes. And I realized that I had told you that none of our *(products)* include *(feature)* as a standard accessory.

Well, I was wrong.

In fact, our model *(model name/number)* does include *(feature)*, along with *(other features)*—*all* standard and *all* included in the price of *($ amount)*!

I should have known this, but, I confess, I did not.

I have enclosed for your review a brochure on this item. If you have any questions, please call me at 555-0000. I promise that I will have *all* the accurate information—because you can be sure that I have now done my homework extra thoroughly on *(model name/number)*!

Cordially,

————————

Dear *(Name)*:

During our recent meeting to discuss *(product/service)*, you asked me about our range of terms, and I told you that it was possible to defer initial payment for *(number)* days, then spread payments over *(time period)*.

This is not strictly true. What I inadvertently omitted to mention is that this plan requires a deposit of *($ amount)*.

I am very embarrassed that I failed to mention this.

The good news, however, is twofold:

1. The deposit amount is nominal—certainly less than a conventional down payment.

2. You have been successfully prequalified for this top-priority, favored-customer credit plan.

I hope that my omission has not caused you any inconvenience. Please accept my apologies.

If you have any questions, do call me at 555-0000.

Sincerely,

I Have the Information You Need

Dear *(Name)*:

I greatly enjoyed our meeting on *(day)*.

You asked me about changes in specifications from our original model *(product)* and our new model. I'm sorry I didn't have the information with me at the time, but here it is:

(list comparisons)

As you can see, the new model represents a significant improvement over the old in terms of performance—and at no extra cost. Your question was so astute that, you can be sure, I'll walk into all future client meetings armed with the above information!

Please call if I can be of further assistance as you review our product.

Sincerely yours,

———————

Dear *(Name)*:

I have prices on those additional quantities of *(product)* you requested:

(list)

As you can see, our run-on discounts are quite generous.

I very much enjoyed talking with you on *(day)*, and I invite you to call me at 555-0000 if you have any further questions.

Sincerely,

Dear *(Name)*:

The answers to your questions are yes, yes, no, and yes.

Now, just on the off chance that you've forgotten your questions, here they are:

1. *(Question and reply)*
2. *(Question and reply)*
3. *(Question and reply)*
4. *(Question and reply)*

Yesterday's meeting with you was a great pleasure, and I hope to be hearing from you soon. If you have any other questions, please call me at 555-0000.

Cordially,

I Understand Your Reservations

Dear *(Name)*:

I enjoyed meeting with you on *(day)*.

You are certainly right: buying a *(product)* is a big step and requires a substantial investment. That is why I sell *(products)* the way I do— by coming out to your office to discuss each and every feature and to help you determine what is best for you.

I understand your reservations about taking the plunge, and I applaud your caution and careful thought. Perhaps, therefore, the following information will be helpful in facilitating your decision:

(list additional information)

And, remember, while *(product)* does require an initial capital investment of *($ amount)*, it will allow you to operate at an annual savings of at least *($ amount)*. If you take into account increased productivity, that savings increases considerably. Most of our customers, including *(list)*, find that the unit had paid for itself within *(time period)*.

I'm not going to insult you by insisting that this decision is really a "no-brainer." But I can state with confidence that this is one investment you will never have reason to regret.

I'm available here at 555-0000 if you have any further questions.

Cordially,

––––––––––

Dear *(Name)*:

I read in a book about sales techniques that a good salesperson is supposed to close the sale with a question: "What can I do to make it possible for you to decide to buy such and such?"

To tell you the truth, I have never liked such blatant high-pressure tactics. The approach I prefer is to present our *(product/service)* as fully and straightforwardly as I can and then leave the rest of the selling to the customer himself or herself. However, because I've not heard from you since *(day)*, when I visited with you, I thought that maybe you had some doubts or reservations or questions I had not addressed. So maybe it *is* time to follow that old book's advice and ask: What can I do to make it possible for you to decide to buy *(product/service)*?

Just give me a call at 555-0000, and I'll be happy to address any lingering issues concerning *(product/service)*.

Cordially,

It's a Big Step, But . . .

Dear *(Name)*:

I'm not surprised I haven't gotten a call from you yet. Sure, we met *(number)* days ago, but I realize that choosing a *(product/service)* is a very big step and one not to be taken lightly. Great as our *(product/service)* is, I never expect people to jump at it. It always takes thought—just like the thought you are devoting to the decision now.

So, choosing a *(product/service)* is a big step.

But it is a *necessary* step. Sooner or later, you are going to need the advantages that our *(product/service)* gives you, including:

(list)

And since you want to get all these benefits, why not get them with the best *(product/service)* available?

I'd be pleased to talk to you further as you continue your evaluation. My direct line is 555-0000.

Sincerely yours,

Time Is Limited

Dear *(Name)*:

If there is one thing that I've learned representing *(Name of company)*, it's that high-pressure sales tactics do *not* work on our typically sophisticated customer. For that reason, I did inform you during our meeting that the prices on our line of *(products)* will rise by an average of *(% amount)* percent on *(date)*. But I did not hit you over the head with that fact.

I'm not going to do that now, either. But I did think that you would appreciate a reminder. The price increase, scheduled for *(date)*, is real, and—unfortunately—it will happen. If you *are* planning to make this key purchase, I urge you to do so before *(date)*.

If there is anything I can do to help you with your decision, please call me at 555-0000.

Cordially,

Confirming Order Details

Dear *(Name)*:

I am delighted that you are seriously considering purchase of *(product)*, and I am pleased to quote you a price. Just to make sure that we are talking apples and apples, kindly confirm the following information regarding specifications and features:

(list)

I also ask that you clarify your requirements as to the following features:

1. Do you want *(feature)*?
2. Do you want *(feature)*?
3. Do you want *(feature)*?
4. Do you want *(feature)*?
5. Do you want *(feature)*?

Feel free to phone this information to me at my direct number, 555-0000, or, if you prefer, fax it to my attention at 555-1111.

I look forward to hearing from you.

Cordially,

———————

Dear *(Name)*:

This will confirm your order for *(product/quantity)*. We will ship *(product)* to *(address)* and bill the purchase directly to *(Name and address)*. As you instructed, we will ship via *(carrier)*.

Thank you for your order, and I know that you will be very pleased with your *(product)*. If you have any questions concerning your *(product)*, including installation issues, please call our technical support staff at 555-0000.

Sincerely yours,

———————

Dear *(Name)*:

Thanks for your call this morning. I'm delighted that you have chosen to purchase our *(model)*. The enclosed purchase order will supply us with all the credit and shipping information we need to expedite shipment of your *(product)*. Please fill out the purchase order and mail or fax it to *(address, fax number)*, marked to my attention.

We appreciate your business, and we'll be here for you.

Sincerely,

Clarifying an Order

Dear *(Name)*:

Well, I know I sold you *something* as a result of our meeting yesterday, but I'm a little hazy on a few of the details. I've got you down for *(product)*, but we have not specified *(model, feature, etc.)*. To make absolutely sure you get what you want, I've enclosed a purchase order with the missing items circled. Just complete it, please, and fax it back to me at 555-1111.

If you have any questions, my voice number is 555-0000.

All best,

Dear *(Name)*:

I neglected one small detail in taking your order yesterday. Do you have a preferred shipping carrier? Here are your choices and the cost of each:

(list)

Why not just phone me direct, at 555-0000, with your preference. If you wish, you may circle what you want above and fax this letter back to me at 555-1111.

Cordially,

Replying to No Response

Dear *(Name)*:

Can I help?

Usually, when I don't hear from a customer for more than *(number)* days after I've made a sales presentation, I discover that I left some questions unanswered. I'd like to help you make a very important purchasing decision, and the best way I can help is to offer as much information as possible. It's been my experience that the more you know about our *(product)*, the easier it is to make that investment in it.

So, let me hear from you. I'd like to get your thinking on this purchase, and I'd like to offer my help as you evaluate our *(product)*. My direct number is 555-0000.

Cordially yours,

———————

Dear *(Name)*:

Can you help me?

My job is to present our *(product/service)* as fully and clearly as possible. Once that is done, my job is to do everything I can to help you evaluate our *(product/service)* in light of your present and likely future needs.

I believe I've done reasonably well with the first part of my job, but I cannot even get started on the second part if I don't hear something from you. To assist you in the decision-making process, I need *your* help: I need some feedback on *(product/service)* and how you see it fitting into your present and future programs, as well as how you see it *failing* to fit in. From this information, I can help you determine just how, why, and when to proceed with your plan to purchase *(product/service)*.

I'll call you next week, if I haven't heard from you by then.

Sincerely,

———————

Dear *(Name)*:

Did I forget to tell you something? Like maybe the one piece of information you need to make your decision on the *(product/service)*?

Often I find that when I don't hear from a customer I've called on, the reason is that some key piece of the puzzle is missing. Usually, it's my job to supply that missing piece.

Please, give me a call at 555-0000 so that we can discuss the purchase. I bet I can help.

Cordially,

Customer Declines to Purchase

Dear *(Name)*:

I'd be lying if I told you I'm not disappointed that you have chosen not to purchase *(product/service)* at this time. However, I am very happy that I had the opportunity to meet you and speak with you. It was good of you to be so generous with your time.

Should your needs change and you do wish to purchase *(product/service)* at a later time, be assured that I'll be here for you.

Cordially,

———

Dear *(Name)*:

Just a note to thank you for seeing me on *(day)* and giving me the opportunity to talk to you about *(product/service)*. While I'm sorry that you've chosen not to make a purchase at this time, I'm happy that we met, and I hope that we will do business in the future.

Sincerely,

———

Dear *(Name)*:

Many thanks for allowing me to meet with you last *(day)*.

If there is one thing I've learned in the selling business, it's how to take "no" for an answer. However, for me, "no" is never the *full* answer until I understand the reasons behind that "no." I'd like to get together—briefly, by telephone—so that I can understand why you chose not to make a purchase at this time. The conversation would be very helpful to me in serving others and in serving you in the future.

I will call you late next week—not with the object of changing your mind, but to know a little more *about* your mind.

Sincerely,

————————

Dear *(Name)*:

I very much enjoyed meeting with you last week, and while I understand that you will not be making a purchase at this time, I do want to make certain that you are aware of the alternatives we offer to the *(product)* I showed you.

Our line of *(type of product)* includes the following, in addition to the *(product)* you and I discussed:

(list)

These offer a wide range of price and feature alternatives, and I would be pleased to discuss any or all of them with you. I'll telephone you next week to set up an appointment, if you like.

Cordially,

————————

Dear *(Name)*:

If you're like me, you get a lot of junk mail. And when you throw that junk mail away, it begets—miraculously enough—even *more* junk mail. Many of these letters begin with something like: "Frankly, I can't understand why anyone would turn down an offer like this!" or "Here's your final chance!"

Well, I won't add to your garbage heap with this letter. *No,* I understand, means *no*.

But that doesn't mean I can't ask you: What would make it possible for you to say *yes?*

Is there anything I can do to make it possible for you to purchase *(product)*?

This isn't *your* last chance. It is *our* opportunity to work together to supply you with a product that will

❑ Increase your productivity

❑ Improve your bottom line

❑ Never become obsolete

I will call after *(date)* to get your thoughts on *(product)*.

Cordially,

————

Dear *(Name)*:

The folks at my office think I'm crazy. I just got off the phone with you. I had a smile on my face.

"Made the sale, huh?" one of my associates asked.

"No. Mr. *(Name)* chose not to buy."

"Then why are you smiling?"

I'll tell you what I told my associate. I don't sell *products*. I sell our company. And what that means is that our relationship doesn't have to end just because I didn't sell you this particular item. After all, I got to meet with you and tell you what we're all about. *That* is valuable to me—and, I believe, it is valuable to you.

As you know, we offer a complete line of *(type of product)*. I've also explained to you our no-nonsense pricing and service policies. I believe I've made it clear that we are a great company to do business with. So, next time you're in the market for *(type of product)*, please know that we'll be here for you.

Cordially,

CHAPTER 4

Judged by Its Cover: Writing Effective Cover Letters

How to Do It

Every small business is a selling business. But it is a mistake to assume that what you are selling is this widget or that framiss or a particular service or a special type of expertise. What you are selling is *your business*. More specifically, what you are selling is your *small* business. You are selling the virtues of smallness as opposed to the vices—assumed or real—of big business. Where a big corporation transforms its customers into mere numbers, your small business treats them like human beings—indeed, like partners in a common enterprise. Selling a small business means selling personal attention, the personal attention of the owner or one of the principals or someone who answers directly to the owner or one of the principals.

When a big company sends out a project proposal, bid, or quotation, it's usually done on a slick form, perhaps in a custom-printed corporate binder. This can be very impressive. But somewhere in the back of the customer's or client's mind are two thoughts:

1. If they can afford something this slick, they must do a million of these things.

2. They sure spend a lot on stationery and printing. How's that reflected in their markup?

The small-business alternative is not to send your bid, proposal, or quotation on handwritten note paper in a wrinkled and recycled manilla envelope. Everything you do should have an air of professionalism. And even a very small business can afford the kind of highly presentable binders and stationery purveyed by "quick-print" and copy shops. But, instead of fretting over superslick binders and fancy stationery, devote your time to matters of more immediate *human* substance: projecting an image, selling your business through cover letters that reach out and personalize each transaction.

Too often, the cover letter is seen as a pro forma insert—something you're just expected to do because that's what is always done. It is a fatal mistake to squander *any* opportunity for communication in this way. Yes, a cover letter is expected. But why stop at what is merely expected? Take your cue from that charming New Orleans merchant tradition and spike each transaction with "lagniappe"—a little something extra and *unexpected*.

This does not require any great wit or effort. The lagniappe is nothing more or less than personal attention, a tone of friendliness. However, it is surprising what a difficult time businesspeople have being friendly in a letter—especially one that is perceived as a pro forma exercise. Some believe that a friendly tone is not "businesslike," while others feel that the client or customer will actually be offended by overfamiliarity. Finally, in our zero-sum-game culture—a culture that stubbornly and unnecessarily posits one winner and one loser for any given transaction—sounding friendly is often mistaken for sounding soft.

The fact is that we can learn something from Middle Eastern merchant traditions. Those who remember the OPEC oil crisis of the 1970s may find it hard to believe, but the Middle Eastern tradition of commerce is founded on a simple maxim: Business is friendship.

Have a hard time looking at it this way?

Just bear in mind that having a client or customer is much like having a friend. You are in a position to help him, and he is in a position to help you. You provide a product or service he needs, and he provides the sustenance you need. Deny it all you want, but you are in this thing together.

The keys to effective cover letters are

1. Friendly, personal tone.

2. Vocabulary of relationship, of commonality, of partnership. Try to use *we* more than *I* or *you*.

3. Courtesy—beginning with thanks and ending with an offer of attention and assistance and collaboration toward a common goal.

— WORDS TO USE —

able	excited	money
advance	expect	new
answer	expected	nominal
answers	expedite	opportunity
anticipate	experience	options
approach	expertise	outstanding
assume	extensive	personal
attention	extra	please
attitude	facts	pleasure
biggest	features	pledge
client	figures	prefer
colleagues	fine	pride
competitive	folks	project
complete	free	promised
confidence	great	prompt
conversation	hope	provocative
customer	impressive	purpose
deliver	improvements	quality
delivery	include	questions
detailed	inclusive	reaction
direct	innovative	ready
discount	inquired	realize
eager	interest	requirements
easier	invite	response
enterprise	key	responsive
exceptional	latest	review

save	specifications	upgrade
send	standard	warranty
service	style	willing
shrewd	support	winner
small	thanks	
special	time	

— PHRASES TO USE —

across the board

as you requested

bear in mind

brand new

competitive edge

complete satisfaction

complete confidence

complete—with absolutely everything you need

comprehensive selection

compelling investment opportunity

cost savings

crystal-clear specifications

customer-support program

deeper level of service

detailed prospectus

discussed with you

drop by our showroom

even more useful

exceptional warranty

experience tells me

extended warranty

free customer support

full range of

give you

great numbers

have just gotten

just came in

just dial 555-0000

just received

key to success

let the document speak for itself

locked in and guaranteed

look forward to

make this project work

many options

may I direct your attention

most popular

my direct line

no unwelcome surprises

not to be missed

nothing in this world is risk-free

our single most important product: ourselves

pass those savings on to you

personal attention

pleased to send

points of special interest to you

pride ourselves

prove it to yourself

ready, willing, and able

right away

risk-free

save you plenty of time

see for yourself

significantly upgraded

special price

special pride

special effort

special highlights

special offers

talking with you

total commitment

trail-blazing

uncompromising quality

very personal

virtually unlimited number of options

walk that extra mile

want very much to work with you

wide range

willingness to help

without risk

your bottom line

your thoughts on

With an Estimate or Bid

Dear *(Name)*:

It is a great pleasure to send you the enclosed bid on your project number *(number)*. You've made my job a lot easier by providing crystal-clear specifications and requirements. Accordingly, our figures reflect strict adherence to them. And that should save you plenty of time and anguish: You can act on our bid with complete confidence that there will be no unwelcome surprises.

Please call me at 555-0000 if you have any questions. I look forward to hearing from you.

Sincerely,

————

Dear *(Name)*:

Many thanks for your phone call yesterday. It is my pleasure to send the enclosed estimate.

Experience tells me that you will find our prices competitive, but what the numbers can't show you is the special, very personal and uncompromising quality of our service. That will mean as much to your bottom line as our great numbers.

Please give me a call—at 555-0000—if you have any questions. I'm here to make this project work for us both.

Sincerely,

Dear *(Name)*:

I've made a special effort to get his estimate to you in a hurry. I think you can guess why: I'm eager for your business.

But maybe you don't realize that it's not just because I need the money. (Though the money wouldn't be all that bad, either!) I've heard a lot about the way you operate that makes me want very much to work with you. Your colleagues—folks in the industry generally—have plenty of great things to say about your style and your approach. I'd like to be a part of these.

Please call me on my direct line, 555-0000, if you have any questions about the numbers or delivery dates.

Cordially,

––––––––

Dear *(Name)*:

I'm pleased to enclose our estimate for *(name of project)*.

We take pride in everything we do, and we take special pride in what we call our competitive edge—not only when it comes to numbers, but especially when we're called on to walk that extra mile to deliver great service.

I'll call you at the end of the week to answer any questions you may have, unless, of course, I hear from you before then. My direct line is 555-0000, or you can fax me at 555-1111.

Sincerely,

––––––––

Dear *(Name)*:

I have enjoyed talking to you about *(name of project)*, and I am enclosing a full proposal and bid. The proposal covers all phases of the project and makes note of a few extras we did not address, but which I believe you will want to consider.

Assuming we receive authorization to begin by *(date)*, we will complete the project by *(date)*.

If you have any questions about our proposal or bid, please give me a call at 555-0000.

I hope that we'll be working together.

Cordially,

Letters to Accompany a Prospectus

Dear *(Name)*:

I am highly pleased and very proud to send you a prospectus for *(Name of company)*. I'll let the document speak for itself, but you might want to look for these special highlights:

1. *(Highlight 1)*
2. *(Highlight 2)*
3. *(Highlight 3)*
4. *(Highlight 4)*

It has been a pleasure talking with you during these past two weeks. I will call you early next week to get your reaction to the prospectus. In the meantime, if you have any questions or comments, please dial me at 555-0000.

Sincerely yours,

———

Dear *(Name)*:

Thank you for your interest in *(Name of company)*. As I promised when we spoke on the phone this morning, here is a detailed prospectus. May I direct your attention to four of its highlights?

1. *(Highlight 1)*
2. *(Highlight 2)*
3. *(Highlight 3)*
4. *(Highlight 4)*

I am, quite frankly, excited about *(Name of company)* and eager to discuss the prospectus with you. Just give me a call at 555-0000.

Cordially,

Dear *(Name)*:

After our conversation yesterday, I expected you'd be asking to see this. The prospectus for *(Name of company)* is enclosed. *(Name)*, this company is a comer, and once you read through the prospectus, you will see why I'm so excited about it.

It is true, as you pointed out, that *(cite potential investor's reservation)*. As I mentioned to you, however, the key to success in *(type of business)* is not *(factor 1)*, but *(factor 2)*.

And that, of course, is what we are all about.

You might also bear in mind a few other highlights as you read through the prospectus:

1. *(Highlight 1)*

2. *(Highlight 2)*

3. *(Highlight 3)*

4. *(Highlight 4)*

As you well know, nothing in this world is risk-free. But *(Name of company)* gives every indication of being a winner. I invite you to look at the prospectus and see for yourself. Then get back to me at 555-0000.

Best regards,

———————

Dear *(Name)*:

Enclosed please find some highly provocative reading: the *(Name of company)* prospectus you requested.

Take your time with it, and do give me a call—at 555-0000—to discuss any points of special interest to you. I'd like to direct your attention to four points of particular interest to *me:*

1. *(Highlight 1)*

2. *(Highlight 2)*

3. *(Highlight 3)*

4. *(Highlight 4)*

Pretty great, huh? Of course, I'm prejudiced, but the combination of *(feature 1)* and *(feature 2)* makes this enterprise a most compelling investment opportunity.

Let me hear from you. I'm eager to get your thoughts on the prospectus.

Sincerely yours,

Cover Letter with Catalog

Dear *(Name)*:

I am pleased to send you our latest catalog, which includes our brand-new line of innovative *(product type)*. We're very excited about the new line—and so is everybody we've talked to in the industry. It includes such trail-blazing features as:

(list features)

One thing that the catalog cannot adequately convey is our single most important product: ourselves. When you buy one of our *(products)*, you don't just buy a fine piece of hardware, you buy our expertise, our willingness to help, and our total commitment to your complete satisfaction.

Please call me directly at 555-0000 if you have any questions.

Cordially,

————————

Dear *(Name)*:

Here's the new catalog you requested—our biggest and most extensive yet. Please take a few extra moments to look through pages *(number-number)*, which feature our special offers. There are real savings here on some of our most popular items.

Please note that any of us here at *(Name of company)* are ready, willing, and able to answer all your questions about the fine products in this catalog. Just dial 555-0000.

Sincerely,

With a Brochure

Dear *(Name)*:

As you requested, here is a brochure describing our latest *(product)*.

The brochure does a great job illustrating and describing *(product)*, but it doesn't tell you much about a very important product feature: the personal attention we give you, beginning with installation and taking you through *(number)* years of free customer support. In fact, our customer-support program is the best in the industry, offering you:

(list features)

If you have any questions, please give me a call at 555-0000.

Cordially,

————

Dear *(Name)*:

When I visited with you the other day, our new brochures were not yet ready. I've just gotten a few advance copies, and I wanted to pass one on to you right away.

Please remember that we offer a wide range of payment plans, including:

(list)

We also offer many options for maintenance:

(list)

If the brochure leaves any of your questions unanswered, please give me a call at 555-0000.

Sincerely,

With a Price List

Dear *(Name)*:

As I promised, here is our latest price list. These prices are locked in and guaranteed through *(date)*, after which I do anticipate an increase, probably in the neighborhood of *(% amount)* percent across the board.

Please note that all prices are inclusive of *(list features/services)*. Expedited shipping is available at a nominal charge.

Please give me a call to place an order or to ask any questions. My direct line is 555-0000.

Cordially,

————————

Dear *(Name)*:

Enclosed is our most recent schedule of prices for *(products/services)*. As I mentioned when we spoke on the phone, we offer a *(percentage amount)* discount for payment with order. This, in fact, is the way most of our customers prefer to do business with us.

I am available to answer any questions you may have. Just dial 555-0000.

Cordially,

With an Accessories List

Dear *(Name)*:

(Name of company) supports its *(product)* with a full range of accessories. I am pleased to send you a list, with the latest prices. If you have questions about any of these items, I invite you to drop by our showroom at *(address)* or just give me a call at 555-0000.

Sincerely,

————————

Dear *(Name)*:

As we discussed when I called on you last week, our *(product)* comes to you complete—with everything you need to

❏ Do *(task)*

❏ Do *(task)*

❑ Do *(task)*

❑ Do *(task)*

❑ Do *(task)*

However, we also offer a comprehensive selection of accessories to make *(product)* even more useful, and, as you requested, I have enclosed a complete list.

Please call me at 555-0000 if you have any questions about any of these accessories.

Cordially,

With a List of Service Options

Dear *(Name)*:

As I discussed with you over the phone, at *(Name of company)* we pride ourselves on offering each of our customers a service package tailored to his or her particular needs. The literature enclosed explains some of our "prepackaged" options—which many customers find just right for them—but you should regard these as starting points only. We can add or subtract features as you wish.

Please give me a call at 555-0000 after you have had an opportunity to review the material.

Sincerely,

———

Dear *(Name)*:

You are a very shrewd customer.

Like you, most of our customers come to us, in part, because of our exceptional warranty and service policy. Unlike you, relatively few think to look beyond that warranty coverage. That's always surprised me, since, after all, *(product)* is designed to last a lot longer than *(time period)*.

So I take pleasure in sending a brochure describing our extended warranty service options. If you order any of these plans before *(date)*, your special price is *($ amount)*, a *(% amount)* percent discount from our standard extended warranty price.

Please call me at 555-0000 if you have any questions.

Sincerely,

Dear *(Name)*:

It will come as no surprise to you that we are a small company. In fact, I assume that's one of the reasons you've called on us. You expect an extra measure, a deeper level of service—service that is personal, prompt, and direct.

Well, we're here to fulfill that expectation

The flyer I've enclosed describes the service options we offer. What it can't fully describe is the attitude with which we perform those services. It is an attitude born of the knowledge that a customer's call is not an interruption in our day, it is *the* purpose of each and every day we do business.

Please call me at 555-0000 if you have any questions.

Cordially,

With a Specification Update

Dear *(Name)*:

My files show that, *(number)* months ago, you inquired about our *(product)*. I replied with a brochure on the item. Now, while you didn't send us an order at the time, I thought you still might be interested in acquiring *(product)*—especially since its specifications and feature list have been substantially upgraded. *(Product)* was outstanding back when you first asked about it. It's even more impressive now.

The enclosed leaflet lists all the improvements, but let me direct your attention to three key items in particular:

(Item 1)

(Item 2)

(Item 3)

Maybe the best news is that *(product)* has actually come *down* in price: from *($ amount 1)* to *($ amount 2)*.

If you have any questions, please call me at 555-0000.

Sincerely,

————————

Dear *(Name)*:

When I sent you the specifications for *(product)*, I mentioned that some changes were in the works. As of *(date)*, *(product)* will feature significantly upgraded

(list upgraded features)

Any order you place now will be filled with the upgraded model. Please note that two product features have *not* changed:

1. Our low price.
2. Our extra-effort policy of full customer support.

I've enclosed a new spec sheet for you to look over. If you have any questions at all, please give me a call at 555-0000.

Sincerely yours,

With an Amended or Corrected Bid

Dear *(Name)*:

As I mentioned on the telephone this morning, I was unaware that you wanted us to bid on all phases of the *(Name of project)*. As you know, the figures I submitted, cover only phases III through V.

Rather than simply add on costs for phases I and II, I enclose a completely revised bid, which *discounts* the prices on *each* portion of the project to reflect the cost savings we obtain by tooling up for the entire project. It is always our policy to pass such savings on to you.

So, what I have enclosed is not just a corrected bid, but a brand-new bid—and one that saves you *(% amount)* percent on phase III, *(% amount)* percent on phase IV, and *(% amount)* percent on phase V, compared to the original bid.

We would be very pleased to take on the entire project, and we are delighted to be able to pass on to you our savings.

Please call me if you wish to discuss any of these items or figures. My direct number is 555-0000.

Sincerely,

Dear *(Name)*:

Not to put too fine a point on the matter: I goofed.

The bid I sent, dated *(date)*, omitted one of the items you asked for, namely, *(item)*. Normally, this would add *($ amount 1)* to the total, but since I'm about to ask you for something—your forgiveness and understanding—I want to give you something else in exchange: a substantial discount. Please add not *($ amount 1)* to our bid, but only *($ amount 2)*, which is our cost for *(item)*. I believe *I* should pay for my mistake—not you.

The addition of *(item)* at the discount price brings our total bid amount to *($ amount 3)*. Please give me a call at 555-0000 if you have any questions.

Sincerely,

CHAPTER 5

Closing —and Opening: Closing Sales by Opening Strong Customer Relations

How to Do It

All of us are in the business of selling—a product, a service, an idea, a point of view—but not all of us are (or consider ourselves) professional sales people. The non-professional may talk of "closing" a sale, meaning getting the order or even getting the check and handing over the goods. The professional, however, knows that "closing" means *asking* for the order. Now, the *super* professional does not stop with "closing" a sale—asking for an order. She uses the closing to *close* a sale and *open* a relationship with the customer.

Why?

Bang for the buck. We tend to think of selling as getting someone to part with money, to invest in a product or service. But we, the sellers, also invest time, effort, expertise, emotion—all of which translates into money, plus the overhead expenses of doing business, which translate even more directly into money. Why mass all these resources toward the object of making *a* sale? Why be satisfied with *selling* a product or service when you can also *acquire* a customer? Why settle for one infusion of revenue when you can create the conditions for virtually unlimited infusions?

Good closing letters not only secure a particular sale, they also open relationships.

There are a great many books on selling. Within this literary—some would insist on the term *subliterary*—genre, there are a great many specialized books devoted to closing. If sales is a function, profession, skill, and art shrouded in a mystic aura, the closing is often treated as if it were some form of out-and-out black magic, which only a few gifted individuals know how to practice successfully.

In fact, the basic principle behind closing a sale is quite simple: assume the order; assume the done deal.

If you flip a coin a hundred times, it will come up heads just about fifty of those times. If you make your presentation—and it is a reasonably good one—then you ask one hundred people, in effect, *Do you want to buy this product or not?* perhaps fifty will say yes. (Other factors enter into the equation—the inherent desirability of the product or service, its cost, and so on; therefore, this is not quite as random a situation as the coin toss.)

But why flip coins for a living?

You want heads? *Hand* your customer the coin, heads up. Not:

"Do you want to buy it or not?"

But:

"Shall I start the project on Tuesday, or do you need to get under way sooner?"

"Which color do you prefer?"

"How many does it look like you'll need?"

Now, in a nice, tidy world, the sales process really would fall neatly into the phases suggested by the first five chapters of this book:

1. Identifying prospects

2. Getting a foot in that prospect's door

3. Following up on the sales call

4. Following up with necessary information

5. Closing the sale

Indeed, sometimes it really does work that way. Sometimes, though, it's even easier. You send out a cold letter, and you get a sale.

Sometimes it's harder. *You* may close by assuming the order, but your customer says, "Whoa! I'm not ready to buy yet." Actually, this is a perfectly acceptable response to the closing. It does not mean that you have failed. The closing is provocative. It is meant to *provoke* a response. If the response is an order, great. If the response is resistance and reservation, that is something, too. In either case, you have succeeded in provoking your customer to tender *something:* cash or a resistance. You know what to do with cash. You *should* know what to do with resistance: overcome it. Either of these *somethings* is better than *nothing:* no tangible response at all.

If the closing elicits resistance, exploit it, mine it, probe it, investigate it, get to the bottom of it, understand it, then overcome it, if possible. If you can get your customer to articulate her resistance, you have already made *a* sale. You have succeeded in getting her to invest time and energy and interest in you and your product or service. The more time and energy and interest a prospect invests, the more likely it is that you will, in fact, make the sale. Use resistance as a learning tool.

But the real world is messier than this, and most professional salespeople subconsciously override the notion of *phases* in a sales *process* by a much simpler thought, a thought as simple as ABC:

Always Be Closing

Professional salespeople gear all steps of the sales process toward closing. Each of their communications conveys the certainty of a sale.

That's what professional salespeople do. Superprofessionals also follow the ABC formula, but they define "closing" as an opening—not just making this particular sale, but opening a relationship with the customer. Each communication, then, works toward establishing and developing this relationship.

— WORDS TO USE —

absolute	assure	comfort
accessories	authorize	competitors
accommodate	authorized	complacency
act	authorization	completion
acute	availability	confident
agree	available	confirm
alternative	benefits	consider
answer	choice	convenient
appreciate	choose	convinced
appropriate	client	deadline
approval	close	debate

decide	liabilities	sale
decision	low	satisfaction
demand	minimum	satisfied
demonstrate	move	save
desire	need	schedule
direct	offer	serve
directly	okay	service
disbelief	opportunities	solve
discuss	option	sophisticated
enjoy	order	style
enjoyable	our	substantial
enjoyed	partners	supply
ensure	percentage	sure
expedite	pleased	talking
experience	pleasure	target
features	possible	terms
final	pressure	testimonial
fresh	price	time
furnish	productive	trust
generous	promise	truth
give	quality	try
guarantee	questions	understanding
help	real	value
immediately	relationship	vendor
information	reliability	winner
inventory	requirement	yes

— PHRASES TO USE —

answer your objections	count on the order
available for immediate shipment	create a new market
beyond my control	demand has been unusually high
challenge the status quo	do yourself a favor
confirm that	do something good for yourself
confirm the availability	don't cut any corners
confirm our understanding	enjoyed talking

exactly what you want	make certain
expect your order	meet or exceed the specifications
extend special terms	no compromise on quality
follow-up	no later than
generous terms	our busy season
give us a try	our situation
go that extra mile	over the long haul
good news	price that's right for you
great product	production times
greatest value for your dollar	proven winner
have no choice	pure pleasure
height of the season	put us on trial
hold the prices promised	put us to the test
hold the quantities promised	ready to ship
I think you'll agree	reaping the benefits
I understand completely	right combination
in the long run	self-indulgent
industry leaders	serve your needs better
lead time	target date
let us help you	to my attention
little room for doubt	very special price
lock in your order	we can
look forward to hearing from you	we don't want you to get shut out
look forward to working with you	
low prices	

Don't Buy Yet!

Dear *(Name)*:

You know what's coming. You know what this is. The Follow-up Letter.

Yes, I enjoyed talking with you on *(day)*, and now it's time to close the sale and take the order. Get you to part with some cash.

But, you know, I've given a great deal of thought to what you said about *(need or requirement)*, and I do *not* think you should reach for your checkbook—yet. Not before you consider *(alternative product or service)*. In view of what you said about *(need or requirement)*, I think that *(alternative product or service)* will serve your needs better in the long run because:

(list reasons)

Now, I hear my salesmen ancestors calling to me from the Great Beyond: *Shut up! You've made the sale! What are you doing?!* But the fact is that I'm less interested in making this particular sale than I am in acquiring you as a customer—somebody I can work with over the long haul. And that kind of relationship can develop only if you are thoroughly pleased. And you will be thoroughly pleased only if I sell you the right *(product/service)*.

So, I have enclosed a leaflet describing *(alternative product or service)*, and I will call you within a very few days to discuss it. If you want to reach me before I call you, just dial 555-0000.

Cordially,

––––––––––

Dear *(Name)*:

Now that we've talked about *(product)*, my *Super Selling Secrets* book tells me that I'm supposed to rush to the "close"—ask you, How many can I put you down for?

Well, I don't always go by the book—and I do *not* want to close this sale until I am convinced that you are ordering just the right combination of *(features)*.

Please look over the enclosed checklist of features and accessories before signing off on the enclosed purchase order. If you have any questions I failed to answer about any of the features and accessories, please call me at 555-0000, and I'll do my best to answer them immediately.

We make a great product at *(Name of company)*, but your complete satisfaction depends on your getting exactly what you want and what you need at a cost that's right for you.

Cordially,

Asking for the Order

Dear *(Name)*:

The good news is that, having reviewed production times for the *(product)* we've discussed, I can tell you that it *is* possible to deliver in the desired quantity by *(date 2)*.

The bad news is: You don't have time to think about it. I need to lock in your order by *(date 1)*. If I let it slip beyond that, I cannot guarantee delivery by *(date 2)*.

If you can give me a purchase order by *(date 1)*, I'll turn right around and lock it in. I'm at 555-0000.

Sincerely,

Dear *(Name)*:

I'm assuming that you've now had sufficient time to decide on *(product)* for your *(business need)*. I think you'll agree that the brochure I left with you leaves little room for doubt: Our *(product)* meets your price, reliability, and availability criteria.

At present I have *(quantity)* ready to ship immediately. Fax me your purchase order now, and I can guarantee you'll have the full quantity by *(date)*. Our fax line is 555-1111.   You can reach me by phone at 555-0000.

Sincerely,

Dear *(Name)*:

When you and I met on *(date)*, you mentioned that you planned to put in your order for *(product)* by *(date)*.

Can I count on the order we discussed? That was: *(list order)*.

Please send the P.O. to my attention, and I will ensure that it gets expedited processing and delivery.

Sincerely,

Dear *(Name)*:

I enclose the photos of *(product)*, as you requested. Please let me hear from you no later than *(date)*. We are seriously under the gun with this item, since demand has been unusually high. It would be a shame if you were locked out.

I'm at 555-0000—my direct line.

Sincerely yours,

—————

Dear *(Name)*:

Thanks for a most productive and enjoyable meeting. As you asked, I enclose complete spec sheets for *(products)*. As you see, all these items meet or exceed the specifications you presented at our meeting.

I'll call you next week for your order.

Sincerely,

Assuming the Order

Dear *(Name)*:

Thank you for a very productive meeting. Based on your requirements as you set them out at the meeting, I am prepared to furnish the following:

(list services)

I can begin on *(date)*, unless you need to get under way even sooner, in which case call me at 555-0000. Assuming the *(date)* start-up, I will need your authorization and a deposit check by *(date)*.

I'll call to confirm that our understanding matches yours. I am very much looking forward to working with you.

Cordially,

Dear *(Name)*:

Following our meeting on *(day)*, I called our warehouse to confirm the availability of the following items:

(list)

I wanted to make certain that you could have them delivered without delay. I am happy to say that all are available for immediate shipment. I can guarantee availability through *(date)*. Kindly call before then to confirm quantities and to authorize shipment.

Sincerely,

———

Dear *(Name)*:

After a most satisfying meeting on *(day)*, I have taken the liberty of pencilling you in for *(service)* on *(date[s])*. My understanding is that you require the following:

(list services)

Please give me a call at 555-0000 to confirm this and to authorize a start-up on *(date)*. As you know, this is our busy season, so I cannot hold this time slot open beyond *(date)*.

Sincerely,

Responses to Objections

NEED MORE TIME TO THINK ABOUT PURCHASE

Dear *(Name)*:

I didn't want to pressure you over the phone, and I won't use any high-pressure tactics now, either. You're too sophisticated for that, and, besides, such an approach is not my style.

However, I do want to point out to you that our *(date)* price-increase deadline is not only real, but beyond my control. My prices are linked to what my suppliers charge me, and their prices, unfortunately, have risen sharply. Based on what I have on hand, I cannot hold the price line beyond *(date)*.

While I cannot, then, indefinitely hold the prices promised, I can accommodate you with rather more generous financing terms, as follows: *(state terms)*. But I urge you to act before *(date)*. My phone number is 555-0000.

Cordially,

Via Fax

Dear *(Name)*:

I wish I had done a better job on *(day)* of making our situation clear. Your target date is *(date 2)*. We require a minimum of *(number)* days' lead time. That means your order must be locked in no later than *(date 1)*—not very much time at all, which is why I've faxed rather than mailed you this letter.

Please, we don't want you to get shut out, especially now, at the height of the season. Call me today at 555-0000, and I can guarantee completion by your target date.

Sincerely yours,

Dear *(Name)*:

If you're like me, you're accustomed to working under pressure, and you've learned to live with it. Pressure, in your line of work, is inevitable. But what you can't tolerate is some salesperson manufacturing additional—and quite unnecessary—pressure.

I understand completely. However, I have no choice but to risk the possibility of rejection—because the pressure we are under is real. *(Number)* of the items you are considering for purchase are in acutely short supply. I cannot guarantee their availability after *(date)*. The truth is that the time to place your order is now—or face the possibility of a delay of *(number)* weeks or even more.

I'm at 555-0000, ready to expedite shipment of *(list items)* directly on your authorization.

Cordially,

Dear *(Name)*:

I understand your reluctance to commit funds to the kind of quantity purchase we discussed, and I would like to be able to assure you that you have the luxury of all the time you may feel you need to make your decision.

Unfortunately, I cannot guarantee you that luxury. Purchasing in the proposed quantity will save you *(% amount)* percent, and, luckily, I am at present in a position to fill your order in that quantity. After *(date)*, I no longer expect to be in that position.

(Name), I am not a high-pressure salesperson. In fact, I'm not a salesperson at all. I'm a manager. And one of the things I must manage is our inventory. Demand is such that I cannot hold the quantity you require beyond *(date)*.

If you have any questions, I urge you to call me without delay at 555-0000. Please—help us to serve you by ordering before *(date)*.

Cordially,

DO YOURSELF A FAVOR

Dear *(Name)*:

One of the things I most enjoy about selling *(product)* is observing the pleasure folks take in the purchase. And, make no mistake, purchasing one of our *(products)* is an act of pure pleasure. It is self-indulgent, there's no denying that.

Maybe that's why you're hesitating. It's understandable. There are a dozen—no, a hundred, a *thousand*—more "practical" things that demand your cash. Why, you don't need to wait a few more *days* to buy your *(product)*, you need a few more months or years, even.

On the other hand, why not just do yourself a favor? *Yourself.*

What an idea! *Do something for yourself.* Now. Today. Especially when *(product)* can be yours at a very special price and on very favorable terms.

Come on. Give me a call, and I'll talk you over any final hurdles. Dial 555-0000.

Sincerely,

BARGAIN PRICE EQUALS POOR QUALITY

Dear *(Name)*:

I make my customers sick. And the disease I give them, if it goes untreated, costs them money and opportunity.

The disease is called the Too-Good-to-Be-True syndrome, and it strikes a certain percentage of my customers when they see the low, low prices I charge for my *(product)*. Its chief symptom is utter disbelief. The victim is heard to exclaim, "How can he charge so little!" Then the fatal complications set in: "*(Products)* this cheap have to be pretty crummy!" And the stricken party finds a vendor who will charge *(% amount)* percent more. Then he considers himself cured. Poorer—but cured.

(Name), I've seen the syndrome before. I know how you feel. But, the fact is that you should be spending less time puzzling over how I can give you such good prices and more time over why my competitors feel the need to charge you so much more.

There is no appreciable difference in quality between my *(products)* and those of my high-priced competitors. There *is*, however, a big difference in price—and that difference goes right into your pocket.

The choice is yours.

Sincerely,

———

Dear *(Name)*:

Why trouble yourself over my low prices? Why not call some of my high-priced competitors and give *them* a hard time. They are spending *your* money on

❒ fancy packaging
❒ fancy offices
❒ fancy retail space

I don't bother with these things, so I save *your* money.

Now, as to quality, I'll admit that my competitors are good. But my products are every bit as good. Where quality is concerned, I don't cut any corners.

The choice, *(Name)*, is yours. You can pay for fancy packaging, fancy offices, and a fancy shop. The packaging you throw in the garbage, and the office and shop you don't take home with you. In the end what you have is a *(product)* that cost you *($ amount 1)* or *($ amount 2)*.

Let me save you some money. How many *(products)* can I put you down for?

Cordially,

PRICE TOO HIGH

Dear *(Name)*:

You won't get an argument out of me, because you are right: our *(type of service)* requires a substantial investment. I won't debate that, because it makes no sense to debate a fact.

What I *will* do is remind you of the far more considerable costs of failing to perform the *(type of service)* we offer. These are the liabilities you face:

(list)

Over a period of *(number)* years, your costs could amount to well over *($ amount)*.

As you know, cost does not exist in a single dimension. It is a function of *cash* and of *time*. Please put both these into your decision equation before you take action—or fail to take action.

Sincerely,

———————

Dear *(Name)*:

I won't attempt to answer your objections to the cost of *(product/service)*. I'll let *(number)* of my clients answer them for you:

(Testimonial 1)

(Testimonial 2)

(Testimonial 3)

(Testimonial 4)

Yes, value requires a substantial investment—as these and other industry leaders know. Why not join them in reaping the benefits of *(product/service)*?

Please call me at 555-0000. I can put you in touch with these or other clients, who will be happy to discuss *(product/service)* with you.

Cordially,

DON'T NEED IT

Dear *(Name)*:

Some folks swear by the old mechanic's maxim: *If it ain't broke, don't fix it.*

My problem is, I'm always asking: *How do you know it ain't broke?*

You didn't get to be the successful businessperson you are by leaving well enough alone. Good enough was never good enough for you. You challenged and continue to challenge the status quo. You equate complacency with failure.

So, that is why I was surprised to hear that you "don't need" our *(product/service)*.

I agree that you can "get along" without it. But you have never been content simply to "get along." Just take a quick look at this short list of the benefits of our *(product/service)*:

(list)

Do you really want to "get along" without these?

I'm at 555-0000.

Cordially,

PRESENT VENDOR SATISFACTORY

Dear *(Name)*:

I can understand your reluctance to leave a vendor you've grown accustomed to, and I wouldn't suggest that you do so if I weren't confident that I can

❐ Supply a superior product

❐ Supply superior service

❐ Give you faster turnaround

❐ Give you better prices

Don't you think that all this makes it worth giving us a try?

I promise you that we are highly motivated, and we will not let you down. Why not give me a call at 555-0000?

Cordially,

BOSS MAKES PURCHASING DECISIONS

Dear *(Name)*:

Thanks for telling me that your boss is the one who makes the final purchasing decisions. If all I were really interested in was making a sale, I would now go directly to him or her. However, I enjoyed talking to you about *(product/service)*, and I believe that we've established an understanding of one another. Certainly, it is clear that you appreciate what we have to offer. So, rather than go to your supervisor, I'd like to give you the opportunity to turn him or her on to *(product/service)*.

Perhaps you might convey:

(list selling points)

I can promise you that he or she will be very grateful for this information.

Sincerely,

BUSINESS IS POOR

Dear *(Name)*:

I know that it's little comfort to you, but you're not alone in suffering through a pretty dismal retail season. That is all the more reason why you need the fresh look our *(product)* can give your operation. We're prepared to take steps to make the purchase easy and effective for you.

To begin with, we can ship *(quantity)* units immediately. Based on experience, I can tell you that your turnover time will be brief, and much-needed cash forthcoming. I am so confident of this, that I am willing to extend special 60-day credit terms to you.

(Name), let us help you out of the doldrums with a proven winner at a great price and on easy terms. Just give me a call at 555-0000 to place the order.

All best,

SEE ME ANOTHER TIME

Dear *(Name)*:

The reason I'm writing rather than calling is that I didn't want to twist your arm over the phone. I know you didn't want to talk business on my last sweep through your neighborhood, but I do want to let you know that we're about to initiate a *(% amount)* percent price increase across the board. I am authorized to offer our line to you at the present low price through *(date)* only.

(Name), unless you don't intend to place any order, I urge you to act now at the present prices rather than delay and get zapped with a *(% amount)* percent increase.

You can call me directly at 555-0000.

Sincerely,

GET FEW CALLS FOR ITEM

Dear *(Name)*:

You're right: It makes good business sense to stock merchandise that's in demand. And I believe you're right about *(product)*. I'm sure you haven't gotten many calls about it.

That is just my point. What we've got here is a chicken-and-egg situation. You don't get many inquiries about *(product)*, because you don't stock *(product)*. You don't stock *(product)* because you don't get many calls for it.

Now, you can keep going on in this vicious cycle, if you choose, or you can let us create a new market for you with our special *(product)* display, which is not only a convenient way to make a modest quantity purchase, but will also ensure that your customers will *see* and *want (product)*.

And that, I submit, is good for us and very good for you.

I'm at 555-0000.

Cordially,

NEGATIVE EXPERIENCE WITH VENDOR

Dear *(Name)*:

When I called you on *(day)* I didn't realize that you had had a bad experience with our firm some years ago. I didn't realize it because I wasn't here at the time. Neither were my two partners. We bought the business back in *(year)*. The name's the same, but that is just about all. The ownership and the management—one and the same—are new.

I would greatly appreciate the opportunity to demonstrate to you just how new. I could just write your business off, but I don't operate that way. I can't rest until I've cleared our name by showing you all that we can do for you.

The fact is, I believe you are putting yourself at a distinct disadvantage by failing to avail yourself of the merchandising opportunities we offer, including:

(list)

Why punish yourself for something somebody else did a long time ago?

We at the new *(Name of company)* are eager to prove ourselves to you, *(Name)*, and we will go that extra mile or two to do it. Please, give me a full opportunity to present our line to you. I'll call next week.

Sincerely,

What Will Make It Possible for You to Say Yes?

Dear *(Name)*:

I could hit you up with another sales pitch, trumpeting the many virtues and benefits of our *(product/service)*. But, it seems to me, there's a more productive step I can take instead.

I've told you, I think, all there is to know about *(product/service)*. Now, let me ask *you* a question: What can I do that would make it possible for you to place an order now?

I'll leave it you. Just give me a call at 555-0000, and I'm ready to deal. I'll do my best to make this order possible for you.

I look forward to hearing from you.

Cordially,

After You've Made the Sale—
Keep Writing:
Following Up a Sale with Letters That
Cultivate Customers

How to Do It

If there are two rules about selling that everyone knows, they are:

1. There's a sucker born every minute.

2. After you've made the sale, shut up.

Like most clichés, these aphorisms contain an element of truth. You *can* find someone to sucker into making purchase. And, once you've closed a sale, you need not risk that particular sale by saying anything else.

But the truth of these clichés is limited to a one-shot concept of selling. The assumption behind both, really, is that you are selling one item to one stranger and then you are getting out of town. You'll never see that person again. The paradigm operative here is defining sales as one-sale-at-a-time, and that paradigm is outmoded, neither cost-efficient, time-efficient, nor energy-efficient. Few businesses can afford to think of sales in terms of a series of one shots. Instead of taking one sale at a time, it is necessary—for economic survival, let alone success—to take one customer at a time. The object of making a sale is not just making the sale itself, but also making a customer, cultivating a relationship that promises to yield many more sales:

to this particular customer and to her friends, colleagues, neighbors, and associates.

The most effective advertising is word of mouth. That does not mean that word of mouth reaches more potential buyers than, say, a television or newspaper ad, but word of mouth is more effective with each of those customers it does reach. Making a great product or rendering a terrific service is essential to generating good word-of-mouth advertising. But why depend solely on the quality of the "thing" you are selling? Extend the value of your merchandise into the realm of human relations by performing effective customer service.

What is at the root of effective customer service? Demonstrating that you *care* about the customer, that you regard him as valuable, a partner in prosperity, something more than a line in your accounts receivable ledger. How do you demonstrate this? First, of course, by being there to take the customer's orders, to ensure that orders are filled properly and promptly, that services contracted for are performed to the customer's satisfaction. Then, by being there to take—and act upon—the customer's complaints, criticism, and cries for help. The basis for these two functions is good communication. We will discuss responding to customer problems, complaints, disputes, and criticism in the next chapter. Here, in this chapter, we will address communication not in *response* to customer issues, but *in anticipation* those issues.

The postsale follow-up is the most neglected aspect of customer communications. Many businesspeople think of it as a frill. Probably many more don't think of it at all. That is a pity and a big mistake, because your present customer is your best customer—a valuable asset and ally. Follow-up letters demonstrate your concern and caring for the customer. They are a way of telling him, *You think that all you bought is a fine watchamacallit? No. For your money, you also get the attention and support of my entire company!*

There are various strategies for conveying this message. Following the sale, you might write any of the following:

1. A thank you

2. A letter of congratulations, reinforcing the sale and assuring the customer that she has made a wise decision

3. An invitation to call if the customer needs assistance or advice concerning the product

4. Instructions for registering the product

5. A reminder about some feature(s) or service(s)

6. Important phone numbers or addresses related to the product or service

7. News about related products, publications, support groups, and so on

8. News of special programs, incentives, promotions, and so on

The follow-up communication may, of course, combine any or all of these strategies. The benefits of the follow-up include:

1. Customer goodwill and loyalty

2. Enhanced satisfaction—and *perception* of satisfaction—with the product or service

3. Repeat business

4. Word-of-mouth advertising

The moral of this chapter is, once the sale is made *don't* shut up—and don't sit back and relax, either. If you succeed in turning a sale into a relationship, both you *and* your customer stand to benefit. A sale is too valuable an opportunity to be wasted.

— WORDS TO USE —

absolutely	better	congratulations
acquire	care	considerate
act	celebrate	contact
activate	certain	continuously
agree	challenging	coverage
anniversary	choice	customers
answer	choose	decision
anticipate	choosing	deliver
appreciate	commitment	demonstrate
appropriate	committed	dispatch
authorize	competitive	efficient
benefit	confidence	enduring
best	confident	ensure

exciting

expect

expectations

expedite

expert

extend

extension

family

favor

features

finest

frank

free

friendly

grateful

gratifying

guarantee

help

hotline

immediately

improve

improvement

intend

interactive

invested

issue

just

maintain

meeting

merit

only

opportunity

original

perhaps

personally

please

pleasure

pride

purchase

recommend

recommended

referral

register

registration

regulars

remember

responsiveness

satisfaction

satisfied

schedule

serve

service

shred

special

support

thank

thoughtful

unlikely

welcome

wise

— PHRASES TO USE —

absolutely everything

activate your warranty

as you requested

complete satisfaction

contact me personally

customer hotline

customer support

detail oriented

enduring commitment

enjoy the peace of mind

established customer

extended warranty service

family of clients

feel free

finest materials

first-class treatment

full benefit

full protection

get back to you

help us to serve you better

here to help

I'll make things right

just a phone call away

let us do the rest

long-term	please keep in touch
look forward	pride ourselves
low cost	quality-assurance program
maintain a very high level	quality-assurance questionnaire
maximum effort	see to it
meet or exceed	self-evaluation
member of our family of customers	serve you most effectively
merit your confidence	stand behind
no later than	take special note
100 percent satisfied	thank you for using
personal account representative	Thank you
personally guarantee it	we will work hard
please be assured	Why not . . . ?

Thank You

Dear *(Name)*:

Thank you for purchasing a *(product)*. I am confident that it will give you years of great satisfaction.

Please remember that you are now a member of our family of customers—and to keep you satisfied, our customer-support staff is just a phone call away, at 555-0000.

Sincerely,

———————

Dear *(Name)*:

Most of our customers kick themselves soon after they buy one of our *(products)*.

That's because they can't believe they waited so long to acquire one!

Many thanks for your purchase, and please remember to confirm your full warranty coverage by mailing in your registration so that we may serve you most effectively.

Sincerely,

––––––––––

Dear *(Name)*:

It was a pleasure meeting with you last *(day)* at your new facility. And, I must tell you, taking your order was a pleasure of at least equal magnitude.

You can be certain that we will deliver the finest *(product/service)* in the industry.

Your personal account representative will be *(Name)*, who will contact you no later than *(date)*. If you have any questions in the meantime, please call *(Name)* at 555-0000.

Sincerely,

––––––––––

Dear *(Name)*:

Thank you for using our *(product/service)*. We appreciate the confidence you have shown in us by making this choice. And we *do* know that, in our highly competitive field, you have many choices. So please be assured that we will work hard to merit the confidence you have invested in us.

Sincerely yours,

––––––––––

Dear *(Name)*:

Thank you for the opportunity to serve you once again. We are always grateful for new business, but new business from established customers is especially gratifying. It is a vote of confidence that we do not take lightly.

As before, your account representative will be *(Name)*, whose direct line is 555-0000.

Sincerely,

Dear *(Name)*:

Thank you for placing your confidence in us. At *(Name of company)*, we take your trust very seriously, and we guarantee to devote our maximum effort to ensure that you always have reason to celebrate your decision.

We maintain a special customer hotline during regular business hours at 555-0000. Please call whenever you have any questions.

Sincerely yours,

Congratulations

Dear *(Name)*:

Congratulations on purchasing the finest *(product)* on the market today—and equipped with what you need to ensure that it remains the state of the art tomorrow.

To get the full benefit of your *(product)*, please be certain to read the Owner's Manual carefully—and, remember, we're here to answer any questions you may have. Just dial 555-0000.

Cordially,

Dear *(Name)*:

Permit me to congratulate you on a wise purchase. Your new *(product)* has been designed with your complete satisfaction in mind. It is made of the finest materials and assembled with pride and care.

(Name of company) stands behind all the products we make. If you have any questions concerning *(product)*—or, in the unlikely event that you have a problem with it—just call 555-0000. We are here to help.

Sincerely,

————

Dear *(Name)*:

Congratulations! You are now in the hands of experts.

You have chosen a detail-oriented *(type of service)*, which requires no second guessing. Now you have the time you need to attend to business. Let us do the rest.

I am here to answer any questions you may have or to address any issues that come up. My direct line is 555-0000, and you may page me at 555-2222.

Thanks for your confidence. It is, I can assure you, very well placed.

Sincerely yours,

————

Dear *(Name)*:

Congratulations are in order. You have chosen to run with a winner.

We promise that we will perform for you as we have for such firms as

(list)

We pride ourselves on responsiveness to our clients' needs. During regular business hours, you may contact me personally at 555-0000. After hours and on weekends, call our Voice Mail Response System at 555-3333. It is continuously monitored, twenty-four hours a day, seven days a week. Even after hours, we will get back to you within *(time period)*.

I look forward to beginning the project on *(date)*.

Cordially,

After Sale, Before Shipment

Dear *(Name)*:

Thank you for choosing *(product)*. It will be shipped to you, no later than *(date)*, at *(address)* via *(carrier)*.

We recommend that the boxed unit be stored indoors at room temperature and humidity. Please instruct your receiving department accordingly.

If you have any questions concerning the shipment, please call 555-0000. Questions relating to installation issues should be directed to 555-3333.

Congratulations on a fine purchase.

Sincerely,

———

Dear *(Name)*:

Thank you for purchasing *(product)* from *(Name of company)*. Shipment of your unit has been scheduled for *(date)*, and it should arrive at your office on *(date)*. Please call immediately after the unit arrives, and we will dispatch one of our installers at your convenience. In the meantime, if you have any questions, please call 555-0000.

We are confident that *(product)* will meet or exceed all your expectations.

Cordially,

———

Dear *(Name)*:

Thank you for your order. We are shipping *(quantity)* *(product)* to *(address)* on *(date)* for arrival on *(date)*. Off-loading requires a minimum of *(number)* square feet of sheltered floor space. Beyond ensuring the availability of appropriate space, no further preparation is required.

Please call me at 555-0000 if you have any questions.

Sincerely,

Dear *(Name)*:

Your order of *(product)* was shipped by air on *(date 1)* via *(carrier)*. It will arrive at your *(facility)* on *(date 2)*. Please call me immediately at 555-0000 if it does *not* arrive by *(time)* on that date.

Sincerely,

Dear *(Name)*:

As you requested, I arranged with the factory to expedite your order. It should now be shipped on *(date 1)* via *(carrier)*, to arrive at your office on *(date 2)*. Our experience with this supplier has been very good, so I don't anticipate any delays. However, in the unlikely event that your order fails to arrive by *(time)* on *(date 2)*, please call me right away at 555-0000.

Sincerely,

Via Fax

Dear *(Name)*:

Your fax requesting expedited shipment of your order has just arrived. Unfortunately, we cannot ship the order on *(date 1)*, as you request. I can, however, get it out to you by *(date 2)*, which is *(number)* days ahead of our original schedule. If you authorize air shipment (at an additional charge of *([$ amount])*), the shipment will arrive at your *(facility)* by *(date 3)*.

Please call or fax by the end of the day with your reply.

Sincerely,

Shipment Delayed

Dear *(Name)*:

Many thanks for your order of *(date)*.

I'm writing to ask for a *(time period)* extension of the promised delivery date to build into the schedule additional approval time. I feel that building in the time now will avoid unpredictable delay later. If you agree, please give me your verbal okay by *(date)*. I'm at 555-0000.

Cordially,

––––––––––

Dear *(Name)*:

Thank you for your order.

My production department has just reported to me that, because of very heavy demand, they are running *(number)* days behind in filling orders. I have directed production to expedite your order, but we are still anticipating a *(number)*-day delay. This means that your order will arrive at your warehouse on *(date)*.

I am very sorry for this unavoidable delay, and I am very grateful for your understanding and patience in this matter.

If you have any questions, please call me at 555-0000.

Sincerely yours,

Welcome to Our Family

Dear *(Name)*:

Welcome to our family of clients!

Here at *(Name of company)*, we don't use the word *family* lightly. We use it because it best describes how we think of you and how we intend to do business with you: in a friendly, efficient, and considerate manner. Truly, we are not satisfied until you are completely satisfied.

Here is my direct line: 555-0000. Feel free to use it whenever you need to discuss any aspect of your account.

Cordially,

––––––––––

Dear *(Name)*:

You are now a member of our family. Welcome!

What does this mean?

It means that you'll always get first-class treatment from everyone here at *(Name of company)*. It means that you will always be welcome here in our offices, and that your voice will be a welcome sound on our telephone. It means that we will do out best never to let you down. It means that we regard your business as a long-term, enduring commitment.

If you ever feel that you are being treated as less than family, give me a call at 555-0000, and I'll make things right.

All best,

Warranty

Dear *(Name)*:

Thank you for choosing our *(product)*.

One of the very best features of *(product)* is the warranty supplied with it, which gives you full protection for *(number)* months and limited coverage for an additional *(number)* months. See your Owner's Manual for details.

But please take special note of the following: You *must* register your *(product)* to ensure that we have all necessary warranty-related information. You will find a registration card at the back of the Owner's Manual. Please take the very few moments required to fill it out and drop it in the mail to us.

Cordially,

Related Products/Services

Dear *(Name)*:

How did the *(type of presentation)* go? I'll bet your reps were wowed by the graphics we produced.

I hope that you will remember *(Name of company)* for all your future graphics needs, including our exciting interactive videos. For many of our customers, video represents the next step up in sophistication from still-frame graphics, and we would welcome the opportunity to demonstrate for you exactly what we can do. Just give me a call at 555-0000.

In the meantime—and to pique your interest—I've enclosed a brand-new video sampler. Enjoy!

And, once again, thanks for working with us.

Sincerely yours,

––––––––––

Dear *(Name)*:

I thought the *(Name of program)* seminar went very, very well. Your people were bright, attentive, and challenging—fully interactive rather than merely passive listeners. You've got a fine group of committed professionals. Thank you for giving me the opportunity of presenting my seminar to them.

As good as your people are, perhaps you have noted one area in which they show weakness. It was, to be frank, certainly apparent to me that improvement is called for in *(area)*. Here is what I believe needs working on:

(Point 1)

(Point 2)

(Point 3)

I can help here. My *(Name)* Workshop is a *(number)*-session program specifically devoted to producing significant improvement in the areas I have outlined, plus:

(Point 4)

(Point 5)

The cost is the same as for the seminar I just gave, *($ amount)* per person, and it includes all workshop materials, among which is a hefty *(number)*-page workbook/manual.

I'll call soon to see if you agree with me that your staff would benefit greatly from the workshop.

Cordially,

————————

Dear *(Name)*:

Your *(product)* is barely *(number)* weeks old, and here I am talking about what happens when you need it fixed.

Of course, you're fully covered for the coming year by one the very best, most comprehensive warranties in the business. But what happens at the end of the year?

Nothing bad—if you act now.

(Name of company) is pleased to offer extended warranty service, which will give you all the benefits of your original warranty for an addition *(number)* years. That's right, you get complete coverage for all the following:

(list)

The cost is only *($ amount)*.

What's the catch?

Only that you must enroll before *(date)* to be eligible for this low-cost extended warranty service. Enrollment is simple. Just send in the enclosed application card, and we will do the rest. If you wish, your payments can be spread over *(number)* months.

Why leave yourself unprotected?

Sincerely,

Dear *(Name)*:

I hope you remembered our anniversary.

The *(product)* you purchased from us will turn one year old on *(date 1)*. And that marks the expiration of the original product warranty.

You can, however, continue to enjoy the peace of mind that comes from full warranty protection by purchasing an extended warranty by *(date 2)*. It covers absolutely everything the original warranty covered, *plus:*

(list additional coverage)

An additional 12 months of coverage costs only *($ amount)*. You save even more by ordering 24 months of coverage at *($ amount)*. If you wish, we will bill you in quarterly installments.

(Name), you have better things to do than to worry about where to turn if your *(product)* requires repair. Why not sign up now—before *(date 2)*—while you are still eligible?

Just mail in the enclosed form. We'll do the rest.

Sincerely,

Are You Satisfied?

Dear *(Name)*:

I want to thank you for purchasing your *(product)* from my store. Your complete satisfaction is important to me; most of our customers, you see, are "regulars" or are new customers, like yourself, who have been referred to us by a "regular." You can well appreciate, then, how vital it is that we maintain a very high level of customer satisfaction.

Kindly do me the favor of completing the enclosed customer satisfaction questionnaire, so that I can continue to deliver the highest quality of service possible.

Sincerely,

Dear *(Name)*:

When you buy a *(product)* from *(Name of company)*, you are also buying service.

We have already rendered two services for you: helping you to select the right *(product)* for your needs, and installing *(product)* in your home. As part of our ongoing effort at self-evaluation and improvement, we ask that you take a few minutes to complete the enclosed quality-assurance questionnaire. It will greatly help us to serve you better.

Please return the completed form in the enclosed stamped envelope.

Sincerely,

———————

Dear *(Name)*:

You've now had just about three months of experience with your *(product)*. We are convinced that our *(products)* are the best in the industry. But, then, we work here. We gotta be convinced.

How about you?

Please let me know, personally, at 555-0000, if you've encountered and problems or have any suggestions for improvements. If you want to call just to tell us you love your *(product)*, well, that would be just fine, too.

Sincerely,

———————

Dear *(Name)*:

I've got a blunt question for you: How do you like the *(product)* we installed in *(month)*?

Is there anything we can do to improve it? Is there anything we should be doing better? Is there anything you need from us?

We want you to be 100 percent satisfied. So, please, keep in touch.

Cordially yours,

CHAPTER 7

As Ye Sow:
Creating Great Customer Relations

How to Do It

Traditional books about business communications would call the letters in this chapter "goodwill letters," and that is a pretty fair description, as far as it goes.

But it does not go far enough.

The trouble with the concept of "goodwill" is that it suggests something extra—something that is very nice, to be sure, but not essential. *Goodwill* sounds like a one-word synonym for *buttering up*.

The letters in this chapter are more important—more *essential*—than that. They address the key issues of customer service. However, there is something valuable to be learned from what is implied by *goodwill* or even *buttering up,* for that matter. Don't think about the definitions of this word and this phrase, but about their connotation. They have about them an aura of quaintness, antiquity, tradition. They connote old-fashioned qualities.

There is a good reason for this. The idea of customer service taps the deepest roots of American business practice. "Old-fashioned" does not mean "outmoded." Quite the contrary. Never have businesses put more emphasis on customer service than they do now. The wide availability of high technology has tended to level the technical and mechanical aspects of products and services. Today, the most significant differences among competing firms tend not to be in technology and price, but in the level of customer service offered.

Goodwill letters—customer service letters—are about accountability, trust, and confidence. The letters in this chapter tell your customer that the proverbial buck stops with you: the accountable, trustworthy human being who wrote the letter.

But that's not all. It used to be that business regarded customer service as a kind of necessary evil. You made a product, you sold a product, and—to a limited extent, at least—you were obliged to support the product. Contemporary business, however, has come to realize that *any* contact with customers is valuable, and they have come to regard customer service not merely as a necessity, but as a potential center of profit. Letters that help customers, that resolve complaints and problems, that transmit product-related information, that make customers aware of your company's pride, performance, and character add the kind of value to your product or service that sells more of that product or service.

The letters in this chapter deal with the following areas:

1. Apologies

2. Responses to disputes and complaints

3. Solutions to problems, answers to questions

4. Warranty and returns issues

5. Maximizing product benefits

If there is one quality that unites all these communications it is that, in essence, they are sales letters. And that includes letters that, for example, respond to customer complaints. I'm not saying that you should respond to a complaint by trying to sell the customer some other product, but that how you respond to the complaint sells your company. Nobody is happy if a product or service fails, but they are grateful to the person or organization that corrects that failure, fixes the problem, and makes things right again. All these letters, then, should be approached positively.

Something goes wrong, and a customer complains. You can:

1. Get defensive.

2. Ignore the complaint.

3. Grudgingly address the complaint.

4. Offer help.

If you want to stay in business, you'll choose option 4, and you'll frame your customer communication to make certain that he realizes you have chosen option 4. It is best to think of a complaint not as evidence that your product or service has failed, but as an opportunity to promote you and your company by offering valuable assistance. The goal of all the letters in this chapter is to impart to your customer the feeling that you and your company care about him. Nowhere is this more critical than in the letter that addresses a complaint or problem. You want your customer to come away from the encounter thinking—and telling others: "Well, I did have a problem with the widget, but Mary at Widgets Unlimited moved heaven and earth to fix it." Get your customer to think along these lines, and you've done more than fix a problem. You've sold your company.

— WORDS TO USE —

absolutely	confirmation	error
accuracy	coordinate	estimate
advantage	correct	examine
agree	customary	exchange
allow	delay gracious	expectations
alternative	delighted	expedite
angry	desirable	experience
anticipate	develop	explicitly inquiries
apology	directness	extensively
appreciate	double-check	flexibility
attention	durability	free
bargain	effective	frustration
business	efficiently	fully
carefully	effort	future
compensate	eligible	gratitude
competitive	enhance	happy
conclusion	enhancement	helpful
confidence	ensure	honestly

honor	please	review
hope	policy	satisfaction
immediate	possible	satisfactory
imperative	powerful	save
important	privilege	service
inconvenience	promise	share
inevitable	prompt	significant
information	promptly	sorry
informative	propose	suggest
miscommunication	questions	suggestion
mistake	receive	suitable
misunderstanding	recommend	test
necessary	rectify	thanks
offer	regret	unavailable
opportunity	reimburse	unavoidable
optimal	reserve	upgrade
options	resolution	upgraded
perfect	resolve	volatile
perform	responsive	wonderful
personal	responsive	

— PHRASES TO USE —

advise me on how you would like to proceed

appreciate the points you raise

appreciate your good humor

as soon as possible

at no charge

attractive price

best option

choice is yours

complete satisfaction

coordinate our resources

decision you will be happy with

direct line

dispatch a technician

earliest possible convenience

ensure that it is given prompt attention

equivalent substitute

exactly what you need

expedite delivery

express my gratitude

extend my thanks

far exceeded our expectations

formulate strategy

free estimate

full exchange value

golden opportunity

great product features

greatly value your business

happy to exchange

happy to help

I agree

I am prepared

in most cases

in accordance with the terms agreed upon

make things right

make every effort

minimize inconvenience

minimum of delay

mobilize all our forces

my attention

nominal charge

offer my apologies

100 percent satisfied

our job is to help

perfect accuracy

personal apology

personal attention

pleased to accept

prompt cash refund

quickly and accurately

rectify the error

sales agreement

scrupulously honest

service at no charge

should resolve the problem

sincere apology

sorry to hear

sorry you find that unacceptable

thank you for calling me

thoroughly test

thoroughly tested

timely and efficient

trade-in value

trouble-free

trust you will find this satisfactory

understand your confusion

up and running

what would you suggest

why not call

you have made a great choice

Apologies

FOR DELAYED SHIPMENT

Dear *(Name)*:

I bet that you're delighted with your *(product)*. And I also bet that you wish it had arrived on *(date)*, when we originally promised.

I could give you that old line about better late than never, but I don't suppose that would be very helpful. What I *will* do is offer my apologies for the delay in filling and shipping your order and also extend my thanks to you for your gracious patience and understanding.

As I mentioned to you, demand for *(product)* far exceeded our expectations, and we had to mobilize all our forces to get the orders out quickly and accurately.

Please call me if you have any questions about your *(product)*.

Sincerely yours,

———————

Dear *(Name)*:

I breathed a sigh of relief when I looked through my memos this morning and saw the confirmation that your *(product)* had been shipped. A combination of shortages from our suppliers and unusually heavy demand has torpedoed our shipping schedules. Fortunately, our suppliers are now up to speed, so I do not anticipate any delays of future orders. As for this order, I thank you very much for your patience and understanding. Especially in a very busy period, such qualities are greatly appreciated.

Sincerely,

FOR PARTIAL SHIPMENT

Dear *(Name)*:

I am very sorry that our having to make a partial shipment to you on *(date)* caused you inconvenience. We always try our best to fill orders fully and promptly, but, in a volatile industry such as ours, this is not always possible. Sometimes we do not anticipate customer demand with perfect accuracy. Sometimes we cannot obtain materials from our suppliers as readily as we would like. In the case of your shipment, we suffered from a little of both problems.

Please let me assure you that we will make every effort to prevent this from happening again. You can help us by ordering as early as possible, since the more lead time we have, the more certain it is that we will be able to ship a full order.

For the present, please let me express my gratitude to you for your patience and understanding.

Sincerely yours,

Letter Included with Balance of a Partial Shipment

Dear *(Name)*:

Here is the balance of your shipment. Your order number *(number)* is now complete.

I apologize for having had to split the shipment in this way, and I sincerely hope it caused you no significant inconvenience.

Sincerely,

Letter Included with Balance of a Partial Shipment

Dear *(Name)*:

This is the last of your order number *(number)*. It is now complete, but let's agree not to let this happen again. When you place an order, you don't want to receive it in batches. We promise to do our best to send you full orders, and you can help us in this effort by ordering as early as possible. The more lead time you can give us, the more time we have to alert our suppliers and coordinate our forces to ensure that you receive everything you want *in a single shipment*.

Cordially,

FOR SHIPPING WRONG ITEM

Dear *(Name)*:

I wanted to write you personally with my apologies for our having shipped the wrong item to you on *(date)*. I'd like to be able to offer you a good reason for our mistake, but the fact is it was nothing more or less than an unvarnished, utterly stupid error.

While I cannot offer any excuse, I can offer my promise that we will take extra care to ensure that we do not repeat the error. Just test us with another order.

I thank you for your patience in this matter.

Cordially,

———

Dear *(Name)*:

I don't have to rehearse for you the whole sad story: How you ordered *(quantity)* of *(product)*; how we shipped *(quantity)* of *(wrong product)*; how you called us about the error; and how we rushed to you an additional *(quantity)* of the *(wrong product)*.

You have every right to be steamed, and I find your grace under pressure remarkable. I am very grateful for your patience and understanding.

Please be assured that we will not let this unpleasant comedy of errors be repeated. Why not put us to the test with another order? The freight for that one will be on us.

Sincerely,

FOR SHIPPING WRONG QUANTITY

Dear *(Name)*:

I owe you an apology, but I'll start off with a riddle.

What do you do with 1,500 boxes of *(product)* when all you ordered was 150?

You ship 1,350 back to me. Not a very difficult riddle, and certainly not very funny, either!

Now the apology. I am very sorry that we added a zero to your order and gave your Receiving Department royal pain—in the head.

Come to think of it, I owe you more than a riddle or an apology. Take *(% amount)* percent off your next order—which, I can assure you, will be filled in the quantity you specify. No less—and no more!

I appreciate your understanding and good humor in this matter.

Sincerely,

Dear *(Name)*:

A good "spin doctor" would come up with a fancy phrase for what happened. But there's no such doctor in our house, so I'll tell it like it is: We messed up.

That's the long, and that's the short of it.

I would be grateful if you would accept my apologies for having shorted you on your last order. I hope that our air freighting the balance of your order minimized any inconvenience.

I am currently investigating how we could have goofed so badly, and I'll get back to you with my findings. For now, thank you for your understanding.

Sincerely,

FOR DELIVERY TO WRONG LOCATION

Dear *(Name)*:

I thank you.

I thank you for your order.

I thank you for not giving in to what must have been a very powerful impulse to scream bloody murder at me after we shipped your order to the wrong place.

I hope that our efforts to expedite transhipment from the wrong location to the right one minimized the aggravation. We will not repeat such an error. That I promise you.

Sincerely yours,

Dear *(Name)*:

The wonderful thing about shipping merchandise to the wrong address is that you get a golden opportunity to enrage *two* people with *one* mistake.

I can endure such a pleasant experience only once, however, and I can assure you that we will not repeat it. Want me to prove that? Just place another order—and the freight (to *your* door) will be on us.

Sincerely,

FOR DAMAGED SHIPMENT

Dear *(Name)*:

Nothing is more disappointing than receiving damaged goods. We make every effort to pack and ship with care, but, unfortunately, accidents do happen from time to time.

I understand that you returned the damaged item and that we shipped you a replacement on *(date)*. I trust that it arrived in satisfactory condition. If you have any questions concerning *(product)*, please give me a call at 555-0000.

I regret and apologize for any inconvenience you may have been caused.

Sincerely,

Letter Enclosed with Replacement Shipment

Dear *(Name)*:

I am very sorry that your *(product)* arrived damaged in shipment.

Please examine the enclosed replacement carefully, and I thank you for your patience and understanding.

Sincerely,

FOR BILLING ERRORS

Dear *(Name)*:

Few things are more annoying than billing errors, and I am very sorry that ours put you to the time and trouble of checking your records and writing us a letter. I apologize, and I thank you for the effort you have made to help us correct our mistake.

We are taking steps to ensure that such an error does not recur.

Sincerely yours,

———

Dear *(Name)*:

Many thanks for pointing out the error in our invoice of *(date)*. A corrected invoice is enclosed, and I hope that you will accept our sincere apology for any inconvenience our error may have caused you.

We appreciate your understanding and your business.

Cordially,

RESPONSES TO BILLING DISPUTES

Dear *(Name)*:

Thank you for your letter of *(date)*.

I appreciate the points you raise concerning the number of hours for which you have been billed, and, accordingly, I have reviewed my time sheets, copies of which are enclosed. As I believe you'll see, I performed all the services you requested and only those services. Moreover, they were completed in a timely and efficient manner.

If, after reviewing the time sheets, you still have questions, please call me at 555-0000. Otherwise, I ask that you render payment in accordance with the terms agreed upon.

Please note that, in the future, you can significantly reduce the time charged to you by sorting and classifying your records before submitting them. Most of my clients find that it is more cost-effective to presort rather than to pay me for doing that task.

Sincerely yours,

————

Dear *(Name)*:

I understand your confusion regarding the total due on our invoice number *(number)*. Note that we have carried over *($ amount)* from the previous billing and have added that to this month's invoice total, which comes to a combined total of *($ amount)*.

Please note that the previous invoice is now past thirty days due and payment would be appreciated.

If you have any further questions, please call 555-0000.

Sincerely,

————

Dear *(Name)*:

Thank you for your call concerning the payment schedule for *(name of project)*.

Our invoice for the billing period of *(date to date)* covers all the items specified in our letter of agreement dated *(date)*. While we cannot modify terms for work already performed, we can modify the remainder of the work and billing schedule, if you would like. Just call me at 555-0000, and I will be pleased to discuss the matter with you.

For the present invoice, I ask that you make payment in full at your earliest possible convenience.

Cordially yours,

Dear *(Name)*:

Thank you for your letter of *(date)* in reference to the terms of our latest invoice to you, dated *(date)*.

The finance charge that you question applies to the unpaid balance due at *(number)* days past our invoice date. As of *(date)*, *($ amount)* was outstanding and, therefore, subject to the finance charge of *($ amount)*.

If I can be of further assistance, please call me at 555-0000.

Sincerely,

Responses to Complaints

MISINFORMATION

Dear *(Name)*:

Thank you for calling me regarding what seems to have been an unfortunate miscommunication between you and *(Name)*, our salesperson.

Following our phone conversation, I discussed the matter with *(Name)*, and we concluded that the source of the miscommunication was her assumption that the *(accessory)* you ordered from her was intended for use in the updated model of our *(product)*. *(Name)* and I agreed that she should have questioned you more closely on this point before filling your order.

To rectify the error efficiently, we are sending the appropriate replacement for *(part)*, and we ask that you ship back to us within ten days the part you now have. Please ship via *(carrier)*, and we will reimburse the shipping costs without delay.

As a result of this misunderstanding, I have instructed our salespeople as follows:

1. Always to double-check and confirm potentially ambiguous orders.

2. Always to ask customers to double-check the model they own.

I apologize for any inconvenience you may have been caused, and both *(Name)* and I are grateful for your understanding and patience.

Sincerely,

Dear *(Name)*:

I thought it important to follow up my personal apology over the phone this morning with a letter. Once again, I am very sorry for having misquoted the price on *(product)*, and I assure you that the misquote was an error and not an attempt at deception.

I greatly appreciate your understanding in this matter.

Sincerely,

Dear *(Name)*:

I am very sorry that you have found your experience with us less than fully satisfactory, but I am grateful that you took the time to write to me with your comments.

I agree that we did not deliver the full measure of our customary service. A minor flu epidemic in our office has forced us to operate temporarily with a greatly reduced staff, and I am afraid that delays have been inevitable and that some phone calls have gone unreturned.

I apologize to you for this, and I should have explained our difficulties at the time. Be assured that our staffing problems have now been corrected and that we will be much more responsive to your needs in the future.

Sincerely yours,

MERCHANDISE CHRONICALLY OUT OF STOCK

Dear *(Name)*:

I can well appreciate your frustration over the repeated unavailability of *(product)*. We are frustrated as well and have communicated our feelings to the manufacturer. Let me share with you what we have learned.

(Name of company) has suspended production of *(product)* while it develops a new and enhanced model. This is expected to become available by *(date)*, at a cost comparable to the present model.

I value your business greatly. For that reason, I am attempting to track down the present model. Alternatively, you may want to wait for the enhanced version.

Please call me at your earliest convenience to let me know whether you want me to continue to search for the present model or to reserve a new model for you.

I thank you for your understanding and patience.

Sincerely yours,

WAS NOT GIVEN PRICE PROMISED

Dear *(Name)*:

When a customer feels he has not been given a square deal, I get very concerned. We at *(Name of company)* live by our word, and it is, therefore, imperative for me to resolve any misunderstandings.

Following your phone call, I spoke to the sales associate who quoted you the price you mentioned. He believes that you misunderstood him, and he pointed out to me the note he had made of the price in his memorandum book. I enclose a photocopy of the relevant page from the memorandum book, which indicates that the price offered was *($ amount 1)*, not *($ amount 2)*.

The terrible thing about misunderstandings like this is that they can quickly damage the soundest of business relationships. *(Name)*, it is not possible for us to extend a price to you that is well below our own cost. We could not stay in business operating that way. However, to make up for the misunderstanding, I am willing to sell you *(product)* for *($ amount 3)*, a price we customarily reserve for quantity purchases.

I trust you will judge this a very attractive price, and that you will accept our apologies for this misunderstanding. You may call me at 555-8000 to place an order at this price.

Sincerely yours,

UNACCEPTABLE SUBSTITUTE

Dear *(Name)*:

Thank you for your letter of *(date)* concerning your recent order.

Our experience has been that, when an ordered item is unavailable, most customers would rather accept timely delivery of an equivalent substitute than wait for the original item they ordered to become available. In view of this, we do specify on our order forms that, unless we are explicitly directed otherwise, equivalent substitutes will be shipped when necessary.

In response to your letter, I have made numerous inquiries in an effort to secure the exact item you had ordered. It is presently unavailable, and the manufacturer was unable to tell me when new production is anticipated.

In view of this, I can offer two options. Retain *(product)*, or return it to me for a full refund, and I will notify you if and when the merchandise you originally ordered becomes available.

I have enclosed a spec sheet describing the substitute item sent to you.

I hope this is of help.

Sincerely,

––––––––––

Dear *(Name)*:

I am very sorry that you find unacceptable the item we furnished as a substitute for what you had ordered. We made the substitution for two reasons:

1. The item you ordered is no longer in production and is unavailable.

2. The substitute is in every significant way equivalent to the out-of-production model.

I can offer three options to you:

1. Retain the merchandise.

2. Return it for a cash refund or full credit toward a later purchase.

3. Exercise option 2 and watch the ads for the availability of a used *(product)*. They do come onto the market from time to time.

Please call me at 555-0000 to advise me on how you would like to proceed.

Sincerely,

DISPUTE OVER MERCHANDISE RETURN

Dear *(Name)*:

Around here, "company policy" is a dirty word—two dirty words, actually. We never use the term, because the only policy we've got is a *people* policy. It's simple: We try to give our customers whatever will make them happy.

I could point out that the sales agreement you signed specifies no cash refunds. But I am more interested in retaining you as a customer than I am in adhering to the letter of our sales agreement. I will make a cash refund as soon as you have returned the merchandise in its original packaging, complete with all accessories and manuals, and in as-new condition.

I trust you will find this satisfactory and will continue to think of us for all your *(type of product)* needs.

Sincerely yours,

PRODUCT COMPLAINTS

Dear *(Name)*:

I am very sorry to learn that *(product)* has not performed to your satisfaction. I can offer two options to make things right.

I can send you a replacement *(part name)*, complete with instructions for replacing the defective part. This should resolve the problem with your unit.

Alternatively, if you prefer, you may return the entire unit to us. We will perform the part replacement and thoroughly test the unit, which will be returned to you with reimbursement for your shipping costs.

If you choose the second option, please take care to pack the unit in its original carton with all the original shipping material.

Just call me at 555-0000 to let me know which option you choose.

Sincerely,

———

Dear *(Name)*:

Thank you for your letter describing the problems you have been experiencing with *(product)*. It is apparent that your unit is defective. You may:

1. Take it to the nearest authorized dealer and describe the problem to him. Please present him with this letter and ask for in-warranty repair/replacement.

2. Pack the unit in its original carton, with all original shipping material, and return it to *(address)*, marked to my attention: *(Name)*. I will ensure that it is given prompt attention.

I am very sorry that you have been inconvenienced.

Sincerely,

———

Dear *(Name)*:

Thank you for your letter of *(date)*. Based on what you report, I must conclude that the *(product)* is not performing properly.

Please call 555-0000 to arrange for a technician to visit your office and test and service the unit. In most cases, we can dispatch a technician within twenty-four hours of your call. Please be assured that we will make every effort to get you up and running properly with a minimum of delay.

Sincerely yours,

––––––––––

Dear *(Name)*:

I have shared your letter of *(date)* with my technician, and, from the information you've furnished, we believe that the *(product)* is not defective, but that it is unsuited to the requirements of your application. For your purposes, *(alternative product)* will work far more satisfactorily. Here are our reasons for having reached this conclusion:

(list)

If you like, we would be happy to exchange the *(product)* for *(alternate product)*. The difference you would pay comes to *($ amount)*. Perhaps you would like to speak with *(Name)*, our in-house technical expert, before making your decision. His direct line is 555-0000.

Sincerely yours,

––––––––––

Dear *(Name)*:

I have been thinking over your phone call of this morning. You are quite right to be dissatisfied with the performance of *(product)*. It doesn't work very well in the kind of heavy-duty tasks you are using it for.

But don't get mad at *(product)*. Get mad at me.

I made the mistake of failing to listen carefully to your particular situation. Had I done so, I would have recommended *(alternative product)* rather than *(product)*. *(Alternative product)* provides *(% amount)* percent greater power, and that is exactly what you need.

I would be happy to rectify my negligence by offering you full value for *(product)* in exchange for *(alternative product)*. Give me a call at 555-0000, and I will arrange the exchange.

Sincerely,

Dear *(Name)*:

I understand your concerns about the durability of *(product)*, but let me assure you that *(product)* was thoroughly tested and was found to be very durable *when used as intended*.

Those last four words are crucial. *(Product)* is priced for light-to moderate-duty applications. It is not designed for the heavy-duty work you describe in your letter. We do offer a product that is more appropriate to your needs: *(alternate product)*.

Unfortunately, *(Name)*, because *(product)* failed as a result of inappropriate use, I cannot agree to a warranty repair or exchange, and if you intend to continue using it as you have been, I would not recommend repairing it, since it will assuredly break down again. Your best option is to upgrade to the *(alternate product)*. Although I cannot extend full exchange value for *(product)*, I would be pleased to accept it in trade—as is—for *($ amount)* off the price of *(alternate product)*. Just drop by the shop with it.

I hope you find this suggestion helpful.

Sincerely yours,

———————

Dear *(Name)*:

I am sorry to hear that your *(product)* failed after only *(time period)*. While I agree that this is far short of the average life expectancy of the *(product)*, it does fall well beyond the expiration date of your warranty. However, it is not my practice to cast my customers adrift. I greatly value your business, and while I cannot honor an expired warranty, I will extend to you a *(% amount)* percent discount on a new *(product)*. Drop by the store any weekday between *(time)* and *(time)* and ask for me.

Sincerely,

———————

Dear *(Name)*:

Thank you for your letter of *(date)*.

Yes, alas, you are right. Your warranty has expired. However, I also agree with you that *(product)* should last much longer than *(number)* months. You say you feel short-changed? Well, I agree with that, too.

Please bring your unit into the shop, and we will repair it for the cost of labor only. I estimate that to be *($ amount)*. There will be no charge for parts.

I hope you find this offer helpful, and I thank you for your understanding.

Sincerely,

––––––––––

Dear *(Name)*:

I was disturbed by your letter of *(date)*, in which you say that *(product)* disappointed you. Quite honestly, it is the first negative response to the product we have received. But it is important to us that each and every customer be 100 percent satisfied with what we make. Therefore, I ask that you jot down whatever suggestions you may have for improving *(product)*. Specifically: What needs to be done to bring it up to your expectations?

You may use back of this letter for your response or a separate sheet of paper.

In exchange for your taking the time to make these comments, please accept the enclosed credit memo, which is good for *($ amount)* toward the purchase of any of our products.

Please mail your response to my attention at the letterhead address.

Sincerely yours,

––––––––––

Dear *(Name)*:

Thank you for your recent letter regarding our advertising.

Let me begin by assuring you that under no circumstances do we attempt to mislead our customers. That's not good business, and we practice only good business.

After studying your letter carefully, I can only conclude that you misread our advertisement. Now, that does not suggest to me that you were careless, but that we may have to revise our advertising copy to prevent such misunderstandings in the future.

For the present, what I can offer is our apologies for the misunderstanding, and, of course, we will make available a full and prompt cash refund, if you wish. Just bring the unit—in its original carton, including all accessories—into the store during regular business hours.

Sincerely yours,

PRODUCT DID NOT PERFORM AS ADVERTISED

Dear *(Name)*:

Our company has always prided itself on informative and scrupulously honest advertising. You can appreciate, then, that I was disturbed by your recent letter.

For me, the key issue is preserving your confidence in our company. For you, of course, the key issue is satisfaction with a product that lives up to your expectations. I can offer two options toward this end:

1. You may return the merchandise for a full cash refund.

2. Alternatively, you might wish to consider the following products, which may be more suitable to your needs: *(list)*

If you wish to purchase any of these, you may exchange your *(product)* at full value.

Sincerely,

REFUND DEMAND

Dear *(Name)*:

Thank you for your letter of *(date)* requesting a refund of the purchase price of *(product)*.

I must point out to you that you purchased the *(product)* on terms that specify no cash refund. Now, this is not a matter of stubborn "company policy," but it is one of the reasons that enable us to price the *(product)* so attractively. These terms are an integral part of a good bargain, the bargain you made with us.

While I cannot, then, make a cash refund, I do want to point out that there is no need to exchange the *(product)* immediately. If you wish, you may return it for full store credit good toward any purchase now or in the future. There is no time limit on this exchange privilege.

I hope that this flexibility enables you to make a product decision you will be more happy with.

Cordially,

––––––––––

Dear *(Name)*:

The *(product)* you returned has arrived, and I enclose a check in the amount of *($ amount)*.

Now, I have a suggestion: Don't cash it. But please read on.

There is an alternative to the cash refund. If you exchange *(product)* for any other item in our catalog, I am prepared to give you a *(% amount)* percent discount on that item. Just return the check to me with your exchange order.

It's your choice.

Sincerely yours,

DEMAND FOR REPLACEMENT PRODUCT

Dear *(Name)*:

I have received your letter asking for replacement rather than repair of the *(product)* you returned.

With a product like *(product)*, which is designed as a modular system, it is neither necessary nor desirable to replace the entire unit. We identify the defective module or modules and replace only what it necessary.

Why is this a benefit to you?

A replacement unit is not tested as extensively as a unit we repair.

It is more economical to replace a single module than an entire *(product)*. Anything that saves us money allows us to remain competitive, and we are able to pass our savings on to you.

Replacing the module automatically renews the warranty on the *entire* unit. You get the same warranty period that you would have gotten with a brand-new—or replacement—unit.

I assure you that your complete satisfaction is important to us. It is the reason we are in business. We are confident that you will be entirely satisfied with the product as repaired.

Sincerely,

IRATE CUSTOMER

Dear *(Name)*:

Why *shouldn't* you be angry? The *(product)* we sold you failed—not once, not twice, but on three occasions.

You probably do not want to hear that something like this is very rare. But rare it is.

Now let me assure you that we will refund the full purchase price, if you wish. Call me at 555-0000, and I will authorize an immediate refund without further discussion.

Alternatively, let us send you a replacement and a technician to install the unit for you and to ensure that everything is operating optimally. This is a service for which we usually charge *($ amount)*. In view of your experience with *(product)*, we will perform the service at no charge.

The choice is yours. Please call me to let me know how to proceed.

Thanks for your consideration.

Sincerely yours,

Dear *(Name)*:

I'd be lying to you if I said that your recent letter didn't upset me. Nevertheless, I am grateful for the directness of your remarks. I have taken them to heart, and I am working with my staff to formulate strategies to prevent what happened to you from occurring again.

In view of this, I hope that you will reconsider your decision not to patronize us again.

Very truly yours,

———————

Dear *(Name)*:

You must be very angry and disappointed to write advising me that you intend to "warn" your friends and colleagues away from our product. To be sure, telling others not to do business with us will give you some satisfaction after a most frustrating experience.

But might I suggest a more thoroughly satisfying alternative?

Wouldn't it be more useful to allow us to work *with* you to resolve the problem?

Would you rather have a measure of revenge—or be up and running productively again?

I propose sending a technician and a replacement unit to your site. She will install the unit and ensure that it is running optimally. She will be available to talk to you about how to get the most out of the product. These services will be performed at no cost to you.

Once you are fully operational, I believe that you will be in a more advantageous position to decide on your next step.

The choice is yours. Please call me with your decision.

Sincerely,

REPLACEMENT ITEM DELAYED

Dear *(Name)*:

I apologize for the delay in shipping the replacement part you ordered. As I mentioned on the telephone this morning, it will not be available until *(date)*. I promise to do all that I can to expedite delivery and, if possible, to better that shipping date.

I will keep you informed.

In the meantime, I regret any inconvenience the delay may cause you, and I thank you for your patience and understanding.

Sincerely,

————————

Dear *(Name)*:

I'm sorry to have to tell you that the replacement of your defective *(product)* will not be available before *(date)*. This is due to an under-stocked supplier.

I regret any inconvenience this causes you, and I am grateful for your understanding in this matter.

Sincerely,

ERROR IN EXCHANGE

Dear *(Name)*:

It is certainly most frustrating to receive a defective part only to be sent the wrong part to replace it. By the time this letter reaches you, the correct part should be in your hands. However, I wanted to write to thank you for your patience and your understanding.

If you have any questions or I can be of further assistance in any way, please call me at 555-0000.

Sincerely,

Enclosure with Correct Replacement Item

Dear *(Name)*:

Here it is! And we got it right—this time.

Please accept my apology for the mix-up, and do call me at 555-0000 if you have any questions.

Sincerely,

UNSATISFACTORY SERVICE/REPAIR WORK

Dear *(Name)*:

I am sorry that you are dissatisfied with the repair work performed on your *(product)*. However, after thoroughly testing the unit, I can find absolutely no problems.

There is a slight possibility that your unit has an intermittent or transient defect, which would not necessarily show up in test results. We can proceed in two ways:

1. I can return the *(product)* to you with every expectation that it will perform properly.

2. You can leave the unit with us for *(time period)* so that we can run a continuous "burn-in" test. This takes time, but it should reveal any hidden flaw.

I'm sorry I can't offer a more certain or a faster solution.

Please call me at *(555-0000)* to advise me on how you would like to proceed.

Sincerely yours,

Register Product to Ensure Proper Activation of Warranty

Dear *(Name)*:

You've made a great choice by purchasing *(product)*. An especially valuable feature of *(product)* is its warranty. Please, if you have not done so already, fill out and return the registration card packed with *(product)*, so that we can confirm your address and other important information that will help us serve you better.

Should you have any questions about your warranty coverage, please call us at *(555-0000)*.

Sincerely,

Responses to Warranty Claims

Dear *(Name)*:

The *(product)* you returned arrived on *(date)*. Please note that the warranty on this item covers durable parts only, not wearables such as *(part)*, which has reached the end of its service cycle.

We do have a replacement *(part)* in stock and can install it at a cost to you of *($ amount)*. If you would like us to proceed, please call me at 555-0000 to authorize the repair. We will bill you for it.

Sincerely,

————————

Dear *(Name)*:

We have received your *(product)*, which you returned for warranty repair. Unfortunately, your warranty expired on *(date)*. However, we will be pleased to repair your *(product)* at a reasonable cost. If you would like us to proceed, please call us at 555-0000. The estimate is free, and we will advise you of all costs before making the repair.

Sincerely,

Dear *(Name)*:

Your *(product)* arrived at our shop for repair. Before proceeding, I wanted to make certain that you realized your warranty on this unit expired on *(date)*.

Repair work will be billed at our standard service rate of *($ amount)* per hour, inclusive of parts. You may authorize the work by phone. Estimates are made at a nominal charge of *($ amount)*, which is applicable to the cost of the repair. Dial 555-0000.

Sincerely,

———————

Dear *(Name)*:

The *(product)* you returned for warranty repair arrived on *(date)*.

I noted that the factory-sealed cover has been opened, which unconditionally voids the warranty.

I can, however, proceed with repair work at our customary rate of *($ amount)* per hour, plus parts. I would be happy to furnish a free estimate before proceeding. Just call me at 555-0000.

Sincerely,

———————

Dear *(Name)*:

I understand and appreciate your frustration with my response to your request for warranty repair of *(product)*. However, *(Name)*, what you ask really is not fair. Your warranty covers manufacturing defects, not damage caused by inappropriate use. A warranty is a guarantee of performance, not an insurance policy against abuse or accident. Indeed, perhaps your best course would be to file an insurance claim with your carrier. I would be happy to furnish a complete technical statement to whomever you designate. I can also offer to repair the unit expertly and quickly, at a reasonable price.

(Name), I am prepared to make as additional offer. If we repair the unit, I will continue your present warranty to its expiration date.

I hope that you can appreciate my position and that you will find what I can offer helpful. Please call me at 555-0000 to discuss.

Sincerely,

Maximizing Product Benefits

Dear *(Name)*:

We make *(product)* so easy to use that you've probably gotten up and running without reading the Owner's Manual. Well, I'm not here to tell you that's a bad thing. But I do want to remind you that the Owner's Manual is a very important product feature, and it was written to help you get the very most from *(product)*.

Why not give it a going over? And remember, if you have a question the manual doesn't answer, just give our Technical Service Department a call at 555-0000. We are happy to help.

Sincerely,

Dear *(Name)*:

If you're like me, you hate junk mail. That's why I'm sending you this letter. You see, *(Name of company)* makes available to its customers late-breaking news about your *(product)* and *(Name of company)*'s other great products. We think you'll want to know about these. But we refuse to send you mail you do not want. Therefore, if you would rather **NOT** be put on our regular mailing list, please tear off the card at the bottom of this letter, sign it, and return it.

If, however, you **DO** want to be kept informed, do nothing. We'll keep you updated.

Sincerely,

Dear *(Name)*:

You paid plenty for *(product)*, and we think you should be getting a lot more out of it.

Here's how.

We have a full range of technical bulletins available on such topics as:

(list)

Why not call 555-0000 to order the bulletins you need? There is no cost for this service.

Sincerely,

———————

Dear *(Name)*:

The time has come.

Your *(product)* is designed for years of trouble-free service, as long as you provide an important minimal level of maintenance.

Our records indicate that you purchased *(product)* on *(date)*. It is now time to service *(parts)*. We recommend that you make an appointment with us at 555-0000 for this important maintenance procedure.

Approximately *(% amount)* percent of the customer service requests we receive are due to failure to perform simple, quick, and inexpensive routine maintenance. Save money, downtime, and frustration by bringing your unit in soon.

Sincerely,

Notice Inserted with Product

Dear Customer:

Our job is to help you. All you have to do is pick up the phone and dial 555-0000.

But not yet!

Before you spend your valuable time with us, take a look through your User's Manual. Most of the time, the answer you need is right there.

Sincerely,

Notice Inserted with Product

Dear Customer:

Yes, you're right. The purposes of registering your *(product)* is to get your name on our mailing list.

And here are three great reasons for putting your name there:

1. It ensures that we have all necessary warranty-related information.

2. It allows you to receive upgrade and other product news bulletins.

3. It makes you eligible for special offers.

Why miss out on three great product benefits? Register today by filling out the attached card and dropping it into the nearest mailbox. We'll do the rest.

Sincerely,

Where Credit Is Due: Writing Letters to Manage Customer Credit Issues

How to Do It

Letters dealing with credit matters should be simple, right? They are, after all, a matter of numbers. Here is your line of credit in dollars and cents. Here are the terms of payments. And so on. Well, maybe that approach will work—when you are responding to a customer credit request by giving him all the credit he wants and on all the terms he desires. But what happens when you have to extend less credit than requested? Or when you must decline credit? You must develop strategies for writing letters that set sane credit limits—or even decline credit—without alienating your customer. But even in the case of wholly positive letters, it is important not to pass up an opportunity to establish or strengthen your bond with your customer.

The key element in such constructive communication is creating a friendly tone. For many businesspeople, this is more difficult than one might think. Many believe friendliness is inconsistent with professionalism. Others feel that the customer will even be put off by overfamiliarity. And how can you be friendly when you are telling a customer that you cannot oblige his credit request?

Establishing a friendly tone has less to do with affection than with recognizing that, when you do business with a customer, you and he are partners. You're in the enterprise together. Begin, then, with simple courtesy. It is usually possible to begin letters with thanks—for placing an order, for applying for credit, and so on—and it is usually possible to end your letter by offering assistance, even if that offer is nothing more than an initiation to call. In between these two points of courtesy, demonstrate to the customer that you are doing your best to furnish what was requested.

Approach credit-related letters in the knowledge that you are not *giving* your customer something so much as you are *enabling* the customer to give *you* his business. Don't fall all over yourself with humble gratitude—after all, you are giving the customer full value in return—but do make it clear that you appreciate the business. If you must give the customer less than he requested, explain the basis for your decision. A partner owes a partner an explanation. Never take refuge in such monolithic concepts as "company policy" or "regulations." Doing so will—quite rightly—drive the customer to seek a company with different "policies" and "regulations." Instead, reveal your decision as a product of human reasoning. Moreover, to whatever degree it is possible to do so, provide room for reconsideration and reevaluation at a later—if possible, specific—time and under specific conditions: *We can give you X amount of credit now. But, after we see your financial statements for the next two quarters, we hope to be able to extend your credit line to Y amount.*

— WORDS TO USE —

accommodate	choose	directly
agree	chose	eager
agreement	community	early
alternative	confident	ensure
alternatively	convenience	enthusiastically
application	convenient	establish
appreciate	current	experience
appropriate	customer	extend
approve	customize	facilitate
arrangement	deadline	favor
believe	delighted	flexibility
best	deliver	generous
choice	direct	goal

great	personal	request
guarantee	plan	requirements
happy	please	respond
help	pleasure	review
helpful	possible	rewarding
history	postpone	schedule
honest	prepared	service
immediate	privilege	settle
interested	profitable	sincerely
invite	prompt	suggestion
issue	propose	tailor
let's	proud	thanks
manage	provide	update
margin	ready	value
negotiated	reapply	viable
oblige	reasonable	we
opportunity	reconsider	welcome
option	references	workable
overhead	relationship	

— PHRASES TO USE —

agreed to verbally	I will
at this time	I wish that I could
be assured	in a position to
cannot afford	in order to make it possible
cash flow	limited resources
credit record	look forward
current obligations	manage cash flow
earliest convenience	mutually profitable
financial situation	net terms
give it another try	open accounts
greatest value	personal attention
I can	please take a few minutes
I hope	promising future

slow payment	we feel
terms and conditions	welcome to our family
thanks for responding	will see to it that
thanks for your order	wish it were possible
too heavily obligated	without excuses
unconditionally guarantee	work together

Soliciting Financial Information

Dear *(Name)*:

Many thanks for your recent order. We plan to ship it on *(date)*. It is always a pleasure to welcome a new customer.

Now I would like to ask you a favor. Please send me copies of your financial statements for *(period required)* so that, as you requested, I can set up a line of credit for you in order to make it easier for us to fill what I hope will be many more orders.

Cordially,

Dear *(Name)*:

Many thanks for your order dated *(date)* for *(quantity)* of our *(merchandise)*. We're proud that you chose *(Name of company)*, and we will see to it that your order is shipped by *(date)*, as you requested.

Since you also indicated that you intend to order from us on a regular basis, I'm sure you will find it convenient to set up a line of credit. Let me ask a favor of you before we fill your next order. Please take a few minutes now to send us a copy of your latest financial statement, which will ensure ready credit with us and prompt, personal attention to all future orders.

Why not mail the statement today? Once again, thank you for your order.

Sincerely,

Dear *(Name)*:

Thank you for your letter of *(date)*, requesting a line of credit with us. In order to make it possible for us to oblige you, we need copies of your financial statements for *(period required)*. You may send these directly to me in the return envelope enclosed for your convenience.

All of us at *(Name of company)* look forward to doing business with you.

Sincerely yours,

———————

Dear *(Name)*:

Many thanks for your order. I look forward to a long and mutually profitable relationship with you, and, therefore, I invite you to open up a line of credit with *(Name of company)*, which will make doing business more convenient for both of us.

To get things started, all we need are copies of your financial statements for *(period required)*, which you may send directly to me in the return envelope enclosed. Please call me directly at 555-0000 if you have any questions.

Sincerely,

———————

Dear *(Name)*:

It is always a great pleasure and privilege to welcome a new customer! You asked about our credit policy. We will be happy to set up a line of credit for you subject to our review of your financial statements for *(period required)*. Please send copies of these directly to my attention, and I will see to it that you are given a prompt decision.

Sincerely,

Extending Credit—and Setting Credit Limits

Dear *(Name)*:

I am delighted to respond to your application for credit. At this time, we are prepared to extend to you a line of credit of *($ amount)*, subject to the following terms, as stated on the application form:

(state terms)

Your current order was shipped on *(date)*.

Welcome to our family of credit customers!

Cordially,

————

Dear *(Name)*:

I am delighted to respond to your application for credit. At this time, we are prepared to extend to you a line of credit of *($ amount)*, subject to the following terms, as stated on the application form:

(state terms)

Your financial statements indicate a healthy business with a promising future. However, we do have to weigh this against the fact that you have been in operation only eighteen months. Once you have crossed the two-year mark, let's review your updated statements and see if we can extend a more generous line.

Based on your current statements, I am confident that we can!

I look forward to your next order.

Cordially,

————

Dear *(Name)*:

Thank you for your application for a credit line of *($ amount)*.

I am prepared at this time to set up for you a line of *(lesser $ amount)*, and I wish that I could oblige with the full amount you requested. However, your financial statements suggest that you are presently too heavily obligated for us to add to that burden beyond *($ amount)*. I suggest that you send us your next quarter's financial statement, and, based on this—together with your payment record, of course—we will review your credit line with an eye toward increasing it as much as we possibly can.

I hope that you find this helpful, and we appreciate your business.

Sincerely,

––––––––––

Dear *(Name):*

I am pleased to set up for you *($ amount)* credit, subject to the following terms and conditions:

(state terms and conditions)

I am confident that you will find that this arrangement makes it more convenient to do business with us.

At your option, you may send us your next quarter's financial statement, and, based on this (together with your payment record, of course), we will review your credit line with an eye toward increasing it.

I look forward to a long and mutually profitable relationship.

Sincerely,

––––––––––

Dear *(Name):*

Thank you for your application for a credit line of *($ amount)*. I'm happy to set up for you a line of *(lesser $ amount)* and only wish that we could oblige you at this time with the full amount requested. However, since you have only been in business since *(date)*, we feel that *(lesser $ amount)* is a more appropriate starting figure.

Let's review financial statements for your next two quarters with the goal of getting closer to the amount you requested.

I look forward to doing business with you.

Sincerely yours,

Declining Credit Without Turning Off Your Customer

Dear *(Name)*:

Thank you for applying for credit with *(Name of company)*.

At this time, your credit record shows a history of slow payment, and, given your current obligations, we feel that it is appropriate to postpone acting on your request for *(time period)* in order to give you the time required to catch up on your open accounts.

For the immediate future, of course, we are delighted to serve you on a payment-with-order basis.

Sincerely,

————

Dear *(Name)*:

Thank you for your interest in *(Name of company)* and your application for credit with us.

Because you have only recently established your business, and in view of our own limited resources, we need a little more experience with you as a "pay-as-you-go" customer before we can set up a line of credit. My suggestion is that you reapply in *(number)* months, after we've worked together for a while on a cash basis.

In the meantime, please be assured that *(Name of company)* will give you the very best prices and service in the industry. We appreciate your business, and we look forward to helping you establish yourself in our community.

Cordially,

Dear *(Name)*:

Thanks for order, which we will ship on *(date)*.

We would very much like to work with you to set up a line of credit; however, the financial statements you furnished at our request indicated that you are at present undercapitalized. This, we believe, would make it difficult for you to meet payments on our terms.

My suggestion is that you find a person or firm to guarantee your open account with us. That would allow us to serve your credit needs as you become increasingly well established.

Alternatively, we invite you to continue working with us on a cash basis and reapply for credit within *(time period)*.

Sincerely,

Dear *(Name)*:

It was great to receive your order of *(date)* and to find that you are still interested in working with us. As you may recall, the last time you placed an order with us, we had some difficulty collecting payment and ultimately had recourse to a collection agency.

That, however, was *(number)* years ago, and conditions certainly do change. We'd be pleased to give it another try. We do ask that you send us a copy of your most recent financial statement and that you provide three current credit references.

In the meantime, we would appreciate your payment in full for the current order, which we will ship promptly on receipt of payment.

Sincerely,

Dear *(Name)*:

I've got a problem. You have applied to us for credit, but, try as I might, I cannot find a way to add you to our list of credit customers at the present time. Your financial statement and your credit record for the past *(time period)* won't allow me to oblige you. Neither of us will benefit by my adding to your present outstanding debts.

So why is this *my* problem?

I value your business, and I don't want to lose you as a customer.

(Name), it's been a hard year for all of us, and as soon as your financial situation turns around, I invite your reapplication for credit. In the meantime, I ask that you continue to consider us as a supplier on a cash-with-order basis.

Sincerely,

Negotiating Credit Terms

Dear *(Name)*:

Many thanks for responding so promptly to our bid on *(project)*.

I wish it were possible for me to accommodate the payment schedule you propose, but our cash flow requirements will not allow us to do so on this cash-intensive project.

Let me suggest two alternatives:

1. Spread the payments as you now propose, but increase the first three payments by *(% amount)* percent, making them *($ amount)* each.

2. Adhere to the payment schedule we originally proposed, but reduce the first two payments by *(percent amount)*, making them *($ amount)* each. Increase the last two payments by *(% amount)* percent over our original figures, making them *($ amount)* each, which includes a modest *(% amount)* percent carrying charge.

Either alternative will facilitate cash flow for *both* of us and will allow you to take immediate delivery on the merchandise.

I'm eager to do business. Please give me a call at 555-0000.

Cordially,

_____

Dear *(Name)*:

Thank you for your response to our bid on *(project)*. Since the work is naturally divided into *(number)* stages, it seemed reasonable to schedule payments accordingly, which would manage cash flow for both of us while giving you ample opportunity to review and approve each stage before proceeding to the next.

I am, then, sorry that you find these terms unacceptable. Let me assure you that your business is highly valuable to us, and I am eager to reach a viable alternative—but, to be honest, I can't think of anything more workable than what I have proposed. Therefore, I invite you to make a counterproposal—perhaps even more than one.

I look forward to hearing from you at your earliest convenience.

Sincerely yours,

————

Dear *(Name)*:

Now that we've agreed on a price, let's see how quickly we can agree on a payment schedule.

We proposed four payments over four months. You want eight payments over eight months. The problem with what you propose is that it puts half your payments beyond the completion date of the project. We are not in a position to carry that kind of overhead. However, we can live with a six-month schedule, the last two payments to include a modest *(% amount)* percent finance charge.

I hope this will give you the flexibility you require. We need to get under way within the next *(number)* days in order to meet your production deadlines.

Sincerely,

————

Dear *(Name)*:

I'm pleased that we're agreed on a price for *(project)*, but I cannot accommodate your request for ninety-day net terms. That amounts to more free financing than we can carry. The alternative I suggest is thirty days net terms, with a nominal *(percent figure)* finance charge on the unpaid balance starting past thirty days. The entire balance, plus the finance charge, will fall due at 120 days.

This arrangement will give us both the flexibility we need. You can extend your payment schedule, and we don't have to cut into an already slim margin.

I look forward to hearing from you and getting the project under way.

Sincerely yours,

Acceptance of Credit Terms

Dear *(Name)*:

We're ready to move!

Enclosed is a copy of our letter of agreement, which incorporates the terms we agreed to verbally on *(date)*. Please sign both copies and return them to me.

It is a pleasure doing business with you.

Best regards,

———

Dear *(Name)*:

This letter, when countersigned by you, constitutes our agreement to the terms of payment for *(product/service)*. As we agreed on *(date)*, the terms are as follows:

(state terms)

If you have any questions, please call me at 555-0000.

I look forward to a long and mutually profitable relationship.

Sincerely,

———

Dear *(Name)*:

It is a pleasure to confirm our agreement to the terms of payment for the *(product/service)* we discussed on *(date)*. You can be confident that we will deliver everything we promised, on time and without excuses.

We look forward to serving you.

Sincerely yours,

————————

Dear *(Name)*:

We're already to begin. A copy of our letter of agreement is enclosed. Please sign both copies and return them to me.

I look forward to a rewarding relationship.

Cordially,

Rejecting Proposed Credit Terms

Dear *(Name)*:

I am pleased that we have reached agreement on prices and delivery dates; however, I am not in a position to offer much flexibility on the schedule of payments.

In a materials-intensive business like ours, cash flow is crucial to accommodate the production schedule you have proposed. Either we need more lead time or you must reconsider the payment terms you have proposed.

Please call me to discuss this final issue.

Sincerely yours,

————————

Dear *(Name)*:

Having agreed on prices and a delivery schedule, I am distressed that we have been unable so far to come to terms on the schedule of payments.

As eager as I am to do business with you on this project, I cannot accept your most recent offer. Why not? The answer is simple: I cannot afford to carry those kinds of costs. You could, of course, turn to a bigger supplier. However, you've come to a small company for the personal service we offer, and I don't think you want to give that up.

(Name), we are so close to a deal that it would be a shame to throw in the towel now. Won't you call me at your earliest convenience to talk this matter over and resolve it?

Let's work together.

Best regards,

————

Dear *(Name)*:

I sincerely wish I were in a position to accept the payment terms you propose. Unfortunately, I am not in that position.

You made a deliberate choice in coming to a small company: to get the personal, efficient, customized service that the bigger suppliers simply cannot deliver. As a small company, however, we do not have access to the kind of funding sometimes available to larger firms. I can unconditionally guarantee that the level of service we deliver will give you the greatest value for your dollars—but the fact is that we must have those dollars on a schedule that will keep us in business.

Let's settle this issue with a phone call. Give it some thought, then call me early next week. I'm confident that we can work this out together.

Sincerely yours,

————

Dear *(Name)*:

I guess there are just some things that are not meant to be. We've negotiated long and in good faith, and, sadly, I must concur with you: We are just too far apart on this one.

I am confident, however, that we can find another project, on another occasion, on which we can come to a happier conclusion. Certainly, I remain enthusiastically interested in working with you, and I trust that you will consider *(Name of company)* in the future.

Sincerely yours,

Let My Money Go: Securing Prompt Payment and Collecting on Delinquent Accounts

How to Do It

Making money is one thing. Collecting the money you've supposedly "made" is another. We hear a lot of people talking about "the good old days," when ten- or thirty-day net terms "really meant something." You identified a prospect, you talked to him, you sold him your product, and he sent you your money. I'm not sure it was *ever* this simple, but the fact is that, "these days," you go through the first part of the process—identifying a prospect, talking to him, selling him the product—and then you wait and wait and wait for your money. It used to be possible to divide customers into those who paid on time, those who were delinquent, and those who were plain-and-simple deadbeats. Nowadays, even your best customers routinely let invoices slide past 30, 60, even 90 and 120 days.

There are plenty of books on the market dealing with collections. Doubtless, many of these are quite good. It's the *subject* that stinks. Collections is a dirty, dreary, thankless business. In our society, the debtor holds most of the cards. You can threaten (without being abusive), you can call your lawyer, you can even sue. But, when all is said and done, the biggest stick you can use against a delinquent account beats you into the ground along with him: *You won't pay. All right. I won't allow you to do business with me anymore!*

In view of this, the following could be a very short chapter, beginning and ending with the phrase: *Just kiss it goodbye.*

But the situation need not be so gloomy.

The trouble with most approaches to collections is that they are reactive rather than proactive. The phone calls and collection letters start *after* the account is delinquent. The proverbial barn door is shut after the proverbial horse has galloped out. A far more effective strategy is to make cash flow a management priority, not a function of damage control. Intervene in cash flow situations before they become crises. Think of collections correspondence as a continuum, a cycle, not a letter or two you fire off when it is—literally—too late. Use collections correspondence not only to repair a malfunctioning account, but to maintain it in the first place.

How to do it?

Consider sending a letter or an insert with your first invoice or—even sooner—with the project proposal. Use this opportunity to offer an incentive to prompt payment—a modest discount, perhaps, a waiver of handling charges, whatever.

Send the first reminder early. But study the models in this chapter carefully. The first reminder should not be an annoying nudge, let alone a veiled threat. It should be informational, presented as a positive service to the customer.

Once an account begins to fall into disrepair, offer your help in fixing it. That's right: *your help.* The most significant secret your delinquent account has is that he *wants to pay.* True, few people or businesses enjoy parting with money, but fewer still relish *owing* a debt. More than likely, your delinquent account would pay you if he could. He wants to. But, for one reason or another, he either cannot or he perceives that he cannot. Communicate with him your willingness to help make it possible for him to pay you.

— WORDS TO USE —

able	expect	program
accommodate	expedite	promised
active	extending	prompt
advantage	fair	promptly
advise	features	proposal
allow	force	proud
appreciate	forced	quality
appropriate	frank	reasonable
assist	friendly	refund
assistance	glitch	reliable
assume	guaranteed	reminder
assured	happy	resolve
attention	help	response
benefit	immediate	satisfaction
budget	important	save
choice	inquiry	savings
choose	investment	scheduled
communicate	invite	service
communication	invited	significant
compel	issue	solve
compelled	latest	special
competitive	maintain	specified
confident	modify	standard
confidential	mutual	substantial
convenience	necessary	talked
cooperate	opportunity	today
cooperation	option	understand
creating	owe	unpaid
current	payment	value
custom	personal	vital
delinquent	pleased	waive
dependable	pleasure	willing
discount	possible	
easier	problem	

— Phrases to Use —

account back on track

added value

alternative payment options

appreciate your business

avoid these charges

bear in mind

best value possible

continue providing

continue serving you

credit privileges

direct line

discount program

establish a pattern of prompt payment

finance charge

formulate a payment plan we both can live with

great customer

happy to hear from you

help us avoid

highest level

in business together

in good standing

legal counsel advises

letter of agreement

making it possible

mutual satisfaction

no additional costs

no hidden charges

not too late

not carved in stone

offer will be good

packed with terrific features

partial payment

payment cycle

payment plan

payment schedule

personal attention

please help

prompt response

prompt payment

remains unpaid

save yourself money

send your payment today

seriously delinquent

seriously past due

service and value

service charges

settle this account

settling the outstanding balance

small-company service

special offer

subject to an additional charge

substantial savings

suffer a blemish on your credit record

suspend your credit

take advantage

thank you for paying promptly

we work hard

without delay

you may reduce

With Bids or Proposals

Dear *(Name)*:

As I promised, here are the prices for the *(products)* you ordered:

(list)

Please bear in mind that these prices include all freight and handling. There are no additional or hidden costs—based on our thirty-day terms. All unpaid balances beyond thirty days are subject to a *(% amount)* service charge. Please help us maintain our low prices by paying promptly.

Sincerely,

————

Dear *(Name)*:

Thank you for your inquiry about *(products)*. I've enclosed our latest price list, which is good through *(date)*.

Our products come packed with many terrific features, and one of the best is a built-in *(% amount)* discount for making payment within ten days after you receive the shipment. It's an added product benefit and our way of thanking you for making our financial lives easier.

To place an order—or to ask questions—please call me on my direct line: 555-0000.

Sincerely yours,

————

Dear *(Name)*:

Many thanks for giving us the opportunity to bid on *(project)*. We appreciate the opportunity, and we are confident that the prices listed below will make you quite happy:

(list)

Good as these prices are, you can make them even lower. We offer a *(% amount)* discount on all accounts paid within ten days of our invoice date. That's a substantial savings to you. The choice is yours.

These prices are guaranteed through *(date)*, and I am ready, willing, and able to expedite your order. Use my direct line: 800-555-0000.

Sincerely yours,

————

Dear *(Name)*:

It is my pleasure to submit our proposal for *(project/service)*. I am confident that you will be pleased with our prices and, more important, that you will be pleased with the value these prices represent. At *(Name of company)*, we specialize in giving our clients a service and value edge—and that begins right now. I invite you to take a *(% amount)* discount on all charges when you pay within ten days of our invoice date. We think you should get something for making it easier for us to continue providing the very highest level of service and quality.

Please call me at 555-0000 if you have any questions.

Sincerely yours,

————

Dear *(Name)*:

I am very pleased to send our proposal in response to your RFP # *(reference number)*, and while I am fully aware of the caliber of competing suppliers, I am confident that you will find that we offer not only the best prices, but the very best value for your investment.

As good as our prices are, you have the option of making them even better. We offer a *(% amount)* discount for accounts paid within *(number)* days of our invoice date. It is our policy to cooperate with our clients in keeping costs down.

I look forward to your response to the proposal and can be contacted at my direct line: 555-0000.

Sincerely yours,

Dear *(Name)*:

It was a pleasure creating the enclosed proposal for you. I have little to say by way of introduction, since our low prices speak for themselves.

We work hard to offer more than our competition does—lower prices and higher value, of course, but also the opportunity for you to decide how much you want to pay.

The prices listed are based on 30-day net terms. If, however, you choose to pay in full within 5 days of our invoice date, you may discount *(% amount 1)* percent from the invoice total. If you send payment after 5 days but before 15, you are invited to subtract *(% amount 2)*. And if you render payment within 20 days, you are still entitled to a *(% amount 3)* discount.

The choice is yours.

Please call me at 555-0000 when you are ready to discuss the proposal further or to proceed with it.

Sincerely yours,

Cover Letters to Accompany Invoices

Dear *(Name)*:

It has been our pleasure to serve you. Our invoice (# *[number]*) is enclosed, and allow me to remind you that you are entitled to a *(% amount)* discount from the total due as our thanks to you for prompt payment. You may take advantage of the discount by choosing to pay the balance in full no later than *(date)*.

Please call me at 555-0000 if you have any questions or comments. I'd be happy to hear from you.

Once again, thanks. Be assured that we look forward to serving you again.

Sincerely,

Dear *(Name)*:

Our invoice *(number)* for *(goods or services)* is enclosed.

I just want to remind you of our special program aimed at saving you money. Subtract *(% amount)* from the total due when you send your payment by *(date)*. There's no secret about the fact that prompt payment benefits us. Why shouldn't it benefit you, too?

We really appreciate it.

It has been a pleasure serving you, and we look forward to doing so again. I am available at my direct line, 555-0000, if you have questions or comments.

Sincerely yours,

Inserts to Accompany Invoices

It's *not* carved in stone!

Take *(% amount)* off the invoice total for paying in full within ten days of invoice date.

Thank you for paying promptly!

———————

Dear Customer:

Don't forget! We invite you to subtract *(% amount)* from the total due if your payment is postmarked within ten days of our invoice date.

It's our way of thanking you for prompt payment.

Sincerely,

———————

(Name of company)

IT PAYS TO PAY PROMPTLY

There are two totals indicated on the enclosed invoice.

The first is the price we originally quoted you. The second—which represents a *(% amount)* discount from that price—is what you pay if you send payment in full within ten days of our invoice date.

It is our way of giving you added value—and thanking you for paying promptly.

Letters to Prevent Payment Problems
(Send these letters two weeks after invoicing customer.)

Dear *(Name)*:

Since this is the first time we've done business together, I thought you might appreciate a reminder about our special discount program for prompt payment. As mentioned on your invoice, we give a *(% amount)* discount for payment received within ten days of our invoice date.

Well, I'm not just writing to tell you that your ten days are up. They are—but because you are a new customer, we'd like to accommodate you by extending that discount period. Send us payment in full by *(date)*, and we invite you to take that *(% amount)* discount.

Sincerely,

———————

Dear *(Name)*:

It takes some nerve to send a payment reminder just two weeks after invoicing! But, despite appearances, I'm not doing that.

Your account is 30 days net, and payment is not due until *(date)*. I do want to point out, however, that you have not taken advantage of our offer of a *(% amount)* discount for payment made within 10 days of our invoice date. That offer will apply on the next order you place with us, so you may want to consider taking advantage of it—next time.

Better yet, if you send payment on the present order by *(date)*, you can still take *(lesser % amount)* off the present order. If your payment is already on the way, I'll send you a check for the difference.

We are *determined* to save you cash.

Sincerely,

————

Dear *(Name)*:

We're sorry to tell you that you've just paid more than was necessary for your recent order with us.

It's not that we made a mistake, but that you chose not to take advantage of the *(% amount)* discount we offer on accounts paid within 10 days of our invoice date.

Although more than 15 days have passed from the date of the present invoice, be assured that the offer will be good on your next order.

Sincerely,

————

Dear *(Name)*:

Here's a friendly reminder that after *(date)* finance charges will begin to accrue on the payment due us for *(products)* shipped to you on *(date)*.

Why not avoid these charges by sending your payment today?

Sincerely,

————

Dear *(Name)*:

Just a note to call to your attention the fact that your account with us will reach the 30-day mark on *(date)*. To avoid scheduled service charges, you have the option of paying the account in full before *(repeat date)*.

Sincerely yours,

Letters to Marginally Slow Accounts

Dear *(Name)*:

Thank you for your payment, which we received on *(date)*. Please note that, while your account is in good standing, your payment was sent *(number)* days after the *(date)* due date and is therefore subject to a service charge of *($ amount)*, which is payable with your next installment on *(date)*.

Please make the next payment by no later than *(date)* to avoid an additional service charge.

Sincerely yours,

Dear *(Name)*:

I could sure use your help.

You have been a great customer for *(time period)*, and that is why I feel I can speak to you frankly. Please take a look at your recent pattern of payment:

(order #) (date payment due) (date payment received)

(order #) (date payment due) (date payment received)

(order #) (date payment due) (date payment received)

(etc.)

As you can see, the payments are not terribly late, but they are consistently late, and your account certainly remains in good standing. However, it would help us to serve you better if you would modify your invoice payment schedule to get the payments in on or before the date due.

If I can assist you in making it possible for you to create the necessary adjustments, please give me a call at 555-0000. I appreciate your attention to this matter.

Sincerely yours,

Cover Letters with Second Invoice: Accounts Past Thirty Days

Dear *(Name)*:

With all you have to do, it's so easy to forget.

Your account with us is now past due 30 days and subject to a *(% amount)* finance charge.

But, as I said, it's so easy to forget. Since you are a new customer—with whom we look forward to doing years of business—we would like to take this opportunity to waive the finance charge if we receive payment in full by *(date)*.

Please call me on my direct line at 555-0000 if you have any questions.

Sincerely,

———

Dear *(Name)*:

Things are starting to get pretty chilly—here on your back burner.

Your 30-day net account with us has gone past 30 days and is now subject to a *(% amount)* finance charge.

I thought that this offer might heat things up a bit: Send us your check today for *($ amount)*, and we will waive the finance charge, saving you *($ amount)*. Payment must be received by *(date)*.

Please call me at telephone 555-0000 if you have any questions.

Sincerely,

Dear *(Name)*:

A friendly note to advise you that your account with us is past due 30 days and is now subject to a service charge of *($ amount)*. You can still avoid an additional service charge of *($ amount)* by paying the account in full no later than *(date 2)*.

But why wait until then? If we receive your payment by *(date 1)*, you may reduce the currently due service charge to *($ amount)* and pay a total of only *($ amount)*.

Please call me at 555-0000 if you have any questions.

Sincerely,

————

Dear *(Name)*:

WAIT JUST A MINUTE! YOU ARE PAYING US TOO MUCH!

At least, I hope you were about to.

(Name), your account with us has now passed the 30-day mark, which means that it is subject to a *($ amount)* service charge.

Because you are a brand-new customer, I'd like to make you a special offer. Pay the account in full by *(date)*, and we will waive the service charge on this invoice only. After *(date)*, the account is subject to the normal schedule of service charges as specified in our letter of agreement.

If you've already sent your payment, including the service charge, I'll write you a refund check for the difference.

Give me a call me at 555-0000 if you have any questions.

Sincerely yours,

Invoice Inserts for Accounts Past Thirty Days

Dear Customer:

Because your account has gone unpaid for more than thirty days, this statement includes a *(% amount)* finance charge. Please pay the full balance due by *(date)* to avoid additional finance charges.

Thank you.

(Name of company)

Dear Customer:

The invoice total includes our standard finance charge for accounts unpaid beyond thirty days. Paying the full balance due by *(date)* will avoid additional finance charges.

Thank you.

(Name of company)

Dear *(Name)*:

Please, don't let us slip between the cracks!

Your account with us has gone beyond our 30-day terms. Won't you, please, mail a check for *($ amount)* today?

Please direct any questions or comments to me personally at 555-0000.

Sincerely yours,

Dear *(Name)*:

You are a great customer, and when a great customer misses a payment due, there's always a significant reason: sickness, cash flow difficulties, even dissatisfaction with goods or services.

Now that the balance due on your account has passed the 30-day mark, isn't it time we talked? If there is a problem, I am confident that we can solve it quickly and to our mutual satisfaction. Please let me hear from you. My direct line is 555-0000. You may, if you wish, leave a confidential message on my voice mail.

Sincerely yours,

Dear *(Name)*:

Enclosed is a duplicate of our *(date)* invoice.

Please note that your payment is now well past our 30-day net terms. We therefore anticipate your immediate payment.

Sincerely,

———————

Dear *(Name)*:

I'm not nervous or worried. All you have to do is place another order, and you'll see that we'll ship it out as promptly as always. But, *(Name)*, it does take money to pay our bills, and that's why I'm writing to remind you that your account has gone beyond our 30-day terms.

You can help us control costs and continue to deliver the best value possible by sending your check today.

All the best,

———————

Dear *(Name)*:

It is always a pleasure to serve you, and we are grateful for your business. However, as the enclosed statement indicates, the outstanding balance on your account is now more than thirty days old. We base our prices on receiving payment in full within thirty days. You can help us maintain low prices and high value by sending the full balance due today.

If you are unable to render full payment now, we would appreciate your calling so that we can agree upon a payment plan.

Sincerely,

Missing an Installment Payment

Dear *(Name)*:

We have not received your payment of *($ amount)*, which was due on *(date)*. It is important that you keep your account with us current. Please use the enclosed envelope to send your payment today.

Your prompt response is greatly appreciated.

Sincerely,

———————

Dear *(Name)*:

A payment of *($ amount)* was due on *(date)*. Please use the enclosed envelope to send us a check today. If you have any questions, please call me at 555-0000 today.

Thanks for responding without delay.

Sincerely,

Serious Delinquency: Past Sixty Days

Dear *(Name)*:

You are about to add *($ amount)* to what you already owe us. It doesn't have to be that way.

If you put your check for *($ amount)* in the mail today, you will avoid a combined service charge of *($ amount)*. It's your call.

Sincerely,

Dear *(Name)*:

You are a very busy person, and, with all you have to do, it's easy to let a bill slip by—even one that's already more than two months old. So I thought you'd appreciate this reminder:

Please send us a check for *($ amount)* today to avoid a finance charge *($ amount)*.

If you have any questions about your account, please give me a call at 555-0000.

Sincerely,

———————

Dear *(Name)*:

Would you be willing to help us out?

Think about it: One of the reasons you do business with us is that we are a small firm geared to deliver a high level of very personal attention.

That's the good part about being small.

The not-so-good part is developing the discipline to operate on a budget lean enough to keep us more than competitive with the bigger firms. Maintaining adequate cash flow is vital to this discipline, and our price to you was based on thirty-day payment terms. *(Name)*, it has been almost sixty days since we invoiced you, and your account remains unpaid.

Help us to continue providing great small-company service at prices you can afford. Please send us your check for *($ amount)* today.

If you have any questions, I'm here to help *you*. Just call 555-0000.

Sincerely,

———————

Dear *(Name)*:

The price we quoted on your order # *(order number)* was made possible, in part, by careful cash flow planning. The price was based on strict 30-day net terms. *(Name)*, the unpaid balance on your account is now approaching 60 days, and we need your help.

If we are to continue providing the personal, custom service you've come to expect from us, we must keep our carrying costs down— way down. You can make this possible by sending the payment due on this account today.

In the event that you are unable to make a full payment at this time, we ask that you give us the opportunity of talking with you about an immediate partial payment and a payment plan we both can live with. Please give me a call at 555-0000 today.

Thanks very much for your help in this matter.

Sincerely,

Invoice Inserts for Sixty-Day-Old Accounts

Dear Customer:

Your account is seriously past due, but it is not too late to help us to maintain our reasonable prices. Just send us your payment in full today.

If you have any questions, please call 555-0000.

Sincerely,
(Name of company)

———

Dear Customer:

The attached invoice includes a service charge of *($ amount)* because your account is past due sixty days.

You can, however, AVOID PAYING this charge IF you send us your check for *($ amount)* before *(date)*.

Sincerely,
(Name of company)

Letters for Accounts Approaching Ninety Days

Dear *(Name)*:

Your unpaid account is now almost ninety days old, and we have received no payment or word from you. The enclosed invoice reflects accumulated finance charges for sixty days. If you do not pay before *(date)*, your account will be subject to an additional *($ amount)*.

Please, avoid these additional charges by mailing your check for *($ amount)* today.

If there is some issue or problem I should know about, call me at 555-0000. I'd like to work with you to settle this account.

Sincerely,

————

Dear *(Name)*:

We quoted you a fair price. How much more do you want to pay? Because your unpaid account is about to go past ninety days, we must charge your account an additional *($ amount 1)*. Unless you really want to pay more than you have to, why not send us a check for just *($ amount 2)* today?

(Name), if you have any questions about your account, please call me directly at 555-0000. Working together, we can successfully address any issues you may have.

Sincerely,

————

Dear *(Name)*:

Your unpaid account with us is about to go past ninety days, which means that it will be subject to a service charge *($ amount)*. Do you really want to let these charges pile up?

There are plenty of reasons not to pay a bill: cash shortage, forgetfulness, dissatisfaction with the merchandise or service.

Please let me know what the problem is, so that we can work together to resolve it and ensure that you do not pay more than you have to. My direct number is 555-0000, and I look forward to hearing from you.

Sincerely,

_____

Dear *(Name)*:

Time is money, and time is running out. Look:

On *(30-day date)* you owed *($ amount 1)* on your account with us.

As of *(60-day date)* you owe *($ amount 2)*

On *(90-day date)* you will owe *($ amount 3)*

Why let this go on?

You don't have to. Just send us a check for *($ amount 2)* today, and save yourself money.

Sincerely,

_____

Dear *(Name)*:

Your account with us for merchandise shipped on *(date)* is still unpaid. Since we have heard nothing from you concerning the shipment or the invoice, we assume that you do not dispute the charges. Therefore, we ask that you pay the balance immediately.

Sincerely,

_____

Dear *(Name)*:

Your account with us for merchandise shipped on *(date)* is still unpaid. Please send us a check for *($ amount)* immediately or call me at 555-0000 to advise me of any difficulty you may be experiencing in settling this account. I'd like the opportunity to be of assistance.

Sincerely,

Dear *(Name)*:

They say silence is golden. But it has been almost three months, and I haven't heard from you.

We shipped your order (# *[order number]*) on *(date)*. The price was based on payment in full on delivery, but here we are, three months later, and we have heard nothing from you. We can only assume that you found the merchandise satisfactory, and, therefore, we ask that you send us a check for *($ amount)* immediately.

If this assumption is wrong, and there *is* a problem, please call me on my direct line, 555-0000, so that I can work with you to settle this seriously overdue account.

Sincerely yours,

Letters for Accounts That Are Repeatedly Late

Dear *(Name)*:

We've been doing business together for *(period of time)*. Because we value you as a customer, I thought it appropriate to let you know that this is the *(second, third, fourth, etc.)* time your account with us has gone beyond the ninety-day mark.

(Name), we are a small company that prides itself on giving our customers personal service. To continue doing that, we must maintain a dependable delivery and payment cycle. This is where you can help by paying all invoices within the thirty-day net period.

(Name), your immediate payment of the current invoice would be especially appreciated.

Sincerely,

———————

Dear *(Name)*:

Accidents happen, and we cannot always pay our bills as promptly as we would like to. I understand and appreciate that. What concerns me, however, is when delayed payment becomes a matter of policy rather than the result of an occasional glitch. *(Name)*, I'm afraid that is what has been happening in the case of your account. For the *(third, fourth, fifth, etc.)* time in *(time period)*, your account has gone ninety days past due.

(Name), I know that you do pay your bills. But I cannot continue offering you prices based on thirty-day terms, then wait for more than ninety days before payment is made. We are a small company, and we are proud of our ability to give our customers fast, personal service at competitive prices. To continue delivering this level of value, we do need to maintain adequate cash flow. And that's where you can help: Please, continue to be our customer, and, please, pay your bills promptly.

Your payment of the current invoice, without further delay, is especially appreciated.

Sincerely,

Letters to the Unresponsive

Dear *(Name)*:

You now have our monthly statements for *(month)*, *(month)*, *(month)*, and *(month)*. We have attempted to reach you by telephone *(number)* times, on *(dates)*. You have received written reminders from us on *(dates)*.

We have yet to receive a response, let alone a payment.

We value and appreciate your business, and we are puzzled about your unresponsiveness. Please communicate with us concerning your seriously late account. If you have a problem with the merchandise you received or with your finances, please let us know so that we can understand the problem and work with you to resolve it. A phone call or letter from you today will help us both. My direct line is 555-0000. You may leave a confidential voice-mail message.

Sincerely,

Dear *(Name)*:

Your account is seriously past due. But, *(Name)*, that's only part of the problem. What makes the situation really difficult is that you have failed to communicate with us for the past *(time period)*.

Very soon, we will have no option but to force communication—by means of our attorneys.

It is best for both of us if we act now to prevent things from getting that far. All it take is a phone call. Just call me at 555-0000 so that we can work out a reasonable plan that will keep us in business together.

I appreciate your cooperation in this matter.

Sincerely yours,

———————

Dear *(Names)*:

I do not enjoy writing this kind of letter. Your unpaid account with us is approaching 120 days. We have repeatedly offered to work with you to help you settle the account. I now have to advise you that, within *(number of days)*, we will be forced to suspend your credit privileges.

It is still within your power to help us avoid this step. If we receive your payment of *($ amount)* by *(date)*, your credit account will remain active.

A postage-paid envelope is enclosed for your convenience.

Why not use it to send us a check today? Please give me a call at 555-0000 if you have any questions.

Thank you for your prompt cooperation in this matter.

Sincerely yours,

———————

Dear *(Name)*:

We don't want to suspend your credit, and we certainly do not want to stop doing business with you. But your account with us is almost 120 days past due, and we must establish a pattern of prompt, reliable payment to continue serving you on a credit basis.

Please pay the balance due on your account today. A postage-paid envelope is enclosed.

If you are experiencing some difficulty, please give me a call at 555-0000. I am confident that, together, we can formulate a payment plan we both can live with, but it is essential that you first communicate with me.

Sincerely,

_____

Dear *(Name)*:

To be honest with you, my credit manager thinks I'm crazy to let this situation go on. For the *(second, third, etc.)* time this year, your account with us is about to go past due 120 days. My credit manager tells me to turn the account over to a collection agency.

But I don't want to do that.

What I'd much rather do is get your account back on track, so that I can continue doing business with you.

We can begin by settling the outstanding balance. Just put a check for *($ amount)* in the enclosed postage-paid envelope.

If you are unable to do this at present, please give me a call at 555-0000. Together, I am confident that we can develop a payment plan that will satisfy us both.

Sincerely,

Credit Suspension

Dear *(Name)*:

Because your account *([number])* in the amount of *($ amount)* remains outstanding after 120 days *(or other period)*, we regret that we must suspend your credit privileges with us.

If you use the enclosed envelope to send us the balance due today, we can, if you wish, develop a schedule for restoring your privileges at a later date.

You may reach me on my direct line at 555-0000.

Sincerely,

Final Notice

Dear *(Name)*:

Make no mistake, this is a "Final Notice." But it is not too late to repair your seriously delinquent account.

Either use the enclosed envelope to send us a check for *($ amount)* today. Or call me at 555-0000 to work out some alternative payment options. You will find us reasonable and flexible.

Whichever option you choose, we must have your response by *(date)* or we will be forced to turn your account over to our attorney for collection.

Please be advised that your credit privileges with us have been suspended until this account is paid in full.

Sincerely,

Warning of Legal Action

Dear *(Name)*:

Our legal counsel advises us to act immediately to collect the balance you owe us on your account (number *[number]*). I would rather not resort to this, but, because we have received no response from you to numerous letters and phone calls, we may have no alternative.

Please send us your payment in full immediately. If this is not possible, you must contact me at 555-0000, so that we can develop a payment plan. I would much rather work with you to resolve this matter rather than work with our lawyers against you.

Sincerely,

Dear *(Name)*:

We are both about to become losers. Your account in the amount of *($ amount)* is 120 days past due, and you have not responded to several letters and notices we have sent you. Now we will have to go to the expense of calling upon our attorney to collect the balance due, and you will have to deal with our attorney and suffer a blemish on your credit record.

Why should we lock ourselves into such a no-win situation? Mail us a check for *($ amount)* in the enclosed envelope today or call me directly at 555-0000 so that, together, we can work out a satisfactory payment plan.

Sincerely yours,

Bounced Check

Dear *(Name)*:

Your check *(number)* in the amount of *($ amount)* was returned to us because of insufficient funds *(or other reason)*. Please give me a call at 555-0000 to let me know whether I should redeposit this check or if you are sending a replacement.

Sincerely,

Promised Payment Not Received

Dear *(Name)*:

On *(date)* we spoke concerning the balance due on your account, which is now *(days)* past due. We agreed that you would send *($ amount)* immediately.

We have not received your payment.

Please use the enclosed addressed envelope to send your check to us today. If there is a problem or if you have any questions, please call me at 555-0000 today.

Sincerely,

Dear *(Name)*:

On *(date)* we spoke concerning your past due account with us. We agreed that you would send *($ amount)* immediately. We have yet to receive the promised payment.

If you have not mailed your check yet, please take this opportunity to do so, using the envelope enclosed. If you have mailed the check, or if you have any questions, please call me today at 555-0000.

Sincerely yours,

CHAPTER 10

Special Promotions:
Announcing Special Events Without
Resorting to Junk Mail Tactics

How to Do It

Here's a flash. The Industrial Revolution is over!

We've grown up with mass production, a theory of manufacturing and marketing that aimed at producing, in effect, one product to suit all people. Today, it is still important to reach large markets, but the approach to these markets is through a variety of products tailored to separate market segments. Successful mailing for special promotions is also following this trend. Direct mail experts lavish great attention and develop expensive graphics for mass promotions. These can, of course, be very effective, but their sheer bulk and their look telegraph the fact that they are, after all, junk mail. Many slick, fat, direct mail appeals find their way directly to the recipient's waste basket, unread.

Owners of small businesses often bemoan the fact that they cannot afford to hire the talent to put together a really "professional" mass mailing. In fact, this deficiency may well be a blessing. Instead of feebly trying to imitate mass-produced mail advertising, create more modest, more personal, more direct promotions aimed at a very specific audience and promoting a specific product or service. Try custom-making your special promotions. Try making them truly special.

The way to do this is not through overstuffed envelopes and fancy graphics—though you can approach the special promotion as a cover letter intended to accompany a brochure—but through establishing a personal tone that conveys the high level of personal craftsmanship and service your correspondent can expect from you. Don't think of these letters as trying to *sell* or *promote* something, but as providing your customers with the opportunity of acquiring a specific product or service at a special price or with special extras. Approach this task with the attitude that you are performing a service by providing information.

— WORDS TO USE —

able	deserve	professional
act	edge	protect
announce	effective	proven
announcing	enhance	provide
answer	ensure	question
approved	established	reasonable
assurance	expectations	recommended
assure	extra	reputation
attractive	extraordinary	request
augmented	feature	response
bargain	final	responsible
capable	free	review
choice	great	rewarding
choose	guarantee	safe
closeout	important	sample
communicate	incentive	satisfying
community	information	savings
competition	invest	savvy
competitive	investment	select
complete	magnificent	soon
complimentary	opportunity	special
convince	personal	specialist
deal	pleased	spectacular
demonstrate	pleasing	sure

tested	try	valuable
thanks	understand	warranty
tough	urge	wise
trial	useful	

— PHRASES TO USE —

about to expire	no obligation, one time only
absolutely free	only the very best
act immediately	our top-selling line
after you have reviewed it	please act soon
all-purpose	professionally rewarding
anniversary sale	prove it to yourself
best-qualified	quantities are limited
cannot afford to miss	response to demand
combine luxury and economy	response to requests
complete information	see for yourself
cost-effective solution	special facilities
discount program	special offer
exclusively to you	substantial discounts
extensive practice	take advantage of this offer
free, free, free	think about it
free of charge	think ahead
here's the deal	this is it
last time	this offer will not be repeated
let me tell you who I am	total confidence
limited time	unique formula
longest established	unlimited selection
look forward to hearing from you	valuable information
move it out of our warehouse	very special
my clients enjoy	wide range
my customers benefit from	you might consider
my direct line	
never again	

Contest

WHAT WOULD YOU PAY FOR $50,000 WORTH OF ADVERTISING?

Dear Graphic Designer:

No, my next question is *not* "Who's buried in Grant's Tomb"? And, no, the answer to the first question is not $50,000.

It's zero dollars, nothing, *nada,* zilch, zippo, free, free, free.

(Name of company), makers of Design Quotient graphics software, is pleased to announce a competition designed to give you an opportunity to demonstrate your talents—and advertise your business—to more than 30,000 major art directors and ad art buyers nationwide.

All you have to do is be a genius—and show it.

Complete the entry form that is enclosed with this letter. Include a 3.5-inch diskette with the best ad graphic work you have created using any of the Design Quotient family of graphics software. Our panel of judges will review all work submitted.

If your design is selected, it will be featured in our August print ad campaign, which is published in the following trade and professional journals:

(list)

Who are the judges?

You'll recognize the names:

(list)

What is the deadline?

(date)

Where do I send the diskette?

(address)

Do I have to use Graphics Quotient software?

You'd be crazy not to. But, to answer the question, in a word: yes. All entries must use Graphics Quotient software. If you don't presently own a Graphics Quotient package, just call 800-555-0000 to speak to one of our sales representatives.

Please note that we cannot return any diskettes submitted.

We look forward to seeing your work!

Sincerely yours,

Special Discount Offer

Dear *(Name)*:

I'm writing to you because, as your firm's travel specialist, you are responsible for satisfying a lot of savvy frequent travelers. They're tough to impress, we know, and we're sure you're tough to impress as well.

But we'll do our best.

All ExtraStep Hotels offer a free morning paper, complimentary overnight shoeshine, valet services, in-room fax service, a computer room on every floor, private dining rooms, and a complete health club. We offer special conference facilities for all purposes and a wide range of accommodations, up through our unrivaled luxury suites.

By now you are thinking: That's what they all say.

And you're absolutely right.

That's why we need to get you and your guests here to prove it. So here's a special offer just to show you how much we want your business.

You guarantee us *(number 1)* nights for the next year in reservations, and we'll give you a *(% amount 1)* percent discount on our extraordinary rooms and our even more extraordinary services. Guarantee *(number 2)* nights per year, take *(% amount 2)* percent discounts. At *(number 3)* nights per year, you and your guests will benefit from a spectacular *(% amount 3)* percent in savings.

Find out how you *can* combine luxury and economy. Just send in the enclosed reply card, and we'll send you everything that's needed to sign up for the discount program of your choice.

Oh, yes. Just what does a *(% amount 3)* savings represent over *(number 3)* nights? About *($ amount)* in a single year.

Worth thinking about, no?

Sincerely yours,

Aptitude Test

Dear *(Name)*:

Do you have what it takes to be a private investigation professional?

If you'd like to find out, please read on.

And if you're reading on, you've already scored high for potential. The single most important quality a private investigator must possess is curiosity.

As to the other aptitude, characteristics, and qualities you need— our simple test, which takes fifteen minutes of your time, will tell you what you need to know.

How do you get the test?

Just send in the enclosed reply card.

How much will it cost you?

Absolutely nothing. And we will send you our analysis of the test results within ten days of your sending in the complete test form.

Why are we doing it?

Because we run the area's longest-established school for training paralegal and private investigation professionals. Now, if you think that means we'll just tell you come on and sign up, you're wrong. Each year, some *(number)* apply to our school, and each year we accept only *(number)*. The test we will send you tells *us* as much as it tells *you*. Just as you want only the very best training available, we want only the best-qualified, most promising students. The quality of our program and the level of our reputation depend on it.

So, if you think you've got what it takes to be a private investigation professional, send in the enclosed card today—and find out for sure.

Sincerely,

Special Advantage Seminar

Dear Systems Professional:

If you're content to set up nodes and terminals, get software up and running, troubleshoot a problem or two, and collect your paycheck, one thing you can cross off your list of things to do in *(month)* is attend our Artificial Intelligence for Systems Managers seminar.

You won't like it. It will be over your head. You'll be bored. So just forget it.

On the other hand, if you see yourself as more than a caretaker and silicon janitor, if you want to give your company the competitive edge in service and data analysis, and if you want to be counted as a key member of your firm's creative team, you cannot afford to miss what may well turn out to be the three most professionally rewarding and stimulating days you have ever spent.

From *(date)* to *(date)*, at the *(Name)* Conference Center in *(City)*, the major players in the application of artificial intelligence to systems management will offer to share their expertise and experience with you. They will address such issues as:

(list)

And they will walk you through dozens of AI scenarios, most of them already up and running in such leading-edge firms as

(list)

Registration is on a first-come, first-served basis. We have room for only *(number)* registrants—and that is all—because we want to ensure that the discussion and the learning is as personal and intense as we can make it.

For information on costs or to enroll, just call 800-555-0000.

Sincerely,

Communication Training Program

Dear *(Name)*:

If I told you I could train your engineers to communicate to the rest of the world, what would you say?

- ❏ I don't need them talking to anyone but each other.
- ❏ I don't have the time.
- ❏ I don't have the budget.
- ❏ I can't let them off the job and have them running out to some seminar.

These are perfectly reasonable answers. Let me offer some even more reasonable responses:

First: Think how much time you would save if you didn't have to translate and buffer everything that went on between your engineering group and your clients.

Second: You don't have to invest any time in the seminar.

Third: You don't have to lay out any money.

Fourth: You don't have to cut into productive work time.

Do I have your attention?

Well, I lied a little. Invest *thirty seconds* of your time right now to fill out the enclosed reply card, and I will send you complete information on how I can work with your engineering group to make them as effective at communication as they are at engineering.

I hope to hear from you.

Sincerely,

Achieve Financial Independence

Dear *(Name)*:

What does financial independence mean?

I suppose there are as many answers to that question as there are people to answer it. But let me tell you what financial independence means to me: It means working only when, where, and if you want to. It means not worrying about pleasing your boss or your clients. It means total confidence that you can provide for your needs and those of your family—for life.

The rest of what financial independence means, I submit to you, is just a matter of details: very pretty details—like how big a boat you want, how many cars you want to drive, how big a house you want to live in, how many vacation homes you want to own. But I'll leave the details—and they are infinite—to you.

Let me tell you who I am. As a practicing professional financial planner in your area for the past *(number)* years, I have been able to create successful plans for financial independence for some *(number)* of your neighbors. I have shown them how to ensure that they have the funds necessary for

❑ Vacations
❑ Business investments
❑ Children's education
❑ Retirement

And so on.

Often, I have been able to structure plans that achieve such goals without radically altering my clients' life-styles. How? I'd like to offer you my free report, *Keys to Financial Independence,* and the in-person presentation that will help you to understand it.

Enclosed is a reply card that will set up a brief—fifteen minute— meeting with me at my midtown office. We'll talk for a bit, and I'll send you home with *Keys to Financial Independence.* After you've reviewed the material, at home and at your leisure, I am confident that you'll give me a call, and I will work with you to set up a plan that will gain you the kind of financial independence you want and you deserve.

Sincerely,

Offer of Free Literature

Dear *(Name)*:

My name is *(Name)*, a *(professional)* in your community. Over the past *(number)* years here, I have developed an extensive practice, and I have found that my clients enjoy receiving *(Name of publication)*, which contains valuable information concerning *(list)*.

The publication also tells you something about my practice and the services I have to offer. Of course, I don't know if I could be of help to you, but I am confident that you will enjoy reading *(Name of publication)*. After you have reviewed it, feel free to call me at 555-0000, and I will be glad to confer with you for one-half hour—absolutely free of charge.

In addition to *(Name of publication)*, I also publish *(books, tapes, etc.)* on *(subject[s])*, which you may find highly useful. When you call, just ask for my publications catalog, and I'll be happy to send you a complimentary copy.

I hope you take advantage of this free offer, and I look forward to hearing from you.

Sincerely,

Free Samples

Dear *(Name)*:

Thank you for taking advantage of our offer of *(trial period)* service for your *(product)*.

You are entitled to *(number)* service calls, absolutely free, except for the cost of any necessary parts. We believe that only by experiencing the level of our service can we convince you of just how efficient and cost-effective retaining a regular maintenance provider can be. Remember, we offer:

(list features/benefits)

We make it easy for you to continue to enjoy the peace of mind that comes with great maintenance on tap seven days a week, fifty-two weeks a year, and twenty-four hours a day. Just call 555-0000 and tell us that you wish to continue service. We'll explain your choice of maintenance plans.

Need more incentive?

How about taking *(% amount)* percent off the cost of any three-month contract? *(% amount)* percent off any six-month contract? Or *(% amount)* percent off of any one-year contract?

These discounts are available only to *(type of)* professionals like you, who have taken advantage of our special free trial maintenance program offer. They're our way of saying thanks for giving us a try.

Sincerely,

One-for-Two Offer

Dear *(Name)*:

We trust you had a great time during your recent stay at *(Name)* Hotel. You were certainly in good company, since it was a record-breaking season for us. You know, we don't always have so many guests. During February and March, occupancy here is down by about *(% amount)* percent—but, of course, the service we offer stays at the same high level as during our busiest season. That's why you might want to consider a return visit when the living's quieter up here.

Enhanced privacy is reason enough to give February or March a try. But here's another incentive. For every two nights you book during February or March, we'll give you one night free.

Think about it. Three nights of our king-sized beds, our in-room Jacuzzis, our award-winning sauna facilities, our fully equipped health club, all in the magnificent setting of *(Name of place)*. Three nights, and you pay for only two.

Call us before *(date)* to make a reservation and take advantage of this very special offer for a very special person—you.

Sincerely,

Out-of-Season Offer

Dear *(Name)*:

Shakespeare said it: "What is so rare as a day in June?" The weather just doesn't get any better than this: mild sunshine, the flowers in bloom, your lawn lush and green.

Only spoilsports and madmen would even *think* about the snows of winter during a season like this.

Well, we don't mean to be spoilsports. But when you see the prices we have to offer on our top-selling line of snow blowers, you might think we're madmen—and maybe you'd be right. Just look at these prices:

(list items and prices)

Sure, you'll buy the machine now and it *will* sit in your garage for six months. But, then, in six months, when this lovely June weather is nothing more than a fond dream and we're all knee deep in the white stuff, you'll be taking care of business while aching backs drive your neighbors to pay *any* in-season price for a blower you paid so little for.

And they'll be lucky if they can find one at all.

Think ahead, and go ahead: Take advantage of us. These prices are crazy, but the madness will not last.

Drop by the store at *(address)*. Crank the top down on the old convertible. The weather's great.

For now.

Sincerely,

Special Trade-in Offer

Dear *(Name)*:

What do you do with an old desktop computer that's too feeble to run today's demanding software applications?

You have three choices:

1. Give it to an employee you don't like very much.
2. Use it as a door stop.
3. Donate it to a local school or charity.

Option 3 is attractive, offering a chance to do your community a service while getting a tax deduction for yourself—*if* you can take the time to find the school or charity that *wants* your machine.

Wouldn't it be simpler if there were an Option 4? If you could just trade your old machine in on a new one, just as you would a used car?

Don't laugh.

From *(month 1)* to *(month 2)*, we're offering you the opportunity to trade in your old computer—no matter how old, just as long as it's in working order—for substantial discounts on any computer we stock at *(Name of store)*. On average, you can expect savings of *(% amount 1)* percent to *(% amount 2)* percent.

But it gets even better.

What do we do with the used machines we take in?

We have taken the time to identify schools and institutions right here in *(Name of community)* who desperately need computers, and we will donate the machines to them.

Think about it: You get rid of your old machine. You get a substantial discount on a new machine. *And* you do something good for your community.

But please act soon. This very special program expires on *(date)*.

Hope to see you at *(address)*.

Sincerely,

Trial Offer

Dear *(Name)*:

The soap chefs at Sparkle Soaps have just created a new line of gourmet soaps in very special shapes and with very special fragrances. We call them our Floral Line: a dozen new soaps in the shape of your favorite flowers, each fragrant with the flower's bouquet. Our rose soap smells like a rose. Our beautifully sculpted lilac sprig bar is fresh with the fragrance of spring lilacs.

I could go on trying to describe these great new soaps—but what's the use? How do you talk about a flower? How do you describe an aroma?

Instead, I'd like to offer you a sampler box of all twelve new soaps. The cost to you is only *($ amount)*, to cover handling.

Sampler boxes are limited to one per customer, but, through *(date)*, we are offering very special prices on quantity purchases:

(list prices)

Call 1-800-555-0000 to order your sampler box today.

Sincerely,

Closeout

Dear *(Name)*:

In response to requests from dealers like you, *(Name of company)* is expanding our line of *(products)*. But expanding also means discontinuing some lines that are similar in style to the new items. As of *(date 1)*, we will no longer be manufacturing the following:

(list)

We will introduce replacements for these by *(date 2)*. In the meantime, we are able to offer the old units to you at very special closeout prices designed to make you as well as your customers very happy. Just look—

(list items and prices)

To take advantage of this closeout, I urge you to act immediately. Quantities are limited. Place your order on my direct line, 800-555-0000, or fax me at 555-555-1111.

When?

Today would be great!

Sincerely,

Overruns

Dear *(Name)*:

I turned the machines on, but nobody told me when to turn them off. The result? We've got *(quantity)* of *(product)* that nobody has ordered.

Normally, inventory like this would take us through *(month)*, but I don't have room to stock all this *(product)*, and I'm in the mood to move it out of our warehouse as fast as possible. So here's the deal: a *(% amount 1)* percent discount on orders up to *(quantity)* and a *(% amount 2)* percent on quantities greater than *(quantity)*. And guess what? I'll pick up the freight.

But, please, act now. I may never make such a stupid mistake again. Maybe.

My direct line is 555-0000.

All the best,

Anniversary Sale

Dear *(Name)*:

(Name of company) is pleased to announce a very personal anniversary sale.

Whose anniversary is it?

Well, it's ours. Not ours, but *ours*.

Okay, here's what I mean. On *(date)*, you placed your first order with us. That's exactly one year ago. To celebrate "our" anniversary, we're holding a special sale. And since it's a very special anniversary, we're offering the sale prices exclusively to you and exclusively for a single day: *(date)*—the day of our anniversary.

A gimmick?

You bet.

But *I* bet prices like this will get your interest anyway:

(list)

So why not come in on *(date)* to benefit from this very special, very private, anniversary sale?

Hope to see you then.

Congratulations,

Electronic Communications: "Paperless" Promotion

How to Do It

THE "PAPERLESS" OFFICE

Let's begin with a modern myth. The electronic office is a paperless office. The creation of documents with a keyboard, CPU, and CRT—that is, the personal computer on your desk—the storage of data on magnetic diskettes (and in some cases, tape cartridges and CD-ROM), and the transmission of that data via modem over the telephone lines have made paper obsolete.

Right?

Not if you examine the evidence: all 775 billion pages of it, which is the amount of paperwork American businesses still generate yearly—each year a stack that would rise 48,900 miles into outer space. It *is* true that office copiers have greatly reduced the amount of *carbon* paper used by today's businesses, but those same copiers are to a significant degree responsible for the proliferation of the paper stack. Not too many years ago, it was an annoying chore to make multiple copies of a document, so, if possible, we made do with the original and nothing more. Now, with a copier in every office corner or even on the desktop, we run off duplicates and triplicates of almost everything—"just to be safe."

In business, communication—truly effective communication—has suffered multidigit inflation. Your colleagues, associates, and customers are drowning in paperwork, most of it electronically generated, which means that an ever-increasing proportion of hopeful and earnestly intended communication goes, as it were, unreceived or, more accurately, unperceived. It just piles up.

True, word processing software for personal computer systems based on the IBM standard as well as on the Apple Macintosh standard—and other operating systems as well—now offers an arsenal of fonts, type faces, point sizes, page layouts, special and graphic effects that would make any job printer green with envy. Well, these things _would_ make the printer envious—if he didn't use them, too. Think of it: the humblest office now has everyday access to the same technology used by the biggest publishing houses to produce what once seemed almost sacred: the "printed page" of The Book. Typewritten correspondence no longer looks like it came from a typewriter. And with good reason. It _doesn't_ come from a typewriter. It issues from laser printers and ink jet printers and 24-wire dot-matrix printers, which produce documents that more closely resemble the "printed page" of The Book than they do the humble sheet from the typewriter.

This has certainly made business correspondence more attractive, but it has done so across the board. There is no longer anything special about a crisp laser-printed letter "set" in 11-point Times Roman, margins fully justified left and right, in contrast to a slightly fuzzy document typewritten in 12-pitch "pica," the right-hand margin ragged as an old comb and the page spotted (like a spackled wall) with "white-out." The laser-printed letter has become the business standard. It is _expected._ Everybody does them. Moreover, it had better be error free, as well as free of the evidence of corrected error—the telltale bird droppings of correction fluid. No, it's not that you're expected to be smarter or even simply better at spelling. It's just that everyone knows that word processing software now comes with spell-checking programs, and it's simply inconsiderate and impolite not to use them. (Of course, you are _supposed_ to run these programs before you print the document, while it is still no more than a glow on your monitor screen. Many—maybe most—of us, however, print the letter out first, glance over it, find mistakes, correct them with a pen or pencil, then go back to the computer, retrieve the document, and print it out again. In this way, we manage to waste additional time _and_ add to the stack of business-generated paper.)

The point is this: To the dismay of any number of futurists, electronic communication has actually multiplied paperwork, has improved the appearance of that paperwork, making each document look more attractive and therefore more valuable but, in the process, has also effectively devalued all documents by encouraging their ad infinitum replication.

If you go to your neighborhood library—not the big central branch, not a university library, and certainly not a library that caters to the needs of business professionals—chances are you will find an old volume or two on writing business "correspondence." Many of these books include sections on using your typewriter to create unusual or "eye-catching" effects: shapes made out of type ("Acme Auto Dealer" repeatedly typed so that it forms the shape of a car) or type wrapped around a special letterhead, or typewritten letters that incorporate some preprinted design or other gizmo. In the Age of the Typewriter, such special effects really were special. Maybe they were corny—but they did attract attention, because they represented an investment of time, effort, skill, and imagination. But, in the Age of the Typewriter, you didn't even have to go so far as to create special effects to project a "special" image. The fact that the letter was well typed—free from errors, erasures, evidence of white-out, the margins not too ragged, the message well centered—was enough to convey a businesslike, professional quality. At minimum, correspondents appreciated clean type (Did you clean up the "a's" and "e's" and "o's" with the little brush that came with the machine, or did you sacrifice an old toothbrush for the job?) and a crisp new ribbon. (Are you old enough to remember when acetate ribbon replaced cotton ribbon as the state of the art in the workplace?)

DESIGNING BUSINESS CORRESPONDENCE TODAY

Correspondence in the age of the word processor and laser printer is *expected* to be letter perfect. Ironically, although these tools also make it easy to achieve special typographic effects—bold headlines, a mixture of typefaces—such gimmicks tend to pack little punch, since they *are* so easy to create. Worse, these devices are all too easy to overuse. Armed with a PC, a laser printer, and a set of fonts, one is tempted to throw a variety of type styles together. The result is usually silly, gaudy, ugly, but, most of all, ordinary.

This does not mean that you should stick with plain old Courier ("typewriter") type. By all means, take advantage of at least some of the typefaces available to PC users. But, in terms of doing business, think about these faces in the same way you think about your business wardrobe. There are really only two secrets of "dressing for success." The first is to be certain that your clothes are neat, clean, and in good repair. The second is to determine what kind of image you want to project—what nonverbal messages you wish to convey—and then dress accordingly.

Likewise, in designing business correspondence, make certain that what you do is neat and clean: crisp paper or stationery (a 24-pound stock is ideal for laser or ink-jet printing; 20-pound stock feels cheap, while anything heavier than 24-pound tends to jam in the printer) and error-free text (use that spell checker); generous margins on all sides; a matching envelope that is addressed either using the computer or a typewriter. This latter point is a problem for some users of word processors. Many people do not want to take the slight time and effort involved in learning how to use their word processing software to print envelopes. Instead, they typewrite the envelopes—an acceptable alternative, but one that often results in a typeface that does not match what was used in the letter—or they handwrite them. The latter expedient is substandard business practice, unless (for special effect or in deference to personal acquaintance) you also handwrite the letter itself. It is far more effective to invest the modest time and negligible effort required to learn how to create envelopes with your computer, word processing software, and printer.

Once you've taken all the steps necessary to assure that your letters will be neat, clean, and crisp, think about the other important elements of your company's image. Do you wish to project a modern look? Traditional? Personal and friendly? Flamboyant? Or some combination of these? Book designers make it their business to use type style and page layout to create the subtle but effective psychological environments in which the message of the book will be received. You may do the same with business correspondence. Here are some basics:

Traditional vs. Contemporary There are two kinds of "traditional" looks. The first, however, may be characterized as more than traditional. It is downright old-fashioned. Simply use Courier or another typewriter-style face and lay out your page with a ragged right margin. It's easy, it's dull—and it works.

A second traditional style works harder at the image and takes advantage of the flexibility in type styles offered by the word processor. Begin with a deliberately traditional type style. Typefaces are broadly divided into two camps: serif and sans serif letter forms. The serif styles have little ornaments at the ends of most letters, and the body of each letter is more or less elaborately contoured:

Aa Bb Cc Dd Ee Ff Gg Hh Ii Jj Kk Ll Mm Nn Oo Pp Qq Rr Ss
Tt Uu Vv Ww Xx Yy Zz

The sans serif styles, in contrast, lack ornamentation and are starker, simpler, cleaner in appearance, with simple letter forms:

Aa Bb Cc Dd Ee Ff Gg Hh Ii Jj Kk Ll Mm Nn Oo Pp Qq Rr Ss Tt Uu
Vv Ww Xx Yy Zz

Within these two basic families is a dazzling variety of typefaces, and an equally dazzling variety of books have been written on type design. It is beyond the scope of this book to enter into a detailed discussion of the subject, nor is it necessarily of great importance and interest to the writers of business correspondence. This noted, however, an excellent single-volume guide for those who use computers to create documents of any kind is *Looking Good in Print* by Roger C. Parker (Chapel Hill, N.C.: Ventura, 1990). For the purposes of the business letter writer, it is sufficient to appreciate the two basic type families and to choose typefaces from them. Note that serif faces have names like Caslon, Garamond, Goudy, and Times Roman. San serif faces include Arial, Dutch, Helvetica, and Optima. For licensing reasons, various font software packages tend to use different names for groups of essentially similar typefaces. The important thing is to begin to appreciate the basic division into serif and sans serif styles. If you become interested in the subject of typefaces (and it *is* a fascinating study that can distract you from the actual job at hand even more effectively than those electronic arcade games you've loaded onto your computer), you will soon notice that there are also "transitional" typefaces, which borrow elements from both the serif and sans serif families.

But let's stick with the two basic families. Choosing a serif typeface in and of itself projects an image of traditional quality and traditional values. Serif faces are classic faces. If you want to reinforce this image, carry over into the layout of the letter another conservative, classic element: a justified right-hand margin. This means that both the left and right margins are perfectly even, in contrast to the "ragged" (that is the technically correct term) right margin that was the Underwood or Royal typist's only choice. Before the PC and word processor, justified margins were available only to professional typesetters creating books, newspapers, ads, and other *printed* materials. Be cautioned that, poorly done, full justification actually looks shabby, especially if spacing between words is uneven. Before choosing a fully justified layout, be sure of the following:

1. Use a "proportional font" as opposed to a "monospaced font." Proportional fonts allow for variations in the spaces between individual letters, so that justification does not force awkward differences in spaces between words. Awkward word spacing—wide gaps between some words and compressed spaces between others—not only looks amateurish, it actually makes the document difficult (and certainly uninviting) to read.

2. Use standard margins. Don't set overly wide margins. The longer your line, the easier it is to achieve even spacing between words.

3. Use a word processing program sophisticated enough to handle "kerning" automatically. Kerning is the art and science of creating well-proportioned spaces between letters so that well-proportioned spaces between words are achieved. The best commercial word processing packages do this automatically and well.

4. Use a printer capable of proportional spacing. All laser and ink-jet printers have this capability. Most sophisticated 24-wire (sometimes called 24-pin) dot matrix printers do it also. Older, simpler, cheaper 9-wire printers often do not. Outmoded daisy-wheel printers never space proportionately.

If you want to project a more contemporary and less formal image, choose from among the sans serif type family. Less formal does not mean less elegant. Think of it this way: well made and beautifully designed modern furniture, with its sleek, simple lines, can be as elegant as traditional designs. Nevertheless, it is undeniable that a room decorated in Danish modern projects a different image from a room furnished with Chippendale pieces. San serif correspondence suggests uncluttered, straightforward modernity, sleekness, and efficiency. If you choose one of these faces, it is probably best to go with a less formal, more dynamic page layout. This means a ragged-right margin rather than a justified one. The ragged-right margin is not inferior to the justified right margin. Indeed, nowadays, book designers often use it to achieve a modern, informal, dynamic look. Now that technology has made it possible for anyone to create fully justified margins, so that they are no longer tokens of special craftsmanship, the ragged-right margin has become a legitimate part of even the high-end design vocabulary, and when you use sans serif type, the ragged-right margin generally suits the image.

Anyone who has poked around in word processors today knows that many more typefaces are available than the basic serif and sans serif styles.

There is a whole range of in-between faces and special display faces, ranging from elaborate script styles, to styles that look like stencils, to cartoon-style type, and so on. These are useful for special purposes, such as ads, announcements, and sometimes in faxes, but, in general, they have no place in business letters—anymore than a neon necktie or a rhinestone tiara have a place in your daily business wardrobe.

Personalized Mailings Another powerful aspect of word processing for the small business is the ability to create large mailings that are thoroughly personalized. These are known as merge letters. Most major word processing programs allow you to create a basic letter with "blanks" that are filled in from a separate document file containing names, addresses, and other items of variable information. In this way, you can personalize direct mail appeals, promotions, and the like. Today, there is really very little excuse for direct mail campaigns in which letters begin with "Dear Customer" or the equivalent. If you have a mailing list, you can create a merge letter, and you can always address your customer by name. Apply a little more thought to the merge letter, and you can accommodate other personalizing variables, such as a notation of the product the customer has purchased from you or the customer's area of special interest. A merge file database not only allows you to generate letters that give your customers the highly confidence-building message that you know them and care about them, this tool actually enables you to know and care about your customers more effectively. The information that goes into a merge letter makes it possible for you effectively to record and track your customers' needs and interests.

And remember, there is no reason for a merge letter to resemble a "form letter." Today, letters for mass mailings can and should be friendly and personal. As to the mechanics of creating merge letters and merge database files, consult the user's guide that accompanies your particular word processing software package. Depending on the program, creating a merge letter *may* seem a bit daunting at first. But persevere. The results can be very rewarding.

A WORD ABOUT ADVERTISING LETTERS

Equipped with an arsenal of typefaces and a laser or ink jet printer—or even a color printer—you can create impressive-looking, eye-catching fliers and advertising letters. The techniques for producing these are similar to those for creating inexpensive print advertisements and are discussed in Chapter Fifteen. But a word about such letters is appropriate here. It is simple: consider a direct mail campaign, using a personalized business letter style, instead of sending a flashier, but less personal advertising leaflet or flier. If you are convinced that a flier is necessary, consider accompanying it with a personalized cover letter. Finally, consider integrating elements of the personalized letter into the flier:

Dear John Smith:

As a long-time user of our Model 500 Widget Detector, you obviously know a good value when you see one. But will you be ready when

OPPORTUNITY KNOCKS

?

You can be, if . . .

. . . and so on.

Remember, your electronic hardware has gone a long way toward leveling the playing field, giving you access to much the same technology as larger firms command. So what? That is what your customers will be thinking: *So what?* The technology can make you look good, and you need to develop the savvy to use it and use it wisely and tastefully. But *everybody* has the technology. What you, as the operator of a small business, have is something the large firms can only simulate: a personal stake in your customers' satisfaction that should very genuinely and immediately motivate a personal approach to communicating with your customers. Instead of using your PC, word processing software, and laser printer to imitate the big firms, learn to use these tools to make the most out of your greatest asset: your *small* size. Think about it. A personal computer allows you to do business on a personal basis. Take full advantage of that.

FAX COMMUNICATION

Perhaps the only workplace relic more poignant than the typewriter is the telex machine. Once a fixture of high-end offices, this device has been wholly replaced by fax machines, which are within the financial reach of everyone, including those who work from their homes and on their kitchen tables. For most users, a fax machine has become an indispensable business tool. Its application as an effective business promotion tool is governed by certain guidelines.

To begin with, it is best to have a dedicated fax line—that is, a phone line exclusively connected to the fax (not shared with a voice phone) and that is published as the fax number on your letterhead, in business directories, and on any publications and advertisements you issue. If you cannot afford a dedicated line, or if, for some other reason, it is impractical to obtain one, hook up any of the variety of "voice-data switches" that are on the market today. These devices, which cost under a hundred dollars, plug into your telephone service wall jack and distribute phone service to your fax, your voice phone, and your answering machine (most newer models also distribute to a computer modem). They monitor the line, listening for something called a CNG signal—the annoying beep a transmitting fax machine emits when it is trying to establish a "handshake" with the receiving fax machine. When the CNG is detected, the voice-data switch "knows" to route the call to the fax machine rather than the voice phone.

The voice-data switch is a reasonably effective alternative to having two telephone lines; however, it is not perfect. Some older fax machines and some inexpensive current fax machines do not generate a CNG. In the absence of that signal, your voice-data switch "thinks" the incoming call is a voice call, and, much to the annoyance of the person trying to fax you, it will route the fax to the telephone unless you happen to be there to route it manually. Also, some voice-data switches have the extremely annoying habit of interpreting the beep of a call-waiting signal as a CNG, which means that your voice call might suddenly be interrupted by the whine of your fax machine trying to respond to a phantom incoming message. Still, if for whatever reason you do not have a dedicated fax line, a voice-data switch is far preferable to informing your customers and clients that they must call you before they fax you. Customers find this extra work highly annoying. The process of unhooking your phone and hooking up your fax is likewise burdensome to you—and you have no choice but to hover around your phone, waiting for the fax to come in and complete itself, unless you want to accept the consequences of leaving a fax machine hooked up to a voice line. If there is one thing more off-putting to customers and clients than having to call before they fax, it is making a voice phone call only to be greeted by the high-pitched whine of an answering fax machine. Not only is this the telephonic equivalent of a whoopie buzzer—and about as welcome and as classy—it will further annoy your customer by sending her to the phone book or Rolodex to double-check your number, which is yet more annoying make-work. All other things being equal, there is a better than even chance that the entire experience will prompt the customer to skip you and head for your competition. If you forget to unhook your fax machine, you effectively block all telephone communication, cutting yourself off from the rest of the world.

Beyond the downright fatal consequences of trying to share fax and voice on a single line, there is the psychological message you are sending the customer: first, that you are an amateur, whose business is so marginal that you cannot afford to install another phone line; second, that you don't care enough about your customers to provide adequate means for them to communicate with you. Remember, a fax machine is intended to be a passive communications tool, serving you and your correspondent by continuously monitoring the phone line for incoming messages without the necessity of any action or intervention on your part. It should be available at all times, twenty-four hours a day, seven days a week, like an answering machine. To use it otherwise is to sacrifice much of its utility—not only for yourself, but, worse, for your unsuspecting customers as well.

Another faxing guideline concerns an often-overlooked feature of fax machines. Most of them have the capability of transmitting a "fax header" and printing it on the top of each page that your correspondent receives. On most machines, this feature may be customized. The fax header functions as a kind of return address, telling the recipient who sent the communication and furnishing such information as your name, your fax number, and your voice phone number. To take advantage of this feature, read the owner's manual that came with your machine (You didn't throw it out, did you?), and program in the appropriate information. You may even have room for a friendly message: "Greetings from the Sally Simpson! Fax: 555-555-1111 Voice: 555-555-0000." The header may also contain the name and number of your intended recipient, and it may feature the time and date of the transmission. All these things are useful to your correspondent, and it is courteous to program your machine to provide them.

It is also a courtesy to ensure that your machine transmits an "identifier" when it "shakes hands" with the receiving machine. This is simply your fax number or (depending on what you set up or what your machine allows you to set up) your name or company name, which shows up on the transmitting machine's LCD display (if it has one) when it has successfully shaken hands with your fax, and shows up on the receiving machine when you transmit a fax. For your customer making a transmission, the appearance of the identifier tells him that he has reached the right person and that the fax is on its way and going through successfully. For your customer receiving a transmission, the identifier provides a preview of the caller—a kind of polite knock on the electronic door.

The fax is, of course, yet one more assault on the myth of the paperless office. Here is an electronic communication medium that starts and ends with paper, right?

Well, in *most* cases this is true. But if you have a personal computer, you should consider installing a fax modem. We will discuss computer communication via modem shortly, but a *fax* modem, teamed with the appropriate software (and most fax modems come bundled with what you need) specifically allows you to send faxes directly from your computer. You create a document using your word processor (or, for that matter, your spreadsheet program, a graphics program, whatever); then, instead of printing it out and taking the hard copy to the fax machine, you use the fax modem to send the document directly from the computer. Most fax software programs make this process as easy as printing a document—except that you "print to" the fax modem instead of the printer. Once you get used to faxing in this way, you will find it far more efficient than generating hard copy and feeding it into the fax machine. An added bonus is that the faxes you transmit will generally be sharper and cleaner than those sent even on a very good conventional fax machine, because your message is transmitted digitally, without the optical intervention of a transmitting machine. I transmit directly from my computer, and I've had clients actually compliment me on the sharpness and crispness of my faxes. Some even ask how I do it. It cannot be a bad thing to have customers praise—and inquire about—the technology you command.

Note that a PC, fax modem, and fax software do not fully substitute for a standalone fax machine. While you can generate documents on your computer and transmit them directly, you cannot transmit hard copy—a piece of paper—using your computer. At least, you cannot do this unless you also own an optical scanner. This is a device for capturing images (including text) for use in your computer. A scanner has many uses, including desktop publishing applications. If you have such a scanner, you can scan a hard copy document into your computer, then transmit it via your fax modem. Generally speaking, this is a more laborious task than simply walking over to the fax machine, feeding in a sheet, and dialing away. You probably should not buy a scanner as part of a system intended to substitute for a standalone fax machine. Moreover, even if you acquire a scanner primarily for other purposes (graphics applications, desktop publishing, and so on), you should also have a standalone fax machine, unless you transmit from hard copy only occasionally. (And once you get accustomed to generating faxes on your computer, you may well find that you resort to hard copy only rarely.)

Depending on how you set up your computer, your fax modem, and your software, you can also receive faxes directly into your computer. Once received, they can be viewed, stored, retransmitted, printed, or any combination of these. Most remarkably, a number of the newer, more advanced fax software packages include an optical character recognition (OCR) feature. The fax that you receive, whether on a conventional fax machine or on your computer, is a picture. It may be all text, but it is really an *image* of text, not a digital representation of text. What this means is that, even though you have captured it in your computer, you cannot edit or manipulate the fax text—at least, not directly. OCR software makes it possible for you to convert the image into digital text you *can* edit and manipulate. What does this mean to you? Let's say a customer faxes you a request for proposal (RFP) with detailed specifications for a project. If you received the fax on a conventional fax machine, you would have to retype the specifications to include them in your proposal document. Depending on the length of the specs, this process is laborious and, of course, prone to error—mistyping. If you received the fax on your PC, and your fax software includes OCR, you can convert those specs directly to text *you* can use in your proposal, thereby saving keyboarding time and labor and reducing the possibility of error.

What's a Fax For?

The fax machine is a powerful communications tool. A kind of hybrid cross between a phone call and a letter, it provides some of the benefits of both and, in some ways, provides even more than either. Like any powerful tool, however, it is subject to abuse. The worst abuse is the unsolicited fax. When these machines first proliferated, businesses were flooded with fax junk mail, prompting the FCC to act to curb the transmission of such unsolicited matter. No law was really necessary, however, since the ill will generated by fax junk mail sent a powerful message of its own: *You tie up our fax line with this garbage, and the one thing you will* not *get from us is our business*. Never send fax junk mail. It will *not* be appreciated. It *will* cause resentment. It *may* even be against the law.

This does not mean that all unsolicited, essentially promotional faxes are taboo. You might find it more effective to send a brief fax in place of making a phone call to inform a customer about a new product or service. Don't blanket the business community with such faxes, but do send them to customers *you know,* who might well be interested in hearing about your latest offering. It is best to put such a fax in the form of a letter or memo rather than make it look like an ad. Keep the fax brief—a single page, perhaps preceded by a cover sheet. Do not send a dozen pages of specs unsolicited. You want to provide just enough information to invite interest and inquiry from your correspondent. You do not want to alienate her by tying up her fax line. You may extend the effectiveness of such targeted fax promotions by using the technique of the "broadcast fax." Many higher-end fax machines and most fax software (for your PC and fax modem) give you the capability of sending the same fax to multiple recipients. You just program in their names and fax numbers, then begin the transmission. Again, it cannot be emphasized strongly enough: do not use this feature to broadcast unsolicited faxes to strangers. But do use it to announce new products or services to selected customers you believe will want to know about the offering.

The Cover Sheet

Whatever the promotional/informational content of the fax itself, it is important not to overlook the advertising potential of the cover sheet. You should include a cover sheet with every fax you send. It functions as a shipping/routing label, providing such vital information as the name of the addressee, the name of the sender, the number of pages included in the transmission (make it clear whether the total includes or is in addition to the cover sheet), a voice number to call in case there is a problem with the fax, and any other special instructions. It makes sense to use this utilitarian document to carry a brief advertising announcement. You might also incorporate graphics, such as a company logo. Examples of cover sheets and cover sheets incorporating ads will be found later in the chapter.

   E-mail and Other Communication by Modem The press is full of stories about how all of us are embarked upon—or about to embark upon—a vast information superhighway. Already, millions of computer users—among them, thousands of businesses—are linked to various computer networks, including such commercial operations as CompuServe, Prodigy, Genie, America Online, and others, and the vast but nebulous noncommercial Internet, which is less a network than it is an agglomeration of thousands of networks. Business users have found, find, and will continue to find many uses for these and other, more specialized networks. They are sources of news, financial data, demographic information, government bulletins, and so on. Through electronic mail (E-mail) links, most of these networks also provide a means of communicating electronically with vast numbers of computer users. Like the fax machine, E-mail is not intended as an advertising medium, and it should not be used as such. However, many on-line services provide electronic bulletin boards that do accept commercial messages. At least one very popular on-line service, Prodigy, sells ad space, complete with graphics capability, which means that your ad can include simple images.

Posting messages or creating ads on commercial on-line services is one thing, but you are looking for trouble if you exploit the Internet for commercial purposes. Loyal users of the Internet jealously guard the noncommercial, nonprofit, democratic nature of the Internet, and an electronic ad in this venue is likely to bring loads of electronic hate mail. (This is likely to change as the government ceases to subsidize various Internet nodes, and the private sector takes them over.)

What, then, is the most effective way to exploit on-line services and electronic bulletin boards to broadcast your message? You can pay for a Prodigy ad much as you would buy print space or a radio spot. Prodigy reaches a huge *general* audience, but proportionately few *business* users. Depending on the product or service you sell, an ad in a general-interest on-line service may be a very good investment—especially if subscribers to the on-line service can order or inquire about your product or service on line. For many small businesses, however, it pays to search out the kind of special-interest and/or regional electronic bulletin boards that proliferate across the country and even worldwide. If, for example, you deal in rare coins, you may want to ferret out the electronic exchanges that consist of networks of coin collectors. Distribute your message through this network. Whereas passive media, like television or radio, are well suited to mass advertising, interactive media are perfectly suited to specialized, niche appeals. Always include in your message a means by which an interested reader can respond to you directly via E-mail.

E-mail is also an alternative to conventional postal service mail (which computer folk refer to as "snail mail"), as well as to the fax and the telephone. Depending on the nature of your business, it pays now—or will soon pay—to subscribe to an E-mail service, get an E-mailbox, and include the number on your stationery and business cards. E-mailboxes are inexpensive to acquire and maintain, and they open up yet one more channel of communication with customers and potential customers. Offer your customers the option of communicating with you electronically.

Business Letter: Formal/Traditional Image

Letterhead, Inc.

1234 Address Road
City, State 01010

Telephone 555-555-0000 Facsimile 555-55 5-1111 E-mail letterhead@bus.sys

Ms. Anna Cleves
President
Customer Bounty Corporation
2345 Welby Street
Terminus Town, State 00001

Dear Ms. Cleves:

Thank you for your recent inquiry about the letter-writing services we offer. I have enclosed a copy of our latest brochure and sample port-folio. I am confident that you will find a letter style perfectly suited to your needs.

We have been serving customers in your field for more than twen-ty years, and we pride ourselves on creating the tasteful and effective let-ters you would write yourself if you had the time.

After you have examined the enclosed materials, I invite you to call me on my direct line, 555-555-0999, so that we can discuss your spe-cific needs at greater length.

Thank you for your interest in Letterhead, Inc.

Sincerely,

Warren Name
Account Specialist

Business Letter: Informal/Contemporary Image

Letterhead, Inc.   1234 Address Road   City, State 01010

Phone 555-555-0000 Fax 555-555-1111 E-mail letterhead@bus.sys

Ms. Anna Cleves
President
Customer Bounty Corporation
2345 Welby Street
Terminus Town, State 00001

Dear Ms. Cleves:

Thanks for asking us about our New Image software package. It is your first step toward creating an exacting new look for your business.

I have enclosed a descriptive brochure and a sampler demonstration diskette, so that you can take the program for a test drive and see for yourself the many benefits it can bring to your business.

After you have had an opportunity to try out New Image, give me a call at 555-999-2626. I'm here to answer any questions—and, of course, to take your order.

We appreciate your interest in Letterhead, Inc., and New Image.

Sincerely,

Warren Name
Personal Account Specialist

Business Letter: Novelty/Special Effect Image

Letterhead, Inc.

**1234 Address Road
City, State 01010
Phone 555-555-0000
Fax 555-555-1111
E-mail letterhead bus.sys**

**Ms. Anna Cleves
President
Customer Bounty Corporation
2345 Welby Street
Terminus Town, State
00001**

Dear Anna:

You've got an image problem! But we are here to **HELP.**

Letterhead, Inc., offers you a full line of business letter service and products designed to help you clarify, refine, or establish your corporate image with each and every letter you write.

I have enclosed our special brochure, which tells you all about us, and I would be happy to tell you a lot more. Just

555-555-1908

All the best,

Warren Name
Account Specialist

Fax Cover Sheets

VIA FAX

To: *(Name)*
Fax: 555-5550
(Name of Company)
(Department/floor)

From: *(Name)*
(Name of company)
Fax: 555-2609
Voice: 555-2525

NUMBER OF SHEETS (INCLUDING COVER SHEET):_____

Comments:_____

_____

_____

_____

_____

IF THIS FAX REACHES YOU IN ERROR, PLEASE FORWARD IT
TO THE NUMBER ABOVE OR CONTACT SENDER. WE APPRE-
CIATE IT!

A FAX FROM

(Name of company)

To: *(Name)*
Fax: 555-5550
(Name of Company)
(Department/floor)
From: *(Name)*
Fax: 555-2609 Voice: 555-2525

NUMBER OF SHEETS (INCLUDING COVER SHEET):_____

Comments:_____

_____

_____

_____

_____

THIS FAX MESSAGE CONTAINS PROPRIETARY INFORMATION
INTENDED FOR THE ADDRESSEE ONLY. IF IT REACHES YOU
IN ERROR, PLEASE CONTACT SENDER IMMEDIATELY.

 **FAX**

For:

From:

Regarding:

Number of pages (including this page):

Facsimile Transmission

To:

From:

Regarding:

Pages (including this page):

*Please hand deliver this important communication
to the addressee!*

A MESSAGE FROM

THE MARK OF ZORRO

Your cutlery specialists.

Dear: _____

The following message consists of _____ pages, including this one.

If any of it is difficult to read, please call 555-5506.

*Remember! No gift makes a bolder
statement than a knife from*

ZORRO

URGENT FAX

From

XYZ INDUSTRIES
CREDIT DEPARTMENT

To

_____

Re

_____

PLEASE DELIVER THIS FAX TO
ADDRESSEE WITHOUT DELAY!

Promotional Faxes

(Date)

To:
From:
Subject: *(Product)* Upgrade

You're on our "A" list for high-priority notification of new and upgraded products, so I took the quickest route to get this exciting information to you.

Beginning on *(date)*, *(Name of company)* will offer the following upgrade features for its *(products)*:

(list)

I'm sure you are already well aware of the benefits of these upgrades—since we are offering them in direct response to what customers like you have told us they want. But here's a capsule rundown of the most important features:

(list)

In most cases, the upgrade can be performed on site, and, as you know from your experience with our service technicians, we work fast, and we don't get in the way.

To arrange for installation, or to talk further about these exciting new upgrades, just give me a call at 555-0000.

(Name of company)

Offers Expanded Customer-Support Hours

I am very pleased to announce that, beginning on *(date)*, *(Name of company)* will offer its clients telephone support *(number)* days a week, from *(time)* to *(time)*.

This is a significant step for us—and a great benefit for our customers. Sure, you can get support hours like this from the bigger firms, but now you can get the kind of super responsive service that sent you to a small company—and get it *(% amount)* percent more hours per week.

Tip: Calling before *(time)* or after *(time)* will ensure the fastest possible service!

(date)

To:
From:
Subject: We're taking orders for improved *(product)*

We thought you would appreciate advance word of the availability of *(product)*, a significantly improved version of the previous model. With *(product)*, you can now:

(list product benefits)

(Product) will not be generally available until *(date)*, but we are shipping on *(date)* to our special customers—like you—who order by *(date)*.

To expedite ordering, you can fax your P.O. to 555-1111. Mark it "ATTN: Priority *(Product)* Orders." If you would like additional information before placing your order, please call me on my direct line, 555-0000.

E-mail to Customer

From:

(Name)—A limited quantity of *(product)* will be available earlier than the date we discussed. I should be able to ship by *(date)*. Interested? You can transmit your authorization by E-mail, and I'll expedite.

From:

(Name): This news is too hot for "snail mail." I thought you'd want to hear about it on line. *(Name of company)* is now offering *(product/service)*, and we're offering it at extremely favorable prices. Here's a sampling: *(list)*.

I'll give you a call before the end of the week to discuss your needs in this area. You can reach me here or by phone at 555-0000.

Electronic Bulletins for Special-Interest On-line Forums

NEW *(PRODUCT)* FOR *(APPLICATION)*

If you've had it with your old *(product)* or are looking for a practical, affordable way to expand into *(application)*, you'll be glad to know that *(Name of company)* now offers a full line of *(product)*, as well as the support that goes with it.

Call 1-800-555-0000 for details, or leave a message here at *(user id)*.

From:

New LOW prices for *(product/service)*

Friends, as users of *(type of product/service)*, you need to know about our line of high-value *(products/services)* before you make a purchase decision.

My recommendation: Turn away from the screen, pick up the telephone, and dial 1-800-555-0000. That is MY direct line—and YOUR direct line to savings.

PART II

On the Phone

The Voice and the Machine

No object in contemporary business life is more used, necessary, loved, and hated than the telephone. It is both a means of communicating with the outside and of shunning the outside. It can make connections with customers and clients, or it can put them off, put them down, and drive them away. It can be a means of providing personal service in an impersonal world, or it can be used as just one more prod by a business that treats people like cattle.

The National Rifle Association used to say, "Guns don't kill people. People kill people. "A customer service professional might paraphrase this for you: "Phones don't kill customers. A bad telephone attitude kills customers."

The varieties of bad telephone attitude—let's call the malady BTA—are infinite, but they all come down to three fundamentals:

1. An unwillingness to communicate
2. An unwillingness to help
3. A feeling that the customer is an intrusion

To cure BTA, these three fundamentals must be changed. You and your staff who deals with customers by phone must develop:

1. A passion for communication
2. A desire to help
3. The conviction that customers are not an intrusion into your business, they *are* your business

The three chapters that follow in this section provide specific methods for curing BTA—or avoiding it in the first place—but let's address some essential objectives and strategies first.

Sales Calls

Depending on your business, "cold calls"—uninvited calls to potential customers—can be effective. Cold calling is, however, hard work and, even more, time-consuming work. Even small businesses often find it cost-effective to hire people to make these calls, although it is also possible to assign the task to secretarial or reception help during slack periods. Small-business managers and owners sometimes make cold calls themselves after hours or during slack spells.

Cold calls have a significant likelihood of being met with resistance, even hostility. You can reduce this likelihood by doing the following:

1. *Call only at reasonable hours.* Early afternoon is good for most calls to businesses. Any time after nine in the morning is good for homes, if you are appealing to people who are likely to be home—for example, full-time mothers. Otherwise, it is best to call after usual dinner times: after 6:30 but before 9. Generally, it is not wise to begin by asking if this is "a good time to call." Such a question invites a no. However, be prepared to offer to call back if the callee tells you he is busy. "I understand. What's a good time to call back?"

2. *Be concise and to the point.* The quicker you make your point, the better. This means *always* using a prepared script. However, rehearse the script so that it does not sound "canned," and maintain flexibility so that you can respond to interruptions and questions.

3. *Present material as information, not promotion.* The most effective sales devices instantly generate desire. However, especially in the case of a business phone call, desire begins with knowledge, with information. By making an uninvited call, you are—let's face it—intruding on another person. Make that intrusion worth her while. Don't let the call be perceived as, "Hi. I'm going to take your time and try to sell you something" but as "In return for a few moments of your time, I am going to *give* you valuable information."

4. *Cultivate a rhythm and tone that are a pleasure to hear.* Some folks are lucky enough to have what is generally called a "pleasant phone voice." If you're one of these people, great! If not—or if you feel that you are not—you can practice and, by practicing, achieve what seems to come naturally to some others. There's nothing mysterious about developing a good telephone voice. Here's what to work on:

   Pace: Slow down. Speak a little more slowly that you normally do.

   Pitch: Lower your voice. Unless you have a deep voice to begin with, consciously pitch your voice a little lower than normal. Lower-pitched voices are usually perceived as more authoritative—whether the speaker is a man or a woman. Generally, the lower pitch will also slow you down and promote more careful enunciation.

Enunciate: Give each word full value. Make certain that you are understood. In and of itself, an uninvited call may or may not irritate the callee, but nothing is more irritating than an uninvited, time-wasting call from some mush mouth who cannot make himself understood. Moreover, careful enunciation and pronunciation convey the message that you are an intelligent human being. If you approach the cold call as providing information rather than promoting yourself or your product, it follows that what you have to say will be perceived as more valuable if it sounds as if it's coming from a person smart enough to be worth listening to.

Targeted Calls

There are cold calls and there are *really* cold calls: positively Arctic attempts to drum up business. You move into an area, rip pages from the phone book, and just start dialing away. Most businesses target their callees more narrowly than this, using calling lists purchased from other firms or from firms specializing in providing leads, or using phone numbers found in appropriate trade directories, and so on. Any seasoned sales professional knows that the best customers a business has are its current customers. These are your most tightly targeted callees. If Customer A has purchased, say, a computer from you, and you now have a special offer available on printers, it's a good idea to call Customer A (and B, C, and D, right on down to the end of the alphabet) to tell him about it.

The same guidelines given for cold calling apply to these calls as well, but you have the great advantage of working from an established relationship. While the particular call is still unsolicited, you don't have to assume it is unwelcome. There is a significant likelihood that what you have to say to the callee will be of interest to her. For this reason, emphasize and highlight the informational purpose of the call.

Follow-up

A cold call or a targeted call may result in

Outright rejection

Expression of a lack of interest

A sale

A request that you call back some other time

Indecision

A request for more information

The last three outcomes require follow-ups. In a business world pressed by hectic schedules, follow-ups are often elusive—something you know you ought to do, but just never get around to. Letting follow-ups slip through the cracks is a serious business error. Precisely because everyone's schedules are so hectic, precisely because most consumers perceive most businesses as impersonal and even careless, the follow-up call is important. In and of itself, the follow-up establishes a relationship between you and the callee. It introduces an element of ongoing stability to what was otherwise a fleeting contact. To the degree—however slight—that you establish a relationship, a continuity, you increase the likelihood of doing business with a customer.

If you are asked to call back, respond by asking for the best time to call back. Then make sure that you call back and call back at that time.

If your initial call is met by indecision, respond by asking the callee something like: "What can I do to help you make a decision?" If this results in a dialogue, great! And if you can supply the answers to the customer's questions, so much the better. If you cannot immediately supply the information necessary to help the callee make a decision, explain that you need to get the information and *agree on a time for your call back to the customer*. Then make certain that you return the call at that time. If you do not have the necessary information by the appointed time, call anyway and report your progress. These last few guidelines also apply if a customer responds to your call by explicitly asking for more information.

Responding to Calls

Initiating calls is one vehicle for promoting your business. Responding to incoming calls is another. The guidelines just discussed concerning rhythm and tone apply here as well, as do the rules for follow-up. In addition, make certain of the following:

1. *Be fast.* Your telephone calls should be answered within twenty seconds. This is not a mystical rule of business. It is plain common sense. If you were calling a friend at home, how many times would you let the phone ring before you assumed he was out or otherwise unavailable? Four, five, at most six rings. Unless they are highly motivated to contact you, most customers will hang up on an attempt at a business call after four rings, after which, quite probably, they will "let their fingers do the walking" down to the next Yellow Pages listing.

2. *Pick up the phone before you speak.* This commandment is not meant to insult your intelligence. Just think: How many times have you called, say, the firm of "Soldier, Tinker, Tailor" only to be greeted with ". . . Tailor"? Pick up the phone, put it to your ear, then make your greeting.

3. *Greet the caller.* This doesn't mean, "Hi! How ya doin?" Whatever it turns out that the caller specifically wants, you can be sure even before she says word one that she wants information. Anticipate this certainty by greeting her with information: "Good morning. This is Acme Widgets, John speaking. How may I help you?" Such a greeting supplies four important pieces of information:

   It tells the caller you are pleasant, polite, and civil ("Good morning").

   It tells the customer that she has reached a specific place. (Acme Widgets).

   It tells the customer she has reached a specific person: you, John.

   Most important, it tells the customer that you are willing to help. It invites dialogue. It strikes up a relationship.

Let's look at the last sentence of that greeting a bit more closely: *"How may I help you?"* This not only conveys a helping attitude, it begins by focusing the conversation. "May I help you?" is better than nothing, but it leaves the caller adrift. "How may I help you?" politely asks the caller to focus his request. It gets the call to the heart of the matter, which saves you and your caller time.

Chapter Fourteen will discuss specific techniques for turning incoming calls into sales and customer satisfaction, but consider the following concept as a general principle for handling all incoming calls. It comes from marketing and customer service consultant Michael Ramundo of MCR Marketing.

He talks in terms of "call ownership," and it is a concept meant primarily to put an end to the runaround many callers get when they call a large organization, only to be tossed from one department to another. However, it can be applied to small businesses as well.

Once you pick up the phone, Ramundo says, *you own the call.*

The call is yours. You must handle it. You must take responsibility for it. You own the call until the caller's question is answered, his issue resolved, or you can "sell" that call to someone else who *can* answer the question or resolve the issue. Thinking in terms of call ownership goes a long way toward creating customer satisfaction.

The Machine

Throughout these pages, you have been counseled not to envy bigger firms. For all *their* power, *you* have, after all, something they can never have: your smallness. You can deliver a level of personal service and direct accountability unavailable to larger firms. Until, that is, you start spreading yourself too thin. And that, alas, is the fate of many successful small businesses. You become a one-person band.

Having said this, I am tempted to write that the last thing a caller wants to hear when he phones your *small* business is an answering machine. But this is not the case. The *last* thing your caller wants to hear is a phone ringing and no one picking it up. If you or another human being cannot be there to answer the phone, it is far better for a machine to pick up than for the call to go unanswered. However, even when it is necessary for a machine to answer, you can still elevate the level of service to something more personal than what the big companies customarily offer. Here's how:

1. *Use one message during business hours and another after hours.* During business hours, your message should greet the caller, giving the name of your firm and your name, then saying something like: "I am away from my desk . . ." or "I am helping other customers . . ." Next, ask the caller to leave a message. Don't just invite a message, be emphatic about it: "Please tell me how I can help you. Just leave a message after the tone, and please include your phone number and the best time to call. I will return your call as soon as possible." Your after-hours message should likewise include a greeting, though it is not necessary to state your name. The message should state your normal business hours, and it

should conclude with an emphatic appeal for a message: "Please leave a message after the tone, and please include your phone number and the best time to call. We *will* return your call." If you have an after-hours number you can dependably be reached at, or a beeper, or an answering service, your message should, of course, provide this information.

2. *Change your daytime message daily.* Even when it is necessary to greet a caller with a machine, you can still let him know that there is a human being living and breathing nearby. Begin your greeting by including today's date: "Hello, this is Jane Smith of Smith Widgets. It's Monday, September 3rd, and I'm with other customers at the moment. Please tell me how I can help you. Just leave a message after the tone, including your phone number and the best time to call back, and I *will* return your call. Thank you." This way, your caller knows there is somebody there—today. Obviously, it is important to remember to update the message each day, and it is also important not to use this message after business hours.

3. *Offer another option, if you can.* If your firm is big enough to warrant a voice mail system, your recorded greeting might offer a "safety valve," a means by which the caller can speak to someone else if you are presently unavailable. Usually, the message instructs the caller to press "0" on the Touch Tone™ pad or to remain on the line until the operator answers.

On Hold

Depending on the size of your business, you will have to decide how many telephone lines to install. If you have only a single line, you will need to weigh the value of a "call waiting" option. Call waiting means that no caller will ever get a busy signal. However, it also means that your current call will be interrupted by a beep or click signaling the presence of another caller. This can be very disconcerting if you are in the middle of a sales pitch or sensitive negotiations. Also, leaving the current caller (even for a moment) to "take another call" may irritate the current caller, suggesting that he is not your primary focus. If, on the other hand, you choose not to pick up the "call waiting" call, *that* caller will hear your phone ringing without an answer. He may assume that you're out—or even out of business.

If you have more than one line, you will encounter situations where you will have to put a caller on hold. You are talking to Customer A, and your other line rings. Say to Customer A, "Will you hold, please?" Then switch to Customer B. Say: "Good morning. This is Name of Company. Will you hold, please?" and return to Customer A. "Thank you for holding."

Notice the phrase: "Will you hold, please?" It is a request rather than a directive. "Please hold," despite the "please," is, in contrast, a rude and peremptory command.

If you are a one-person band, and you usually get a lot of calls, you should consider either hiring help or installing an automated response unit (ARU), which will pick up the other line when you are busy. This unit will answer with a message asking the caller to hold. You also ought to consider a system that plays music while the caller is on hold. True, you may find some people who complain about listening to music—but it is better than dead silence, which leaves the caller wondering if she's been disconnected or forgotten. Another useful device plays a recorded message at intervals to let the caller know that you are aware of his call and that you are working as fast as you can to help him. Avoid a recorded message that says something like "Your call is important to us." This phrase is calculated to create anger and resentment: *If my call is so blankety-blank important to you guys, why am I sitting here on hold?* Better to give the message that you are aware of the call and that you will speak to the caller just as soon as possible.

At times, you will have to put a caller on hold not to answer another call, but to handle the caller's request; for example, you might have to look up a customer record or recover some other item of information. In this case, explain what you need to do and *ask* permission before you put the caller on hold. Tell the caller about how long she will be on hold: "I need to pull the service record on that item. May I put you on hold? It will take about two minutes." If the delay unexpectedly becomes longer, get back to the caller and inform her: "I need another couple of minutes. Thanks for your patience."

The important point about using the telephone and the various devices that extend its usefulness is that all these things are merely instruments, neither good nor bad in and of themselves. Whether you are speaking face to face or over wires and through silicon, it is what you say and how you say it that either builds rapport or destroys it, that creates a positive or a negative relationship, that promotes your business customer by customer or takes it apart—customer by customer.

Person to Person:
Preparing "Spontaneous" Telephone
Sales Calls

How to Do It

You can use the telephone in two ways to make sales. There is the fully scripted solicitation, in which you or a staff member reads a written pitch. This approach, which is treated in the next chapter, is usually the most practical method for conducting full-scale sales and promotional campaigns. If the script is well written and, equally important, well delivered, the approach is not only practical, but effective as well. But there are many other telephone occasions when a prepared script is inappropriate. For example, you've come out with a new service. Draw up a short list of current customers (current customers are always your best prospects) who you are reasonably certain will be interested in the service. Give them a "spontaneous" call.

Indeed, *any* call can turn into a sales call, especially if you learn to listen to your customers. You call a customer who is late with a payment:

"I'm sorry," he says. "Your invoice just slipped through the cracks."

"I understand perfectly. In fact, are you aware that we have a software product to keep that from happening?"

"Really?"

"Yes, it's . . ."

Few abilities are more admired in business than the faculty of thinking on your feet. Maybe you believe that this is a talent you either have or don't have. To a degree this is the case. However, it is also a skill that can be acquired. The most important requisite for this skill is full knowledge and thorough familiarity with the products or services that you are selling. You can't launch into a spontaneous sales presentation without knowing what you are selling. The second requisite is enthusiasm about the products and services you are selling. It really helps to believe in what you sell. It really helps to like—if possible, to love—your work and to take pride in the range of merchandise and services you offer. Beyond this, you can prepare "crib sheets" or "fact sheets" or "cue cards" listing the most important sales points of the merchandise or services you offer. Keep these handy by the phone.

What is handy?

You could prepare a loose-leaf binder, with tabs, arranged alphabetically or with the hottest products up front. You could use a 4 × 5 or 5 × 7 card file, again arranged in logical order for quick reference. If your office is equipped with PCs, you might prepare data sheets using any one of the many database software package available, so that whoever takes or makes a call can, with a few keystrokes, "pop up" the relevant product or service, complete with information on features, pricing, and so on. Whatever strategy you adopt, the idea is to convey to the customer not only that your knowledge of the product or service is thorough, but that you yourself are so completely sold on the merchandise that you have the information on it uppermost in your mind at all times.

How exhaustive should your prompt cards (or whatever format you choose) be?

They should be just comprehensive enough to interest—to "hook," if you will—your customer. You should not risk boring him with details he doesn't want to hear. In advance, distill the selling points for each item to their essentials. If the customer expresses interest, you can always ask him to wait a moment while you get the full spec sheet. Not only will your customer not mind waiting a moment or two, he will appreciate the effort you are making to serve him.

There is more to "spontaneous" sales calls than knowing and communicating the selling points and features of your products or services. Sales techniques are subject to many variations, but you can't go far wrong if, whatever approach you take, you bear in mind the following steps:

1. Get your caller's/callee's attention.

2. Identify a need your caller/callee has.

3. Show that you can fill this need.

4. Persuade the caller/callee to buy.

5. Get the caller/callee to act.

The strategies that follow are based on accomplishing these three steps.

Lukewarm Calls

Note: "Cold" calls are virtually shots in the dark. They are calls made to people you don't know. Perhaps the callees are selected from special-interest lists you have purchased or leased. Perhaps the list is based on your own research. Perhaps the list is nothing more specialized than the names in the local telephone directory. Calls following up hot leads, in contrast, are calls to established customers or to others you know have an interest in your product or service. Somewhere in between these two extremes is what I am identifying as the "lukewarm call." Generally, these are calls to established customers or others you have some reason to believe will be interested in your product or service. In general, these are reasonably good candidates for prepared "spontaneous" sales calls. You should not waste time—your's and the callee's—by using this "spontaneous" approach in cold call situations. Cold calls should be scripted. Items on hand:

1. Short list of potentially interested customers to call concerning *(new product)*

2. List of selling points, beginning with points that specifically answer the question: *Why should I be interested in new product/service?*

The call is unscripted, but might go something like this:

Caller: Hello, *(Name of callee)*. This is *(Name of caller)* at *(Name of company)*. I'm calling because you mentioned to me a while ago that you were looking into *(type of product/service)*. Well, we've just developed a new *(product/service)*, which, I think, would fill the bill for you just perfectly. And we are offering it at a very special introductory price.

Are you interested?

Callee: Yes.

Caller: Great! Let me tell you a little about it.

First, you had mentioned that *(repeat requirement[s] customer had mentioned)*. Well *(new product)* can do all that and more. For example, *(list features)*.

Second, installation is not the hassle it used to be with units like this. Ours has a special feature that *(explain)*.

Third, there's the price. This will surprise you—pleasantly. The base price is *($ amount)*. With the options I think you'll want—such as *(list)*—the total comes to *($ amount)*. Now, that's our regular price. Our introductory price, with the options package, is only *($ amount)*.

And one last point: our warranty. Industry standard is *(number)* years. *Ours* is fully guaranteed, parts and labor, for *(greater number)* years.

The introductory pricing period ends in *(number)* weeks. I'd really like the opportunity to demonstrate the unit to you. I can drop by your office, if you like. When would be a good time for you?

Note how, within an informal context, the presentation follows the basic steps of selling. It begins by getting the callee's attention and establishing her need. In this case, the caller's task is not to create a perception of need or to persuade the callee that she has a certain need, but to build on information previously obtained. This is why it is important to become sensitive to your customers' evolving needs, to make note of these needs, and to create a system that allows you to review and recall these needs as required. The caller goes on to show how he can fill the need. At this point, in this particular presentation, it is not appropriate to proceed directly to a closing, but, instead, to set up a sales call. So the fourth step here is to persuade the callee to allow the caller to make a full-scale sales presentation. The call concludes by getting the callee to act: Not *Why don't you give me a call some time so that we can discuss the product?* but *When would be a good time for you?* Always conclude a sales presentation, whether "spontaneous" or scripted, with an inducement to and instructions for a specific action.

LUKEWARM CALL BASED ON CUSTOMER REFERRAL

Any seasoned sales manager knows that a company's best prospects are current customers. Current customers—provided they are satisfied customers—

are also a company's best salespeople. No form of advertising is more effective—more likely to result in a sale—than word of mouth. When a current customer furnishes you with a lead to new business, follow it. If your informant tells you that So-and-so definitely wants the product and is ready to buy *now,* congratulations, you have been gifted with a *hot lead.* But, as is more often the case, when you learn that So-and-so is simply a likely prospect, then a "lukewarm" call is appropriate. The most valuable tool you have in the lukewarm sales situation is a relationship—the personal connection established by the fact that a current customer gave you the name of a prospective customer. This knowledge and the confidence it conveys give you the competitive edge. Begin your "spontaneous" sales call by invoking that relationship.

Caller: Hello, *(Name of callee).* This is *(Name of caller)* at *(Name of company).* Your good friend, *(Name of reference),* thought you would want to hear from me about a solution we offer to your *(identify/describe need). (Name of reference)* tells me that you've been looking for *(product)* and that, so far, you haven't found anything that lights your fire. Is that the case?

Callee: Yes.

Caller: Well, then, I'm glad that *(Name of reference)* put me in touch with you, because we have a new product that, if I understand your needs correctly, will give you precisely what you want. It also allows for future additional applications, so that you'll be protecting your investment, and—since I know you've been shopping around—I believe you will find our prices very competitive.

Would you like to hear more?

Callee: Yes.

Caller: *(List the selling points from your card or computer file.)* If you're eager to get a system installed, I can personally demonstrate the product in your office. What would be a good time for you this week?

Lukewarm Call Based on Casual Market "Research"

It is difficult to decide whether these calls are lukewarm or tepid. Certainly, they verge on cold. If you are investing in formal market research, you should also invest in carefully scripted sales calls. But not all market research is formal. For example, you hear that So-and-so is in the market for a service you happen to offer. This is not an outright referral, but intelligence you happen to gather. Or, while talking to your widget repair technician, you learn that he's just made his umpteenth service call to So-and-so. "It's about time So-and-so either got a new unit or thought about outsourcing." And a light bulb goes on in your head.

Now, it is usually appropriate to be discreet about how you use such information. You do not want to give your callee the impression that you are spying on her, nor do you want to put your casual informant in the position of seeming to be a spy or of betraying a trust. Nor do you want to make your caller look foolish: *I hear your stupid widget broke down again. Boy, are you an idiot!* If, upon reflection, you see absolutely no harm in revealing your source, it is best to do so. If, on the other hand, you have any reservations about revealing it, simply make the call. In either case, such calls, based on casual research or information gathered simply by keeping your ear to the ground, do not require full-scale scripting. They are spontaneous situations.

> Hello, *(Name of callee)*. My name is *(Name of caller)*, and I own *(Name of company)*. We specialize in *(service)*. I was talking to one of our clients yesterday—he happens to be an associate of yours, *(Name of source)*—who mentioned that you were looking for *(service)*. I thought you might find a call from me useful. We offer a full range of *(service)*, including *(highlight list)*.
>
> Would you like to hear more?

If the response is positive, use your crib sheet to hit the high points in somewhat greater detail. Close by directing an action:

> I'm glad I called. You are probably quite anxious to get the ball rolling on this project. I can come out to your plant as early as *(day)*. How does that look to you?

Here is an approach to use when you are acting on intelligence from a source you do not wish to reveal:

> Hello, *(Name of callee)*. This is *(Name of caller)*. I run a company that supplies *(product/service)*. You know, we've been in the business for *(number)* years, and yet I've not had the opportunity of speaking with you about your *(product/service)* needs.

Is this a good time for us to talk a bit about how I can help you with *(product/service)*?

If your intelligence source was accurate and your call prompt enough, the callee will spark at your question: *Yes. I really am glad you called.* Or: *You've called at just the right time.* If the callee is not interested, no harm has been done, and you have not compromised your source in any way.

Lukewarm Call to New Business

If you are predatory by nature or just given to cynicism, you might observe that any new business entering your community is fair game for a sales call. True enough. But rather than look on the new kid in town as your quarry, why not see him as a neighbor who needs all the help he can get to succeed in your community? This way of looking at things is not intended to get you into heaven, but is, in fact, more potentially productive than the hunt-down-and-nail approach. Be the first in your community to welcome a new business. Let the newcomer know how you can help him—by selling him your goods or services.

How do you prepare a "spontaneous" call to a newcomer? The one thing you want to avoid is any appearance of calling with a "canned" or scripted spiel. The new business gets a lot of sales calls—most of them, to one degree or another, canned. To avoid this in your call, prepare by exercising your sympathetic imagination. Think back to what it's like to be new in a neighborhood, to be just starting up. What do you want to hear? What kind of help can you use? Begin by greeting the newcomer as a new neighbor. Then go on to identify yourself not so much as a vendor with something to sell, but as a source with *helpful* products or services to offer: the very merchandise the newcomer needs to establish himself, to make the transition to the new location easier, to succeed.

Hello, *(Name of callee)*. This is *(Name of caller)*. I run *(Name of company)* at *(location)*, and I wanted to be one of the first to welcome you to our community. This is a great place to do business. I've been here for *(number)* years, and I'd be happy to share some of my experience with you, if you like.

I know what it's like to be the new kid on the block—with a million things to do to get up and running, so I don't want to take up your time. But you do owe it to yourself to take a break and try out *(Name of restaurant)* for lunch as soon as possible. I'd like to take you to lunch, maybe answer some questions you may have about the community, and suggest some ways in which my company might help you get established. We offer a full range of *(products/services)*: all designed to flatten out the learning curve and let you hit the ground running.

I'm sure your schedule must be pretty hectic. But can you break for lunch, say, tomorrow *(or other day)* at *(time)*? There's no better introduction to *(Name of community/neighborhood/area)* than eating at *(Name of restaurant)*—especially when you can get the other fella to pay.

RESPONDING TO INQUIRIES

The potential customer who calls you to inquire about your products or services is doing two things:

1. Shopping
2. Calling for help

The caller may tell you—and may even believe—that he is only seeking information. But don't, therefore, be tricked into supplying mere information. To satisfy the underlying motives of the call, respond by selling and respond by helping. If your product or service is as good as you can make it, the two activities are really one and the same.

In the introduction to this section of the book, we have discussed strategies for answering the phone. Use those strategies here:

1. Pick up the phone.
2. Do not begin to speak until you have picked up the phone and have it to ear and mouth.
3. Greet the caller. Give your company name, and give your name.
4. Then focus the call: *How may I help you?*

The phrase is not "May I help you?" Or "What can I do for you?" But "*How* may I help you?" This gently but firmly prompts your caller to define her request, saving both of you time and setting up a positive context in which the chances for misunderstanding are minimized from the outset. Ideally, the phrase will evoke something like: "I'm looking for such-and-such a product."

Now it's your ball. What will you do with it?

Begin by assuring the caller that she has come to the right place: "I can help you with that."

Next, make certain that you have enough information. Seasoned businesspeople know that failure to satisfy the customer almost always begins with misunderstanding, and misunderstanding is born of inadequate, insufficient information. However, even experienced businesspeople tend to blame this on the customer. It was all well and good for department store pioneer Marshall Field to declare as his motto, "Give the lady what she wants." But the lady—or the gentleman—doesn't always *know* what she or he wants or is unclear about expressing it.

True enough. But instead of fixing blame on the customer, why not prevent the problem? And that is too important to leave up to the customer. Work to prevent misunderstanding by making certain that you are asking enough questions to *help* the customer get what he wants or to get the product that best fills his needs (the two are not always the same). This process takes some effort, but, even more, it takes a certain amount of courage, for the all-too-common "wisdom" of selling emphasizes convincing and persuading. Often, salespeople are trained to *avoid* asking questions. The idea is to create the impression that you, the salesperson, knows what the customer wants even before the customer knows what he wants. In fact (some salespeople believe) it is actually dangerous to ask questions, because, once *you* start asking questions, the *customer* may start asking questions, including *Why am I buying this?*

If your goal is to sell one item to one customer, the received wisdom is good enough. Yes, by all means, talk the person into buying whatever you want him to buy—then you might as well pack your bags and get out of town. You've made a sale, but you haven't acquired a customer. All businesses—but especially *small* businesses, which must cultivate each and every customer as a precious asset—literally cannot afford to make sales at the expense of making customers. It is not enough to sell the product. Your responsibility is also to create satisfaction. Do that, and you will make a sale (yes, maybe the hard way) as well as establish a relationship with a customer. That customer will be a source of future sales as well as a potential generator of word-of-mouth advertising, testimonials, and referrals.

Any businessperson soon learns a law as immutable as gravity: *There is no reward without risk.* It is well worth risking an immediate, cut-and-dried sale by asking enough questions to ensure that the customer is buying what he wants and what he needs. Besides, there is an *immediate* upside to this approach as well. Customers are justifiably leery of salespeople who try to "talk them into" buying more than they want: the superdeluxe model at $XXX instead of the merely deluxe model at $XX. No matter how tempting, you should resist "talking the customer into" an unwanted upgrade and thereby squandering the opportunity offered by a customer inquiry. But, by asking the right questions, you may well create the context in which the customer *convinces himself* that it is appropriate to spend more money to get the superdeluxe model he hadn't realized he wanted before you helped him determine the exact nature of his needs and requirements. Those who make their living in the persuasion business—novelists and actors, for example— quickly learn that the essence of their craft is to *show,* not to *tell.* By nature, human beings are most persuaded by what their own senses and judgment tell them. Your job is to create the context in which the customer's senses and judgment will tell him what *you* want to tell him.

Asking the right questions is so important to creating the kind of satisfaction that builds relationships as well to making sales, that part of your "ad lib" preparation might be a list of product-related questions to ask callers. Don't ask the questions as if you are reading them, of course, but use the list of questions to ensure that you cover all the bases (You pick up the phone):

You: *(Name of company).* This is *(Name).* How may I help you?

Caller: I am looking for *(product).*

You: I can certainly help you with that. We offer a wide variety of *(products).* Let me ask you a few questions to make sure that we zero in on precisely the *(product)* that's right for you. *(Use list of questions.)*

Based on your needs, I would suggest that you consider either *(product 1)* or *(product 2).* Both will do *(list functions based on answers to questions),* but *(product 1)* will also *(list additional functions).* The price of *(product 1)* is *($ amount 1),* compared with *($ amount 2)* for *(product 2).* You have to ask yourself whether the additional features are attractive enough to you to spend the additional money. Certainly, if you want *(functions),* the additional cost is actually highly cost-effective.

Where you go from here depends on the customer's response. It never hurts to end by asking: "May I take your order for *(product 1)* or *(product 2)*?" If the customer expresses hesitation or is simply not yet ready to order, ask how you might help him decide: "Is there any more information I could supply to help you make your choice?" And, incidentally, "choice" is a word that is preferable to *decide* or *decision*. It sounds less momentous and implies less pressure. *Decision* conveys a sense of compulsion, whereas *choice* suggests empowerment and freedom. It places in a positive context the action you are trying to prompt.

Often, turning customer inquiries into sales—while creating satisfied customers—is a balancing act. If the customer has a clear idea of what she wants and needs, your task is straightforward. The same is true if your customer wants product X and you offer only one variety of product X. Your task: Sell product X, of course. But what happens when your customer is unclear about her needs? Or when product X comes in a wide range of variations? You have several choices:

1. You can simply try to sell the caller *some*thing.

2. You can explain that the decision is complex and offer to send a catalog.

3. You can bombard the caller with questions, so that she wishes she never called and loses all interest in acquiring product X.

4. You can work out, in advance, strategies for leading callers through the available choices.

The "correct" multiple-choice answer is probably obvious. Alternative 1 may produce a sale, but it is far less likely to produce a sale *and* a satisfied customer; therefore, it squanders a valuable asset. Alternative 2 risks losing a sale; while you don't want to railroad your customer into making a purchase, you do want to motivate action, not postpone it. Alternative 3 makes the buying experience unpleasant; overwhelmed with choices, the customer is likely to reject the product or service as too complicated—he may choose to postpone a decision or may decide not to buy at all. Alternative 4 requires preparation and clear thinking on your part, but it is worth it. If the purchasing choices that must be made are indeed complex, you might consider drawing up a "decision tree" or a "flow chart," with the yes and no responses branching from one decision to another. Another creative way of presenting complex alternatives concisely is to combine the telephone with the fax machine. Offer to fax—right now, while you're still on the line—a checklist or chart that will aid the customer in making a decision.

Strategies for Focusing

Approach this process not as a salesperson desperate for a sale, but as counselor, as one who is willing to work with the customer to ensure that her needs are met and met optimally. The truly successful sales scenario is one in which the customer perceives the selling process itself as value added to the purchase. Construct a set of questions tied to intended use. Once this area has been addressed, turn to cost. You should preface the questioning with a "helping" remark: "Let's take just a few moments to work through your requirements together." Or "Let's work together to determine just what product will be best for you." Or "Take a few moments to work with me so that we can connect you with just the right product."

The key here is patience. If the customer perceives you as impatient, he will not only become anxious, but will, in fact, become impatient as well. Remember the motto of any successful business: *The customer is not an interruption of your business day; the customer is the reason for your business day.* You must invest whatever time is necessary. Don't, however, spend time persuading the customer that he needs this or that product. Instead, invest time leading him through the process. If you keep the process interactive, your customer will not feel that his time is being wasted but, rather, will be grateful to you for investing so much time in his needs. Furthermore, it is a rule of thumb in any negotiation—and, ultimately, that is what a sales presentation is—that the more time both parties invest in the negotiation, the more likely that it will be consummated and consummated to mutual satisfaction.

TAKING ORDERS

Sometimes—in some businesses, *most* of the time—a customer calls knowing what he wants. He doesn't want you to sell him anything. He just wants to place an order. Even calls that require a lengthy question-and-answer process end—if they end successfully—with the taking of an order.

This is one task for which you should always have a prepared form with explicit blanks for all necessary information. Making a sale is always exciting, but don't get so excited that you record information inaccurately. Repeat back to the customer the particulars of the customer's order. Make certain you have them all right.

Before the call is concluded, assure the customer that the order will be shipped promptly or that whatever special handling or option was specified will be attended to. Resist the impulse to reassure the customer that he has made a good decision. Such reassurance after the purchase usually has the opposite of its intended effect. However, when appropriate to the merchandise, you might say something like, "I know that you will enjoy using your *(product)*." Finally, end by asking the customer if you can help him with anything else, and be certain to thank him for his order.

OVERCOMING RESISTANCE

When you make a lukewarm call, it is important to recognize the difference between a definite "no" and a highly qualified "no"—that is, resistance. If the customer tells you flatly that he or she is not interested in what you have to offer, cease and desist, concluding the call with something like: "Okay. Thanks very much for your time, and I hope you'll keep us in mind should your needs change."

In contrast to an out-and-out *no,* resistance is characterized by "I don't know" or by certain sets of assumptions that you must overcome:

"Isn't that terribly expensive?"

"The cost would be prohibitive."

"I've heard those things don't work."

"I've always used such and such."

"I don't have the staff to operate it."

Resistance may also take the form of postponement:

"Can you call me about it later?"

"I've been too busy to think about it."

"I'm not ready to buy yet."

The first variety of resistance must be overcome with education. It is not your task to argue with the customer or his preconceptions, but to show him alternatives. For example:

Customer: It's just too expensive.

You: I agree that *(product)* requires a substantial investment. However, our experience has shown that it is cost-effective. On average, in installations for companies the size of yours, the initial investment is amortized within *(time period)*. As the old saying goes, it pays for itself. Recognizing this, we can offer you a wide range of financing plans.

Overcome resistance by showing your customer how to overcome resistance. When you encounter an obstacle, point out the way around it.

The second class of resistance—postponement—is not overcome with coaxing or heavy-handed persuasion. The customer feels burdened by uncertainty and indecision. Therefore, offer to take on some of the burden yourself:

"What can I do to help you make your choice?"

"What additional information will help you move on to the next step?"

"How can I help you define your options?"

In the midst of the sales process, you may feel that you need all the help you can get. The fact is, your *customer* often feels much the same way. If *you* don't offer her that assistance, who will?

CHAPTER 13

No Hangups:
Fully Scripted Telephone Solicitations

How to Do It

Telemarketing expert Robert J. McHaton observes: "The shortest distance between a salesperson and a prospect is the telephone line." The telephone is a powerful communications tool. Old-time, door-to-door salesmen (and they were invariably men) had to work to get a "foot in the door." The telephone is virtually an *automatic* foot in the door: few people can resist picking it up when it rings (though, increasingly, voice mail and answering machines are used to "screen" incoming calls). The telephone is also a great leveler of the competitive playing field. It is available to the smallest, most modestly capitalized of businesses as well as to the *Fortune* 500 giants, and, increasingly, it is those blue-chip firms that are making most extensive use of telemarketing. If you wish to consider telemarketing as a business in itself rather than as a business technique, then, surely, telemarketing is one of today's fastest-growing industries.

The preceding chapter covered the "spontaneous" sales calls (which, as we saw, should never *really* be all that spontaneous). These are most effective when used in "lukewarm" or "hot" selling situations: situations in which you have already established some form of contact or relationship with the target customer. The present chapter covers strategies for making "cold" calls; that is, calls to prospects who are total strangers to you and with whom you have no relationship.

STRATEGIES FOR MAKING "COLD" CALLS

You have four basic choices for making such calls:

1. Winging it
2. Following an outline
3. Following a full script
4. Using an ADRMP

WINGING IT

There are people in the world who certainly seem to be "natural born sales-people." And there are people who just love to talk on the phone. Put these two personality types together in a single human being, and, chances are, you have a telemarketer who can make sales without a script or outline of any kind. If you're convinced that you are such a person, then all that need be said is, *Well, bless your heart,* and you need not read on.

Most of the world, however, lacks this kind of talent—just as most of the world can't play basketball like Michael Jordan or play the fiddle like Isaac Stern. For those folks, winging cold calls (as distinct from lukewarm and/or hot calls) is

Exhausting

Demoralizing

Time-wasting

Ineffective

So why do it?

FOLLOWING AN OUTLINE

Creating and following an outline, which you keep before you as you make your calls, allows you or your *experienced* and *knowledgeable* sales staff to cover the bases with a prospect without, however, sounding "canned." It allows a good salesperson to imprint each sale with his or her own personality, yet it helps to ensure that:

1. All relevant product/service benefits are covered.

2. All terms and conditions are covered.

3. No promises are made that cannot be kept.

4. The product/service is not misrepresented.

Outlines also tend to increase the volume of calls over the number that can be achieved through spontaneous calls. Less time is wasted. Having that outline in front of you makes calling less of an emotionally demanding experience and, therefore, keeps your energy level higher, which results in more calls and more effective calls.

The outline should consist of selling steps and product/service benefits. You will need to include at least nine steps in the outline and as many key selling elements (especially product/service benefits, terms, conditions, etc.) as required.

1. *Verify the prospect's name.* Why? Who cares, if it's a cold call? Getting a name at the very beginning of the call gives the call a purpose. It tells the caller that you are calling him or her—not just anybody. It also allows you to use your prospect's name, an act that, in and of itself, breaks some of the ice of a cold call by establishing a rudimentary relationship between you and the callee.

2. *Identify yourself and your firm.* You can't "trick" your prospect into listening to what you have to say by withholding the fact that you are calling from a company that is trying to interest him in buying something. It doesn't work that way. In fact, failure to be upfront about who you are and where you are calling from will trigger instant suspicion, resistance, impatience, and a desire to hang up. Give your name and the name of your firm: "This is John Doe, calling from XYZ, Incorporated."

3. *Then tell the callee why you are calling.* Don't delay on this point, either. But be aware that certain words are *poison* in most selling situations and in a cold call situation particularly. These lethal words include:

buy	contract	deal
cheap	cost	decide
		sell

Announce the purpose of your call, but use *positive* words to do so. For example:

alternative	gain	taste
benefit	inform	test
breakthrough	information	touch
choice	money	trustworthy
choose	new	value
desirable	opportunity	wanted
distinctive	option	win
easy	prove	wise
family	see	
free	smart	

In short, combine telling your prospect why you are calling with a good reason for the prospect to take your call and to listen to you.

4. *Ask a "test" question.* Many sales professionals have a prejudice against questions. They want to do the talking and let the customer do the listening to reduce the risk of being shut out. Cold callers actually experience relatively few out-and-out hangups. Most people find it difficult to hang up—even on an unwanted sales call. Instead, often, they will listen to your pitch (at least for a while), even if they are not remotely interested in what you are selling. True, you haven't been shut out. But you have wasted time you could have devoted to a more promising prospect. It is, therefore better to launch out with a test question. But, like a good-hearted teacher, give your callee every opportunity to "pass" the test. Ask an appealing, inviting, intriguing question. Frame it to highlight benefits. Don't start out by poisoning the well with something like "Would you be interested in buying . . ." This is like asking, "Would you please reach into your pocket and give me some money?" Begin by testing your customer. Just make sure you ask a question that invites a yes. Often, it helps to make a statement, then simply ask for confirmation. "I have reason to believe that you would be interested in hearing about a new *(product)* we've developed, which

(briefly describe benefit). Is that the case?" A test question structured in this way not only launches your sales pitch, it also invites a yes—yet it allows the customer to say no, if he really and truly is not interested. The negative response will allow you to say, "Thanks for your time and have a nice day," hang up, and go on to the next prospect.

5. *Make the presentation*. We will cover this in detail using examples. In an outline, this section should clearly list all selling points, always emphasizing product benefits rather than product features. We will discuss promoting benefits versus features more fully in Chapter Fifteen, The Power of the Press, but let's anticipate that important distinction here. The features of a product or service are what it does. The benefits are the good things the product or service will do for the customer. Usually, benefits are intimately linked to emotion and feeling. "Acme detergent will clean your dishes better than any other detergent" describes a product feature. "Acme detergent enhances your dining experience because you and your guests feel as if you are dining with brand-new, pristine china" describes a product benefit.

6. *Overcome objections*. Your outline should anticipate customers' objections to buying your product or service, and it should provide quick-reference strategies for overcoming those objections. Experienced telemarketers put their outline (or their script) on a clipboard, using a short sheet of paper. Beneath the outline or script sheet or sheets is a longer sheet, labeled at the bottom (so that the label is clearly visible) with a type of objection: "TOO EXPENSIVE." When you turn to this sheet, you find an outline strategy for countering this particular objection. Clipped beneath this sheet is an even longer one, labeled at the bottom with another usual objection: "TOO DIFFICULT TO INSTALL." Beneath this is yet a longer sheet of paper labeled "TOO DIFFICULT TO USE," and so on. In this way, responses to objections are "tabbed" and immediately accessible. You might consider using computer software to create the electronic equivalent of the tabbed clipboard, with responses to objections that can be "popped up" readily on your monitor screen.

7. *Ask for the order*. When you counter an objection, don't ask your prospect if you answered his question. Former New York City mayor Ed Koch was famous for his familiar tag line, "How'm I doin'?" Well, that worked for Ed, but it's not the right message to send to your prospect. Instead, immediately follow your counter to his objection by asking for the order.

"Asking" does *not* mean "Would you like to order one?" This asks for a yes *or* no. Instead, ask for the order by giving your customer a choice that invites only a positive response. "Would you like to charge your order on a major credit card or would you prefer C.O.D.?" Or "Would you like the upright or horizontal model?"

8. *Verify information.* Make sure your outline includes a checklist that asks for verification of the customer's name, billing address, shipping address, and credit information. Make sure the outline prompts the salesperson to read back the order to the customer.

9. *Thank the customer.* Don't leave this to chance. The outline should remind the salesperson to thank the customer for the order.

FOLLOWING A FULL SCRIPT

If you want to exercise maximum control over how your product or service is telemarketed, you must create a fully scripted presentation. This simply takes the outline to the next level, making the same points, achieving the same goals, but fleshing out the skeleton. Use the nine outline steps just listed to guide you in creating a script. Keep it within 300 to 500 words in length—a maximum of about ninety seconds of telephone time without rushing.

The verbatim script has the following advantages over the spontaneous approach and the outline approach:

1. It can be used effectively by the experienced as well as the novice "telemarketing communicator." This means that you can hire low-cost telephone help (retirees wanting to earn extra money, students, aspiring actors, and so on). With low-cost help, your time is freed up for other tasks, and you can put more people on more phones to increase call volume.

2. Verbatim scripts ensure adherence to your selling goals and policies.

3. Verbatim scripts reduce misunderstanding and the possibility of misrepresentation by well-meaning (or, for that matter, ill-meaning) overzealous sales personnel. In this way, the scripts can increase customer satisfaction.

4. Verbatim scripts reduce training time and expense.

Are their disadvantages to verbatim scripts? Yes, there are:

1. A poor, unexpressive, lackluster telecommunicator will make the customer feel that he is being read to, that he is being subjected to a canned spiel.

2. Working from a script may reduce the individual initiative of the telecommunicator.

3. If an inexperienced telecommunicator attempts to depart from the script—to answer a question, for example—he may falter and become confused.

4. If adherence to the script is rigidly required, it may be difficult or impossible to meet customer objections and counter resistance.

BULLETPROOFING YOUR SCRIPTS

Most of the potential disadvantages of telemarketing scripts can be anticipated and overcome by taking four steps:

1. Prepare an effective script.

2. Include tabbed responses to objections.

3. Get through to the right person.

4. Work on your delivery and voice.

An effective script should follow the same steps as an effective outline, with these additions:

Use language that talks *to*—not *at*—your customer.

Wherever possible, use *you* rather than *we, I,* or the *company*.

Formulate a strong opening statement that gets your prospect's interest.

Incorporate questions into the script that are designed to get and keep your prospect involved.

Use questions that can be answered either with a "yes" or that prompt a positive choice among positive alternatives.

Sell benefits, not features.

Use descriptive language.

Use testimonials and examples, especially examples of success.

End with an "action closer"—prompting the customer to act now.

Address objections.

As in preparing an outline presentation, anticipate potential customer objections and provide responses to them. Using a clipboard with labeled and tabbed objection responses is a good way to handle this in a fumble-free manner. If you are equipped with personal computers and appropriate software, you can create responses to objections that can be "popped up" on your screen. As you gain experience selling your product or service over the telephone, compile a list of objections you actually encounter. Formulate responses to each of these objections and incorporate them into your script material.

In general, it is ineffective to attempt to counter an objection with an argument. Disputes generate hostility, and hostility does not produce sales. If your customer protests that the merchandise is "too expensive," your saying "No, it is not" won't help. A better strategy for countering objections and resistance is to put the issue back on the customer, by asking a question or by obtaining more information from him to get him to tell you just what would allow you to make the sale. If you do want to present what is, in effect, a counter*argument,* do so by supplying genuine, useful information rather than simply telling the customer that he is wrong.

Let's return to the "too expensive" objection. You might respond with: "What do you pay now?" Then work with the answer—"Does that price *include* freight?" Or "What quantities do you have to buy to get that price?" Or "Are you really satisfied with the quality (the warranty, the color, the variety, the service . . . whatever)?" Or "When you say 'too expensive,' what are you comparing our product with?" You might also present an *informative* counterargument, turning the objection into an opportunity to amplify your pitch: "'Too expensive'? Not when you consider the quality—we used eighteen-gauge steel throughout, 30 percent heavier than the competition—and the service. We're on call 24 hours a day, seven days a week."

What if your prospect hits you with a flat "I don't want it"? How can a scripted presentation handle *that?*

Don't agree. Don't surrender. Don't hang up. Respond: "Please tell me why you don't want it?" Notice that the question is framed as a polite request, not a demand ("Why don't you want it?"). Many objections can be met similarly:

I don't like it. "Please tell me why you don't like it."
I don't need it. "Please tell me why you don't need it."
And so on.

Two very common objections are the put-off—"I'm not interested now. Maybe later"—and the assertion of policy: "I never buy on the phone." You should have responses prepared for these. If the customer says "not now," respond that the offer is limited and may not be available later. Alternatively, ask the customer when you should call back: "Okay. May I call you back this afternoon, or would tomorrow morning be better for you?"

If the customer asserts that she never buys on the phone, ask her why:

"Please tell me why you don't do business on the phone."
"I understand your hesitance. Have you been burned in the past?"
"Please tell me why you don't trust me."
"A large number of *Fortune* 500 companies now do most of their purchasing over the phone."
"Do you get a better guarantee from another supplier?"

Get through to the right person. One objection you might encounter is that the callee needs permission to make a purchase or is not the person responsible for purchasing. Don't respond with frustration. Use this objection as an opportunity to identify the right person to call: "I see. Can you, please, tell me who makes the decisions regarding purchases?" Better yet, ensure that you call the right person to begin with. Before dialing the phone, take the time and effort to identify the person who makes the purchasing decisions, and start with her.

Work on delivery and voice. Telemarketing does not require the highly trained voice of a television or radio announcer, but it does call for a person who can deliver the scripted presentation clearly, smoothly, with clear pronunciation, with conviction, at an even pace, and with enthusiasm. Pace— don't rush, *ever*—and enthusiasm are the two most important qualities. Pace is a matter of practice, of training yourself or your staff to read the script at a moderate tempo. Enthusiasm is best developed from a genuine understanding of and enthusiasm for whatever it is you are selling. Silly as it may at first sound, you should also make the presentation with a smile. True, the callee cannot see you, but if you smile, chances are that all the positive inflections of voice and verbal delivery that go with a smile will be transmitted over the telephone wire.

The script itself does much to foster enthusiasm. Keep it simple, and keep it positive. Write in a way that encourages a positive, enthusiastic, smiling approach. This is not as difficult as it may at first seem. Simply take a potential negative—

"I must secure credit approval before I can ship."
and turn it into a positive—

"I'll ship that right out as soon as your credit approval arrives."

One surefire way to convert a potential negative into a real positive is to shift from "I" to "you":

Not
I think that
But
You will discover that
Not
I need to point out that
But
You will be interested to know that

USING AN ADRMP

There is an alternative vehicle for the delivery of the fully scripted telephone sales presentation. The automated dialing-recording message player (ADRMP) automatically dials preprogrammed telephone numbers and plays a recorded message to whomever answers the phone. The advantages of the ADRMP?

1. A machine is a tireless caller that, like the mechanical bunny used to promote a certain brand of batteries, keeps going, and going, and going, and . . .

2. A machine presentation ensures absolutely unvarying presentation of your prescribed sales presentation.

3. A machine will never lose its temper.

4. A machine permits you to record a professional voice, perhaps even the recognizable voice of a well-known celebrity.

Disadvantages? You bet there are:

1. Many people resent a "computer" intruding on their privacy and will slam down the receiver without listening to *any* of the actual sales presentation.

2. Even those customers who do listen to the recorded message may resent being treated like a target for an electronic dart.

3. Using an automated means of reaching customers may suggest that you intend to treat your customers like machines.

4. A machine cannot respond to customer questions or counter customer resistance.

5. ADRMPs are under attack in some states and jurisdictions and are subject to restrictive legislation or may even be illegal.

In general, an ADRMP is a poor choice for small-business promotion, mainly because it works against the greatest asset a small business has: a size and scale of operation that promote personal service and one-on-one contact with customers. ADRMPs do have a future, but they will probably prove most consistently useful for follow-up. For example, a mail-order fulfillment operation might program the phone numbers of customers who have placed catalog orders, and the ADRMP may call them to confirm that the order arrived—asking the customer to call only if the order has failed to arrive. For such follow-up tasks, the ADRMP is actually perceived as a positive customer service asset, an extra service. An ADRMP is also a good choice for initial collection "reminder" calls. Customers who have neglected to make a payment will be less embarrassed by a machine reminder than by a human caller and, therefore, less likely to resent the reminder.

Generating Leads

SCRIPT 1

Good morning/afternoon. This is *(Name)* from *(Name of company)*. Could you please give me the name of the *(owner, manager, etc.)*?

Thanks.

Would you connect me, please, with *(Name of owner, manager, etc.)*?

Thank you.

(Name of owner, manager, etc.), this is *(Name)* from *(Name of company)*. I am calling you today to give you some information you will want to have: *(Name of company)* has just developed a *(product)* that will *(identify key benefit)*.

Do you currently use *(type of product)*?

Are you aware of the full benefits of *(type of product)*?

Let me ask you, if I may: Do you currently *(describe activity)*?

Then you will definitely benefit from *(product)*. And I would like to tell you exactly how:

(list benefits in detail)

May I suggest that we have one of our representatives call on you to demonstrate for you the competitive edge *(product)* will give you? Who should our rep contact?

What would be a good time for our rep to visit?

In the meantime, would you like to see our literature?

Thank you very much for your time, *(Name)*, and have a good day.

SCRIPT 2

Is this *(Name of callee)*? Good morning/afternoon. My name is *(Name)*, and I'm calling from *(Name of company)* because I would like to know a few things about your *(type of product/service)* needs. Can you take just a moment or two to help me?

Great. Thanks.

Do you currently use *(type of product)*?

No? Would you tell me, please, why you don't?

Are you aware that using *(type of product)* can increase your revenue from *(type of operation)* by *(% amount)* percent or more?

Let me tell you how. *(Explain key points.)*

Would you like to learn more about *(type of product)*, what it costs, and what it can do for you?

Great.

I would like to set up a visit by one of our account representatives. Does *(time period)* look good for you?

Okay. What day during that week? We'll need no more than *(number)* minutes of your time. Is morning or afternoon best?

It's been a pleasure talking with you, and *(Name of representative)* will see you on *(repeat day and time)*. Thanks very much for your time, and have a good day.

Setting Up a Sales Call

Hello. May I speak with the *(manager, owner, etc.)*, please? Thank you.

Hello, *(Name of manager, owner, etc.)*, this is *(Name)*. I'm calling from *(Name of company)* this morning to introduce you to our new line of innovative *(products)*.

To introduce our new line, I can offer you a very special price on *(product)*.

Can you tell me, please, what brand do you use now?

How much do you pay?

Well, here's what you get with any of our *(products)*:

(list benefits)

Now ordinarily you would pay from *($ amount)* to *($ amount)* for quality like this, and, based on your long-term satisfaction, you would find these prices quite reasonable. But, for a limited time, I can offer you discounts of *(% amount)* to *(% amount)* percent off these prices.

One of my field reps will be in your area during *(time period)*. I can arrange for him to call on you, if you would like, to take advantage of this offer.

Terrific!

Let's set it up now. *(Secure details of time, place, etc.)*

(Name of rep) will see you, then, at *(time)* on *(day)*. It's been great talking with you, and have a good day.

Making the Sale

SCRIPT 1

Good morning/afternoon. My name is *(Name)*. May I please ask the name of the person who handles purchasing for *(department)*? Thank you very much.

(Name of right person), this is *(Name)*, with *(Name of company)*. We manufacture *(products)* for a wide variety of companies like yours, including *(list three big-name customers)*.

Do you currently use *(type of product)*? What brands? What are you accustomed to paying?

Well, then, you will be interested to hear what I have to offer.

Our *(product)* is unique and highly cost effective. It provides *(list benefits)*, and every firm that has used it, including *(list three big-name customers)*, has voiced great enthusiasm for it. For example, *(Name)* at *(Name of customer company)* has reported that *(brief quotation relevant to product benefit)*. At *(Name of another customer company)* revenues have increased by *(% amount)* percent because of *(product)*.

(Name of callee), *(product)* is fully guaranteed for *(period)*. What kind of guarantee do you have at present?

I'm sure you will agree that our guarantee offers quite an advantage. And, remember, service is available—on-site—daily.

We ship in quantities of *(quantity)*, and the price for each unit is *($ amount)*. With your approval, I will send *(quantity)* to you. Would you like express delivery—ship date *(date)* for a charge of *($ amount)*—or standard at *($ amount)*?

Do you require a purchase order?

[Customer responds: *(Yes)*.]

Do you have a fax number? Great. Go right ahead and fax the P.O. to *(company name, fax number, etc.)*

[Customer responds: *(No)*.]

Fine. Then let me make sure I'm spelling your name correctly. And your title is? And now, *(Name)*, let me just confirm *(quantity, price, shipping mode and date)*.

Thank you, and have a great day!

SCRIPT 2

Hello. Is this *(Name of callee)*? Hello, *(Name of callee)*. I'm *(Name)*, calling from *(Name of company)*. I am calling to let you in on an opportunity to improve your bottom line on *(type of business)*.

Am I correct in assuming that you would like to increase your share of this market?

Great. Then I'm speaking with the right person.

(Name), do you currently use *(type of service)* or do you handle this in-house?

It has been our experience that few business professionals can find the time to do a cost-accounting study to determine just how much in-house *(type of service)* costs. So let me offer you the results of our survey of *(number)* of businesses that are similar to yours. We find that in-house *(type of service)* operations consume *(number)* hours per week and cost a minimum of *($ amount)*, but can run as high as *($ amount)* in some cases.

You agree that such costs are unacceptable?

So why accept them? We can fulfill all your *(type of service)* needs for *($ amount)*.

You heard right, *(Name)*. For *($ amount)* per *(time period)* you get: *(list services)*. And that means you save *($ amount)* each and every *(time period)*, and you also get *(additional benefits)*.

Now it will take us *(time period)* to set up your account, so it will be to your advantage to place a service order with me today. I can expedite processing and get you on the system no later than *(date)*. All I need is some basic information: *(list)*.

You will be booked into the system *(number)* days after we receive your first payment of *($ amount)*.

Let me just make sure I'm spelling your name correctly. The title of your position?

If you send *($ amount)* to *(Name of company and department, address, etc.)* today, our field representative will call on you by *(date)*, and you will be on the system no later than *(date)*, which means that, this month alone, you will save about *($ amount)* in *(type of service)* costs.

I am very happy that I spoke with you today, *(Name)*, and we look forward to serving your *(type of service)* needs. Have a great day!

Off the Hook:
Making Adjustments, Explanations,
and Apologies by Phone

How to Do It

It is possible to think of this chapter as a necessary evil. It is necessary because accidents happen, and therefore, you are obliged to explain, apologize, and make adjustments by telephone. It is evil because nobody likes to be in the position of explaining, apologizing for, or having to rectify errors. But, then, this is a book about *promoting* your small business, and I prefer to look on this chapter as yet another set of strategies and models for doing just that: promoting.

That's right. Start by thinking of accidents, errors, and instances of customer dissatisfaction not as disasters to be dreaded, but as opportunities for promoting your business by building better relations with your customers. Look at it this way: Think about your friends, your *best* friends. Sure, you enjoy the good times, when things are going just great. But what is the real test of affection, loyalty, and friendship? The acid test of the relationship?

Not the good times, but the bad. Dare I say it? I dare: *A friend in need is a friend indeed*.

How friends relate to one another—and help one another—in times of crisis and stress not only tests the relationship, it builds and strengthens it—that is, unless one friend fails the other. In a crisis situation the stakes are high, but while we tend to focus on the risks in such situations, the potential rewards are great, too.

Here is a situation that, I believe, has happened to any number of us. You buy a personal computer with the express purpose of "increasing your productivity." You set it up. You install the software. And something goes wrong. You pore over the manuals to no avail. You become frustrated, maybe even a bit panic stricken—especially if deadlines loom or irreplaceable data hangs in the balance. How do you feel about the PC manufacturer or the software vendor? Well, right now, you hate him. You're thinking, *Why did I ever buy Brand X? I should have bought Brand Y. Please, Lord, if you just give me another chance, I'll never buy Brand X again. And I'll go on a personal crusade to see that nobody, nowhere, and never ever buys Brand X again. Just, please, help me out.*

Help me out.

Then you remember the technical assistance phone number in the back of your owner's manual. You make a call. Maybe a recorded voice leads you through a few touch-tone number punches, and, at last, a friendly, confident voice greets you: "This is Technical Support. Susan speaking. How may I help you?" And—together—you sort out your problem and resolve your crisis.

How do you feel about Brand X now?

You feel like telling your friends and associates about how the company stands behind its product. How supportive they are. How helpful they are. You tell your friends that a tech support person named Susan saved your life—entirely forgetting, of course, that her company's product put your life at risk in the first place.

Maybe it would have been better—for you and for Brand X, Inc.—if the problem had never occurred. A PC, after all, should work transparently, without your having to think about it. But, then, maybe not. The glitch caused panic, despair, and loathing. But the resolution of that glitch transformed temporary dissatisfaction with a product into long-term satisfaction with the company that made the product, and this is likely to translate into future sales.

Unfortunately, many of us have also met with disappointment and disaster when we call tech support lines. It's often difficult just to get through to a technician: the phone rings and rings and nobody picks up; you get an endless busy signal; more often, you are put on hold and asked to wait for the "next available agent"—as if James Bond were lurking in the wings. Or you get a surly, impatient, and uncommunicative tech support person. Or you get one who chides you for failing to read—or understand, or take to heart—The Manual.

Such encounters turn a crisis into an unmitigated disaster, both for the customer and for the company. For if word-of-mouth advertising is the most effective advertising, tales of dissatisfaction travel even faster and farther. Lose one customer through a failure of customer service, and you are likely to lose ten or twenty. You'll never know how many potential customers were sacrificed.

Depending on the size and volume of your business and on the size and competence of your staff, customer support can be a serious challenge, both expensive and time consuming. Yet it is necessary and—on the upside—valuable: another means through which you can build and promote your business.

The introduction to this section of the book has already discussed the perils and benefits of electronic aids to handling telephone calls. What bears repeating here is that you need to develop some system for answering calls within twenty seconds or so. Promptly answering a customer who has a problem in and of itself goes a long way toward solving that problem. Conversely, keeping that customer waiting substantially exacerbates the problem with each passing second. When you do answer, remember to aid the caller in focusing his issue by asking, "How may I help you?"

Obviously, the most important objective in handling calls concerning problems with a product or service or billing or delivery—whatever—is to arrive at an action that resolves the problem. But almost equally important is *how* you arrive at that action. It is important to build rapport with the caller in the course of the conversation. To help a caller, there are things you need to know. Begin to establish rapport by taking care to avoid asking for the necessary information with words that convey command or demand. "What is your account number?" or "Account number?" do not build rapport. Whereas "Do you have your account number handy?" or "Do you happen to have your account number with you?" do build rapport. Request information. Do not demand it.

Another means of building rapport is to transform the "you" and "I" at opposite ends of the phone line into a single, connected "we." You could say something like, "I need to get some information from you." But it is far more effective to say, "Let's fill in some information together." A customer has a problem, you can fix it, so you might be tempted to declare—heroically—"I can fix that for you." Still, it is better to say something like, "We can work that out together without any difficulty at all."

Finally, the single most effective way of building good rapport with your caller is to let her in on what's going on and to include her as far as possible in decisions and actions. The telephone is a wonderful instrument, but it leaves you blind. How many times have you called a company, been asked for information, and then endured a silence punctuated, perhaps, by the faint clack-clack-clack of a computer keyboard? Better to tell your caller what you are doing: "I'm just entering some information about your system into my computer." Or "I am looking up your order. It will take me just about thirty seconds." And note that, whenever possible, give your caller duration estimates. Tell her what you are doing and how long it will take. If you need to put the caller on hold, ask her permission, always explaining why you need the time. "I have to go over to the other filing cabinet to pull your original invoice. That's going to take me less than a minute. Would you be willing to hold? "Then, by the way, you really should put the caller on hold—not just lay the phone down on the desk so that she hears background noise. You can't, after all, control what people around you might say, especially if they believe they are alone.

The foregoing, as well as the example scenarios that follow, will help you transform "problem" calls into promotional events. But if you take away nothing else from this chapter, try this much:

Very, very few customers who have a problem call a business to complain. What, after all, is the point of that? What they are really calling for is help. And, if you can give them that help, you become a hero, and more important, your company becomes a source of satisfaction.

It would be nice to end this part of the chapter on that note. But we must take a look at a small—a very small—but nevertheless significant minority of callers: the irate customer.

Dissatisfaction with a product or service can cause rage. A feeling that one is being taken advantage of often triggers a downright primal bluster and posturing: *YOU CAN'T DO THAT TO ME!* Probably even more often, rage produced by dissatisfaction or a perception of having been cheated is really the proverbial last straw. Mr. Smith argued with Mrs. Smith last night. Traffic was murder coming into work this morning—and some so-and-so cut in front of him at the toll line. Then another miserable lowlife parked in his supposedly reserved spot—and he had to walk an extra two hundred feet through the pouring rain, ruining his brand-new two-tones in a mud puddle. He walked into the office, managed to say good morning to his boss, who replied, "I want to see you. Ten-thirty. *Sharp.*" So then he remembers that he meant to call you about a billing error. He picks up the phone, you answer, and you find yourself on the receiving end of Mr. Smith's bad day.

You cannot control all the stressful and enraging factors in your customers' lives. You can recognize, however, that it is fairly difficult for a caller to maintain his rage in the absence of an enraged response from you. You can adopt some strategies for regulating your response and thereby keeping a potentially explosive situation from actually blowing up. Of course, you cannot regulate all the stress in your own life, either. But you can at least learn to recognize and regulate your own flash points by bearing in mind one law of business: *Irate customers become former customers.* You can also try to reduce or eliminate some factors that increase your own potential for responding to rage with rage. Maybe you should be getting more sleep. Fatigue reduces your patience and tolerance, rendering you vulnerable to angry outbursts. Maybe you should try to handle difficult calls after breakfast or after lunch. There is a good reason why warriors of certain Native American cultures ritually fasted for a day before doing battle. Hunger made them fiercer in a fight. Maybe you should cut back on your intake of coffee. Caffeine mimics many of the physiological changes anxiety and rage bring on. Maybe you should turn up the air conditioning. It is no secret that heat makes most people more irritable. Think about the worst, most infuriating traffic jam you've ever been in. Chances are it took place on a sweltering August afternoon. Finally, try to do something about any of the dozen little things that annoy you: the fluorescent fixture that buzzes, the clock that ticks too loudly.

Now: you answer the phone, put the receiver to your ear, and you get blasted. What do you do?

You begin by doing almost nothing. But, make no mistake, that *can* be difficult. Allow the irate caller to let off steam. Try to hear what the problem is, but avoid the temptation to respond to the customer on his level. Let him sputter and shout and expend his energy. Don't argue. Don't take offense. Don't tell the caller to calm down.

Once the initial onslaught has passed, try to repeat to the caller the gist of his message—minus, of course, the outrage: "If I understand you correctly . . ." Or "What I hear you saying is . . ." Or "Let me make certain that I understand you . . ." Whatever else rage is, it is a desire to be heard and understood and attended to. Don't feed the rage, but do satisfy the underlying desire.

Next, you have two alternatives. If you are certain that you have a highly satisfactory solution to the caller's issue, propose it. If, however, you are less certain about the resolution, put the ball in your caller's court. "How would you like to resolve the problem?" Or "What would you like me to do about this?" Rage is often a response to a feeling of powerlessness. By asking the caller to tell you what he wants, you empower him and, therefore, summarily eliminate a chief motive for anger. And here's a special bonus: Very often, the customer has a perfectly good solution to offer *you*—a better solution than you might have come up with, especially on the spur of the moment and under the pressure of an irate call.

If you can agree to your caller's solution, fine. Take the necessary action. If you are unsure about it, reply that you need a certain amount of time to think about it. Tell your caller that you will get back to him *at a specific time*. Before you hang up, agree to that time. Finally, if the caller's solution is unfeasible, negotiate another solution. Don't simply reject the proposal by saying something like, "I can't do that" or "That's impossible." Flatly rejecting a solution you yourself solicited is likely to reignite the rage—and understandably so; it's an infuriating thing to do. Instead, make a counteroffer, phrasing it in positive terms: Not, "I can't do," but "Here's what I can do." Begin to work as a team.

If relatively few callers are irate, even fewer are downright abusive. But it does happen. You should never be obliged to take abuse. Don't *fight* back, but do give fair warning: "Mr. Smith, I really want to help you so that we can resolve this problem. But if you continue to use this kind of language, I'm going to have to end the conversation." Delivered calmly, such a warning will—usually—bring a dramatic change in the customer's language and attitude.

— WORDS TO USE —

able	confirmation	help
accommodate	convince	important
agree	convinced	information
agreeable	delighted	majority
alternative	disappointed	mistake
apologize	double-check	optimal
appreciate	encouraging	optimum
assure	expedite	patience
benefit	expedited	performance
choice	experience	privilege
choose	explain	promise
confident	frustration	prompt
configuration	grateful	promptly

reason	respond	support
refund	responsive	together
reimburse	satisfy	unavoidable
replace	serious	understanding
replacement	sorry	willing
resolve	sorry	

— PHRASES TO USE —

answers will help me determine

apologize for the inconvenience

apologize personally

appreciate your understanding

as promised

best case/worst case

bottom line

do everything possible

Do you happen to have your order number handy?

either/or

expedite shipment

good afternoon

good morning

grateful for your understanding

How may I help you?

I am calling to check

I estimate

I fully understand

I want to thank you

if you like

I'm sorry to hear

Is that agreeable?

Is there anything else I can help you with today?

it will take

it's your call

leave the choice to you

let's work together

my error

my mistake

necessary steps

on behalf of

resolve the problem

shared your letter

sorry you had a problem

sound reasonable to you

take comments like yours very seriously

thanks for your order

that information will speed things up

up and running

up to you

we make every effort

we'll proceed accordingly

whatever is necessary

Which option would you prefer?

Which would you prefer?

within my power

you can be certain

you can help us

your satisfaction is our primary concern

Calling to Advise That a Shipment Will Be Delayed

Hello, *(Name of callee)*. This is *(Name of caller)* at *(Name of company)*. One of our suppliers has experienced some manufacturing delays, which, unfortunately, means that we will not be able to ship your order before *(date)*.

I'm very sorry for this delay, but it is unavoidable. I am confident of the revised date.

Is there anything you would like me to do to help you accommodate to the revised ship date? We could do *(list of helpful steps)*, if you like.

I appreciate your understanding, and I'm here at *(555-0000)* if you have any questions.

Calling to Advise of a Partial Shipment

Good morning, *(Name of callee)*. This is *(Name of caller)* at *(Name of company)*.

We are shipping out your order on *(date)* as promised. However, I wanted to alert you to the fact that *(number items)—(list)—*will be shipped to you at a later time. These have been back ordered, and I am confident that I'll be shipping these by *(date)*. I knew you would want to get a partial shipment on time rather than have me hold up delivery to wait for a few items.

I will do everything I can to expedite shipment of the balance of your order.

(Name of callee), I am grateful for your understanding and patience. Just give me a call here at 555-0000 if you have any questions.

Apologies for a Delayed Shipment

Good afternoon, *(Name of callee)*. This is *(Name of caller)* at *(Name of company)*.

I am calling to check in on your *(product)*. I trust that you are up and running now.

Customer: Yes.

Great!

I also want to apologize to you for the delay we had in filling and shipping your order, and I want to thank you for being so understanding about it. I know how important it was for you to be up and running as soon as possible. If at any time you have questions about your unit, you know that you can reach our technical support staff during business hours at 555-0000.

Hello, *(Name of callee)*. This is *(Name of caller)* at *(Name of company)*—just calling because I was relieved and delighted to have received confirmation from our warehouse that the *(product)* you ordered was shipped.

I am sorry for the delay. Demand was just extraordinary—and, I have to admit, totally unexpected. You made my life much easier by being so gracious and understanding.

Did the installation go smoothly?

Customer: Yes.

I'm not surprised. If there's anything else I can help you with, you know that I'm just a phone call away. Thanks again.

Apology for an Incomplete Shipment

Hi, *(Name of callee)*. *(Name of caller)* here—from *(Name of company)*. My assistant, *(Name)*, tells me that our having to split up that last shipment caused you some problems.

First of all, let me apologize again for the inconvenience, and let me ask you if there's anything you'd like to tell me. Is there anything I can do—now—to help you cope with whatever difficulties the split shipment caused?

I want you to know that we make every effort to fill orders promptly and completely. But this is a highly volatile business, and we don't always hit the target in anticipating customer demand. You can help us by ordering as early as you possibly can. The more lead time I have, the more maneuvering room I have to make sure that you get what you want when you want it.

Again, I'm sorry you were inconvenienced, and I thank you for your understanding.

Apologies for Shipping the Wrong Item

(Name of callee), good morning. This is *(Name of caller)* at *(Name of company)*.

I don't enjoy sitting here with my face all red, and I wanted to apologize personally for having shipped the wrong item to you.

Before I picked up the phone, I was trying to come up with some excuse to make the mistake look less stupid, but I just couldn't — for the simple reason that it was just a plain old ordinary stupid mistake. So instead of offering an excuse, let me make a promise: that I will do my best to ensure that we don't ever inconvenience you again.

I appreciate your understanding—and thanks for your order.

Hello, *(Name of callee)*. This is *(Name of caller)* at *(Name of company)*.

If you're not overjoyed to hear my voice, I can forgive you. I hope you have forgiven me. But, of course, you have every right to be angry over the mix-up in orders. That kind of thing is very frustrating.

I'm very anxious to redeem myself, so I hope you'll test us again with another order. When you do, I'll give you an automatic *(% amount)* percent discount.

Apologies for Shipping the Wrong Quantity

Hello, *(Name of callee)*. This is *(Name of caller)* at *(Name of company)*.

I hope you'll resist the impulse to hang up on me—after your receiving department had to cope with an avalanche of unwanted *(product)*.

Somebody—that really means *me*—typed an extra digit on the form we faxed to the warehouse, and the net result was a whole lot of extra *(product)* shipped to you. I am very sorry that my mistake caused you a headache.

In addition to my apologies, I'm giving you a *(% amount)* percent discount on your next order with us. You can also be sure that I'll double-check the quantity of that order.

Thanks for being so very understanding.

———————

Hello, *(Name of callee)*. This is *(Name of caller)* at *(Name of company)*.

You know, one thing I'm happy about is that we don't live in ancient Egypt. I remember reading somewhere that merchants who were caught shorting their customers ended up nailed by their ears to the nearest door. I *am* sorry, though, that we shorted you on that last order, and I hope our having expedited shipment of the balance of the order minimized the aggravation and inconvenience.

I appreciate your understanding.

Apology for Delivery to the Wrong Location

Good morning, *(Name of callee)*. This is *(Name of caller)* at *(Name of company)*.

I bet you're surprised that I could find your phone number when, apparently, we couldn't find your warehouse.

I'm sorry for that, and I am very grateful that you didn't bite my head off when your order turned up where it shouldn't have.

I want to assure you that I won't make the same mistake again. Thanks for your patience.

Apology for Damaged Shipment

Customer: I just received my *(product)* from you. *(Describes damage.)*

I'm very sorry to hear that, *(Name)*.

We can handle this in one of two ways. Either return the damaged item to me by *(carrier)*, and I will immediately transship a replacement and will reimburse you for freight, or I can send someone out with a replacement on *(day)*, and he will pick up the damaged unit. Which would you prefer?

Customer: (Expresses preference.)

Okay. We'll proceed accordingly.

(Name), I am, again, very sorry that this happened, and I appreciate your patience and understanding.

Responding to a Disputed Invoice Amount

Good morning, *(Name of callee)*. This is *(Name of caller)* at *(Name of company)*.

I received your letter of *(date)*, and I fully understand and appreciate the questions you raise concerning the number of hours for which you have been billed. What I've done is carefully review the time sheets for the project, and I must tell you that I am convinced we have performed all the services you requested, and that we did so in a timely and efficient manner.

I'm putting into the mail a complete set of photocopies of our time sheets. They're meant to be internal documents, but I believe they are self-explanatory. My suggestion is that you review them for yourself, and if you still have questions, we can go over the time and charges item by item.

Does that sound to you like a reasonable way to proceed?

————

Hi, *(Name of callee)*. This is *(Name of caller)*, here at *(Name of company)*.

I just received your note about the total due on our invoice—that's invoice number *(number)*. I understand why you are questioning the total. The present total includes *($ amount)*, which we carried over from the previous billing. That gives the current invoice total a grand total of *($ amount)*.

To date, we have not received the balance due on the previous invoice.

Apology for Billing Errors

Good afternoon, *(Name of callee)*. This is *(Name of caller)* at *(Name of company)*.

I've just gotten your letter concerning your *(month)* invoice. You are right: We are wrong. And I am very sorry, not only for our error, but for having put you through the trouble of checking your records and writing a letter. I'm sure you had better things to do with your time.

On behalf of all of us here at *(Name of company)*, I apologize.

The payment you made is correct, and I will immediately forward to you a corrected invoice marked "paid in full."

Thanks for your order. Thanks for your vigilance. And, most of all, thanks for your patience and understanding.

Apologies and Adjustments for Defective Merchandise

Customer: I just bought one of your *(products)*, and it *(describes malfunction)*.

I'm sorry to hear that.

You can be certain that we will do whatever is necessary to ensure that *(product)* works to your satisfaction.

If you would, please help me resolve the problem by giving me some information. Can I have your full name?

Customer responds.

And your address?

Customer responds.

Daytime phone number?

Customer responds.

Great. Now, you have already described the problem. Let me just ask a couple of additional questions, which will help me determine the exact cause of the malfunction. *(Asks questions.)*

Customer responds.

What your answers tell me is that we will need to replace the unit. I will put that into motion right now. Do you happen to have your order number handy?

Customer responds.

Thank you. That information will speed things up.

Okay, I have just made out an order for a replacement *(product)*. When you receive it, please open the box carefully, because you will use that box to return the defective unit to us. I will include prepaid freight and a prepared shipping label. All you have to do is paste on the label and call the carrier.

(Name), I'm very sorry you had a problem with *(product)*. I'll expedite shipment of the replacement, and you can expect to receive it on *(day)*.

Is there anything else I can help you with today?

Customer: (Describes problem with product).

I understand, and I'm sorry you're having a problem. It sounds like your unit is defective. Now, we can proceed in one of two ways. Either take the unit to the nearest authorized dealer and describe the problem to him. If you give me your address, I will tell you who the dealers are in your area.

The second option is for you to pack the unit in its original carton, with all original shipping material, and return it to us at *(address)*. If you mark it to my attention—*(Name)*—I will see that it is given prompt attention.

Which option would you prefer?

Customer responds and is given the appropriate information.

Okay. We will see to it that the unit is serviced—or replaced, if necessary—and we'll get you up and running as soon as possible. I estimate turnaround time to be *(number)* days.

Let me double-check your address and telephone information. *Does this.*

Again, I am very sorry that you have had difficulty with the *(product)*. Is there anything else I can help you with today?

————————

Hello, *(Name of callee)*. This is *(Name of caller)* at *(Name of company)*. I just received your letter concerning your new *(product)*, which arrived with "scratches and abrasions." I am sorry to hear that.

Now, since the cosmetic problem doesn't affect performance of the unit, I don't think it makes much sense for you to return the unit for repair. So what I propose to do is ship out to you a new body shell, along with instructions for replacing it yourself.

Is that agreeable to you?

Customer responds positively.

Great! Then you should receive the part by about *(date)*. I don't believe you'll experience any difficulty replacing it, but you can always call Technical Assistance for help, should that be necessary. Their number is included with the part. There's no need for you to return the damaged body shell. Just discard it.

I'm sorry for the inconvenience, and I am grateful for your patience and understanding.

Product Failed to Perform as Promised

. . . I am very sorry that you are disappointed with *(product)*. Let me respond by assuring you of two things. First, the overwhelming majority of our customers are quite satisfied with *(product)*. Second, we will either see to it that you are likewise satisfied, or we will refund your money.

Now, with that in mind, let's work together to make certain that you have the unit installed and configured optimally. *Asks series of questions. Determines that unit has not been properly configured. Gives instructions for proper configuration.*

Okay. I am confident that you will find performance far more satisfactory now. Go ahead and give the new configuration a try and do give me a call if you still have a problem. But I believe you'll experience quite a difference now.

Is there anything else I can help you with today?

New Model Is Inferior to Old

Hello, *(Name of callee)*, this is *(Name of caller)* at *(Name of company)*. I'm calling to talk with you about your comments on our new model *(product)*. I want to tell you, first, how much I appreciate your taking the time to write to us. However, I was sorry to read in your letter that you found the new features less satisfactory than the old.

We take comments like yours very seriously, and, for that reason, I have shared your letter with our marketing and our research and development staff.

Now, *(Name)*, your satisfaction is our primary concern. As you are probably aware, *(product)* is sold with a thirty-day "no questions asked" return privilege, and you do have the option of returning it for a full refund. However, I am willing to extend the return privilege for an additional thirty days if that will persuade you to try a little experiment: Try using the new model and the old model side by side for another couple of weeks. In all honesty, customer response to the new model has been generally very positive.

Perhaps you might benefit from giving the new model a little more time to "grow on you."

What do you think about that?

Demand for Cash Refund for Product Purchased on an Exchange-Only Basis

(Name), I certainly appreciate your frustration with *(product)*, but let me explain the reason behind the exchange-only terms on which your purchase was based. This is not just a matter of stubborn "company policy." We don't set much store by words like "policy." The exchange-only terms are a big part of the reason we were able to offer the *(product)* to you at such a highly competitive price. We

operate on a narrow margin, and we must maintain cash flow so that we can continue to keep our prices low.

Now I can offer you this alternative: There is no need for you to exchange the *(product)* immediately. You can return it for full store credit good toward any purchase now or in the future. We believe this option provides the flexibility you need to make a choice of a product you will be happy with.

Will this option help you?

Customer Says She Will Never Buy Another Product from the Company

(Name), I don't blame you for being angry about the performance of our *(product)*. It's clear that the original unit you purchased was faulty, and, worse, so was the replacement we sent you. It's enough to make anyone feel pretty disgusted.

Now, I'm sure it isn't much help in this situation, but I feel obliged to tell you anyway: It is rare that a defective unit gets by us, and it is downright uncanny that *two* would fail like that.

Of course, the bottom line is that it happened, and it happened to you.

Here is what I can do. If you wish, I will refund the full purchase price of your *(product)*. The alternative is to give us one last chance to please you. If you would like, I will come out to your plant—at absolutely no charge—to install the *(product)* myself. This way, I can ensure that it is operating in an optimal environment.

I am very, very serious about not losing you as a customer, and I want to see to it that you are satisfied with our product—and with our service.

I leave the choice to you.

PART III

In Print

The Fourth Estate

Parts III and IV of *The Do-It-Yourself Business Promotions Kit* are chiefly concerned with advertising, that is, with promotion via the most familiar media avenues. If owners and managers of small businesses envy the copywriting, graphics, and fulfillment resources of big businesses in the direct mail arena, they positively burn with jealousy over the clout big firms wield in the media, both print and broadcast.

The Small-Business Advantage

Better to stop burning and start thinking—of ways to exploit the small-business *advantage* in "big-time" media. And that kind of thinking begins by thinking about why I put quotation marks around "big-time." Without doubt, the print and broadcast media industries are giants. Yet, paradoxically, their product is an intimate one, reaching into homes, and living rooms, and bedrooms, and—yes—even washrooms. In short, these media touch individuals and families. Because of this, the small business enjoys an opportunity to exploit the image of personal, direct, human service that comes naturally to a *small* business, but that big firms have to invest their fortunes to mimic.

Perhaps even more important is to recognize that a big business, to survive, must appeal to the largest number of potential customers possible. A big business needs the newspaper and magazine giants. It requires expensive campaigns broadcast on the national networks. And it must employ—at great cost—major advertising agencies to coordinate all this. A smaller business, however, need appeal only locally or to a select group of potential customers. Advertising in local newspapers, in neighborhood publications, and in such special-interest periodicals as trade journals and bulletins is far cheaper and less complicated than mounting a national media blitz. Radio, too, offers many venues for local advertising, and, nowadays, cable television holds great potential for precisely targeted, eminently affordable local appeals. Small-business promotion in the broadcast media will be discussed in Part IV, On the Air. In the next two chapters, we will look at strategies and models for inexpensive and effective print ads and for virtually cost-free press releases.

Before we turn to these two areas, however, we need to look at some advertising basics that are common to all advertising, regardless of medium.

The Basics and the Options

The first question you must ask is: *Do I need to advertise?* More precisely, *Do I need to advertise differently?* For you are already advertising, whether you know it or not. Every service you perform, every client you satisfy (or fail to satisfy), every product you sell, every phone call you make, every letter you send— these are all advertisements. They may, in fact, be sufficient advertisements. Some of the strongest businesses are local firms that have "built" their reputation over time through word of mouth, which is the most cost-effective and case-for-case effective kind of advertising. Why? Your customer, Customer A, loves your product. His telling this to his friend and associate, Potential Customer B, sends a far more credible message to Potential Customer B than any newspaper or television ad you could create. Of course, the problem is that this particular message reaches only Potential Customer B. The rest of the alphabet are strangers to Customer A, so he can't reach them. Moreover, you can't buy word-of-mouth advertising. You earn it. You build it. And that takes time.

Once you have decided that you want or need to advertise, you have three broad options:

1. You can hire an advertising agency.

2. You can hire advertising professionals—writers, designers, photographers, a video production unit, whatever—and direct their efforts yourself.

3. You can create your own ads.

It is possible to expand these options by some combination of options 2 and 3, and it is also true that many newspapers and radio and television stations offer varying levels of assistance in the creation of your ads.

Just how many "professionals" you use depends on your budget, the kind of advertising you want or need to do, how much time you have to devote to creating advertising yourself, and how well you feel you understand the nature of the message you want to create. In figuring cost of services, be certain to think beyond the simple terms of the wad of cash you have to plunk down on the table. Yes, an advertising agency will cost you X dollars. And, yes, you can save X dollars by not hiring the agency. However, what is the cost of the time and effort you will have to spend if you do not hire the agency? And are you confident that the result you produce will be equally—or more— effective?

The Art of Positioning

No matter what option you choose for creating advertising, you need to invest some time and effort in self-reflection and, perhaps, in research as well. Look out on the big-business landscape today. Is it a chaos of unfamiliar names and obscure products and services?

No.

Coca-Cola, McDonald's, Walt Disney—and on and on. The landscape is dominated by familiar presences, logos, and brands that have become cultural icons and that provoke an almost knee-jerk public knowledge of what each company does. You don't stumble into a McDonald's hoping to find a four-course candlelight dinner. You *know* what to expect.

The companies that are household names in America and the world have attained that status, in large part, by *positioning*. "Positioning" is not so much what a company does or makes or is, but what a company's customers perceive it to be. This is not meant as a cynical statement. It does not mean that you can turn out a poor product and somehow bully your customers into perceiving it as a good product. President Lincoln's time-honored adage applies: *You can fool all of the people some of the time, and you can fool some of the people all of the time, but you cannot fool all of the people all of the time.* Yet—and it happens all of the time—you can produce a widget with specifications identical to that of another company; you can charge the same for your widget as the other fellow charges for his; but if you have positioned your company so that it is perceived as a terrific manufacturer of widgets, whereas the other fellow has positioned his company so that it is perceived as a fine maker of framisses, the great likelihood is that your widgets will outsell his. (You might want to stay out of the framiss market, however.)

Before you invest time and money in advertising, reflect on your positioning. Define it by answering three questions:

1. What benefits does my product/service offer?

2. Who is my target customer?

3. Who is my competition?

Some definitions are offered here to help you answer these questions and make productive use of the answers. "Benefit" is not necessarily the same as "use" or "purpose." A good vacuum cleaner has one "use": to suck up dirt. Its benefits, however, are many and, to some extent, vary from customer to customer. Let's zero in on one: *A good vacuum cleaner will leave my house clean, so that I can be proud of the way I live, and feel comfortable inviting my friends over.* Or, to state it rather more negatively, *I need a good vacuum cleaner or else people with think I am a filthy, loathsome pig.* The benefit of a product, then, is the *emotional* needs it addresses. If my sole purpose in purchasing a vacuum cleaner is to suck up dirt, you will have a hard time persuading me to part with $500 for your superdeluxe brand when I can pick up a different machine for $100. However, if my purpose in buying a vacuum cleaner is to create the impression that I am a tidy human being fit to live in civilized society, then I will be far more receptive to a discussion of the *benefits* of your $500 model as opposed to the $100 bargain brand.

Make a list of the benefits—not the uses—of your product or service.

Second, your *target* customer is your best potential customer.

What separates a successful author from a failed scribbler? A good agent? Luck? Meeting the right folks at the right cocktail party?

Maybe. But far more important is the writer's knowledge of her audience. A successful writer never begins to write without first imagining a reader. You don't speak to your daughter the same way that you speak to your client. They constitute two different audiences. A medical textbook writer doesn't bear in mind the literary cravings of the reader of romance. Similarly, you need to create a clear picture of your target audience. Here are the key features of such a picture:

1. *Client population.* Who currently buys your product? And who currently does not buy your product? We will suggest some inexpensive research methods for assessing this. Related to this dual question are the three areas of inquiry that follow.

2. *Demographics.* This sounds as if it would involve technical knowledge available only at great cost. Not true. Demographics is nothing more than census data, including age, marital status, sex, income, race, home ownership as opposed to renting, and so on.

3. *Psychographics.* That's what advertising and marketing professionals call life-style, which includes opinions, beliefs, and spending habits.

4. *Media preferences.* This may be considered a subgroup of psychographics, but for advertising, it is important enough to list in its own right. You need to know what media your target audience watches, listens to, or reads. In some cases, this is a very simple question to answer. If, for example, your company creates fly-fishing lures, you will want to advertise not in *The New York Times,* but in *Fly Fishing Times.* The question becomes more complex when you are dealing with products and services of less readily definable appeal.

Using information relative to these four areas, you should be able to define your target customers in terms of the product *benefits* they seek, and which your advertising should therefore promote. This information should show you how closely the benefits of your product or service as you perceive or intend them correspond to the benefits as your target audience perceives them.

Your third major task is to study your competition. Learn from them. Learn who their customers are. Learn what they are doing effectively that you are not. Study their product and their promotional material.

What do you do with this intelligence? Decide how what you have to offer fits into the context created by the competition. Essentially, you need to determine whether or not there is room in the marketplace for your product or service. If you are selling something that commands little brand loyalty—let's say, metal fasteners—then claiming a juicy share of the market will involve a combination of attractive pricing, quality service, and appropriate advertising. If, on the other hand, you are attempting to compete in an area dominated by brand loyalty, you will have to mount a major advertising campaign designed to erode that loyalty and win it over to you, or you will have to combine such a campaign with a significantly improved product or service (one that offers a benefit your competition lacks), or you will have to make the decision that it is more cost-effective to seek a different market with a different product or service.

If you determine that you are competing in a category that is not dominated by brand loyalty—marketing and advertising specialists call this a "substitutable category"—you should decide just how you want to increase your sales volume. There are three major ways:

1. Increase your outreach. If your business is well known in Chicago, should you also reach out to Milwaukee to the north and Peoria to the south?

2. Increase the volume of purchases among your current customers. Current customers are always also your best potential customers. Let's say you are selling compact discs. Sending direct mail letters to your current customers and/or advertising to them in the local newspapers you know they read, perhaps combined with other incentives (buy three get one free), is very likely to increase your volume. Obviously, if you are selling certain high-ticket merchandise—automobiles, for example—it may be more difficult to increase the number of current customer purchases.

3. Get a bigger piece of the pie by beating out your competition in terms of price and/or quality and benefits.

The foregoing should enable you to define three elements of an equation that will motivate and shape your advertising: benefit, target, and competition. Now, take these three elements, and express them in what mathematicians call an "elegant" equation: an expression that is concise but comprehensive, that tells it all. Here's an example:

> (*A*) For the business professional who needs to write business letters but doesn't have the time, Jack Griffin's *New Handbook of Business Letters* (*B/C*) provides effective model business correspondence that will make more time for success (*D*).

Where *A* is the target audience, *B/C* is the product and its implied competitive category (a letter book competing in the category of letter books), and *D* is the product benefit. As in any equation, the variables are, well, variable. You can formulate your positioning statement by filling in the blanks:

(*A*) For _____ ,
                                    (target)

(*B*) _____ is the
                                    (product)

(*C*) _____ that
                          (competitive category)

provides/makes/creates/enables (D) _____

_____.

(benefit)

This positioning statement should motivate and focus all your advertising. It is the essential message you want to get across.

Research

Big companies invest huge sums in market research, often hiring high-powered marketing consultants or maintaining their own substantial research departments. Smaller firms lack the capital for such undertakings, but they usually enjoy the advantage of already knowing their market more intimately. This knowledge can be expanded and supplemented by a variety of inexpensive research methods.

You can create a survey and make phone calls. You can mail a survey. You can distribute a survey in your store or place of business. It is often helpful to accompany the survey with a modest incentive—perhaps a discount coupon or a free sample—and it is always most effective to keep the survey brief. Questions you will want to ask might include

Have you ever bought *(type of product)* before?

How often?

Have you ever bought *(your company's product)* before?

How often?

How did you find out about this product? (Yellow Pages? advertising? brochure? referral? other?)

Were you satisfied with this product?

Would you buy *(product)* again?

Please tell us a little more about yourself:

Sex: M   F

Marital status: Single   Married   Separated   Divorced   Widowed

Age: Under 20, 20s, 30s, 40s, 50s, 60s, over 70

Children: None, 1, 2, 3, more than 3

Home: Own   Rent

Household income: Under $20,000

$20,000–40,000

$40,000–60,000

Over $60,000

Interests: *(list choices relevant to product or service, such as sports, television watching, etc.)*

THANK YOU FOR YOUR TIME AND YOUR ATTENTION!

Another low-cost research method is test marketing. This does not have to be a large-scale distribution campaign. It can be as simple as asking one or more of your regular customers to try out a product for a specific period of time and report to you her evaluation of it. If appropriate, you can reward the customer by giving her the product or by offering it to her at a substantially reduced price.

Large companies very often use "focus groups" as a controlled method of testing out new ideas. Eight to a dozen participants are assembled in a room and are asked to respond to a set of ideas, statements, packaging, products—whatever. The format is often discussion oriented, and the effect is that of a brainstorming session with your potential customers. Cash investment in such research can be quite modest. You may wish to rent special facilities for conducting the focus group activity, so that you can record it on audio and video tape. You will also need to pay participants a small fee, give them a sample of your product, or treat them to some sort of reward. However, focus group activity should not be related to any sort of contest or compensation based on level of performance. These will skew the results.

What to Do with All This

After you have positioned your product or service and tested that positioning through some form of research, you should be in a position to make some basic advertising decisions:

1. What medium or media to use

2. Who you want to reach

3. What your advertising priorities are

Very simply, these priorities are what you want your target customer to know about your product or service in order of importance. If, for example, you are introducing a brand-new product, your number one priority may very simply be telling your potential customers the name of the product. Plant this single item in enough minds, and you have gone a long way toward successfully launching the product. Second to this, with a new product, may be a description of what the product does and, third, what benefits it delivers—the emotional satisfaction the customer will derive from the product or service. Truly successful advertising conveys all three priorities.

Now, regardless of medium used, there is one additional basic to be resolved: paying the piper.

How much should you spend on advertising?

I'll begin the answer with a timely evasion. *This is something you need to figure out for yourself.* Advertising budgets vary widely and are dependent on such factors as the size of the business, the size of the market, the cost of the product, the nature of the product—et cetera and so on. In short, the budget depends on just about every variable that bears upon your business. However, there are at least labels you can attach to whatever budgeting approach you choose, and these labels are a start toward helping you think clearly about budgeting matters.

Many companies—and for that matter, individuals—base their budgets (not only for advertising, but for just about everything) on history: what was spent in the past. If you allocated $15,000 for advertising last year, and you are doing pretty much the same kind of business this year, you might allocate $15,000 again. It sounds perfectly logical, but, of course, if you stop to examine the "historical method," it is actually based on the irrational premise that what worked before will work again—an especially irrational proposition if you have never really tested whether that $15,000 could more effectively have been $10,000 or $20,000.

Another evasive "method" is simply to decide what you can afford to spend on advertising, and then spend it. Maybe that number will be whatever is left over after you pay for rent, materials, salaries, and other overhead items.

More sophisticated budgeting techniques tie advertising dollars to sales revenue. You establish a percentage amount of sales revenue and set it aside for advertising. If sales go up, so will advertising dollars—though the percentage remains constant. How much of a percentage should you allocate? Well, again, that is for you to decide. However, most businesses plan on allocating a higher percentage to introduce new products, then notch the number down into a "maintenance mode" once the product is established. For a new product, you probably need to count on allocating for advertising at least 10 percent of *projected* sales revenues. If it is a major product/service launch, you may plan on investing as much as a third of projected revenues. Once the product is up and running, you might allocate 10 percent or even less of sales revenue to advertising.

Another way of looking at the allocation of advertising dollars is the objective-, goal-, or task-oriented approach, which can also be combined with the preceding three methods. You divide your advertising campaign into its constituent objectives or tasks, such as building awareness of a new product, maintaining awareness of the product, expanding the market for the product, generating repeat purchases, and so on. Then you divide and allocate you budget accordingly, projecting the *full* amounts necessary to achieve each task or objective.

Whatever budgeting method or methods you use, it is important to discipline yourself to adhere to the budget and to monitor the cost-effectiveness of your advertising. All businesspeople know the power of impulse buying for certain products, and they package certain products expressly to provoke impulse purchases. Be aware that those who sell advertising—whether they are agencies or media ad sales reps—are highly conscious of the fact that their clients are themselves also susceptible to impulse appeals. If Campaign X has resulted in a 10 percent increase in sales of Product Y, they may suggest that you take "a quick look at what this full-page, four-color ad in *Blitz Magazine* can do for you! Act now, and you can gain another 2 percent!"

The ad looks really terrific, but, of course, it will also put you way over budget, and you have no idea whether many of your customers read *Blitz*. Restrain yourself from acting impulsively when buying advertising.

The Power of the Press: Creating Inexpensive and Effective Print Ads

How to Do It

Print media include a wide variety of newspapers and magazines. Except for space in the classifieds, advertising space in major city newspapers is costly. Space in major national magazines is even costlier. If you have the budget to invest in these, you should also have the budget to invest in professional copywriters and designers. Probably, you should also be leaning on a good ad agency to coordinate these professionals. Simply put, this kind of space is so expensive and provides such exposure, that it attracts ads of a very high caliber. A less than professional message will not only prove cost-ineffective, it is likely to be an embarrassment, actually detrimental to your company's image. If you are looking for alternatives to agencies and other advertising professionals, look to the classified sections of major newspapers and also buy space in smaller, more precisely targeted newspapers and magazines. Exploit the potential of trade papers and journals. Think about various publications targeted to special-interest groups: working mothers, computer users, antique collectors, and so on. Use community and neighborhood papers. Make use of club publications. Investigate the opportunities offered by weekly "shoppers" and "bargain finders," which are often distributed free of charge, either by mail, route delivery, or in the entrance vestibules of stores and shopping malls. For the small business, which packs the punch of personal identification, these special-interest papers and magazines usually present the most affordable and cost-effective vehicles for print advertising.

Print advertising enjoys a number of advantages over advertising on radio or television. If your product has a well-defined target audience, chances are that a publication exists that is targeted to that audience. This may substantially increase your "hit rate"—the proportion of ads that generate business for you.

An interested customer can take all the time he wants to ponder your ad, whereas a radio listener or television viewer is generally limited to a few seconds. You can also present more detailed information, including such practical essentials as how to get to your store (including a map). If you provide a phone number on the radio or television, you have to hope that the interested listener or viewer either has an awfully good memory or happens to have a pencil and paper nearby. In newsprint, you can give the necessary phone numbers, and the interested reader can simply tear the ad out.

Producing newspaper and even modest magazine ads is almost always cheaper than producing ads and buying time on broadcast media. Newspapers are also often willing to accept last-minute changes, corrections, and additions.

On the other hand, print ads do have some drawbacks. They are very easy to ignore. Television and radio commercials intrude themselves on the customer uninvited. Even if he is deliberately trying not to pay attention, some of the message inevitably leaks through. Newspaper ads, in contrast, are easy to ignore, especially if your ad appears on a page cluttered with others. Depending on the kind of publication you are dealing with, reproduction may be quite poor, especially of fine-line artwork and photographs, making your product look less attractive. Finally, general-interest newspapers tend to appeal to readers who are somewhat older than the national average. Depending on what you are selling, this may or may not be a good thing. Keep in mind also that the person most likely to spend the most time reading the paper is the older reader. In general, older consumers change their buying habits less frequently and less readily than do younger consumers.

WHAT DOES IT COST?

The all-important question of cost is, not surprisingly, one of the most difficult to answer. It depends on a number of other questions:

1. What is the circulation of the newspaper?
2. How big is the ad?
3. How complex is the ad?
4. Are illustrations used in the ad?
5. Is it in color or black and white?
6. Will you use an agency?
7. Will you hire copywriting and design professionals?
8. How extensively will you use your copywriting and design professionals?

Nor are these questions always so easy to answer. Remember, cost is not simply calculated by the amount of money you withdraw from your pocket. If you have no interest in writing ad copy and designing an ad, then trying to get along without hiring a copywriter and a designer will prove the costliest alternative. You will waste your time on producing an ineffective—maybe even self-destructive—ad. In fact, if you are really averse to creating advertising, you are probably best off investing in the services of an agency.

For those who have the skills or are willing to develop the skills necessary to create their own advertising, it is helpful to know the ground rules governing the purchase of space. Magazine and journal space rates vary widely, but newspapers usually price ads by the column inch: the number of vertical inches the add takes up multiplied by the number of columns it crosses horizontally. An ad that is 6 inches tall and that runs across three newspaper columns is said to be 18 column inches in size. Some newspapers base their charges on a variant of the column inch called the agate line. There are 14 agate lines per column inch, so it is easy to convert the agate-line rate to the column-inch rate for comparison purposes: just multiply the agate-line rate by 14.

You can expect to pay anywhere from $7 to $20 per column inch to run a weekday ad in a small-circulation paper, up to about $100 per column inch in large-city dailies. National papers charge several times this amount. Even in dealing with large-circulation city papers and national publications, it is often possible to save money by choosing "zoned coverage" or, in the case of national publications, placing the ad in regional editions. Many big-city newspapers publish sections that vary with the suburb or even the neighborhood in which a particular edition of the paper is sold. You may choose to restrict your ad to a zoned section and thereby save significant money. If your business has local appeal, this money-saving strategy does not even represent a compromise, but actually focuses your campaign. The same is true for an ad you place in a regional section of a national publication. Why pay for national advertising if you do business only in one section of the country?

WHAT TYPE OF AD?

In virtually all newspapers and in many magazines, you have a choice of placing three types of ads:

1. Display

2. Display classified

3. Classified

Many newspapers offer a fourth option: the free-standing insert, or FSI. Sometimes called "advertiser preprints," these are slick, usually four-color inserts, often multipage, which generally come cascading out of your Sunday paper if you hold it the wrong way. Many magazines offer their own version of a free-standing insert, the "blow-in card." These are the postcard-size combination ads and reply cards that fall out of several magazines, especially such special-interest, consumer-oriented publications as personal computer magazines, hobbyist publications, and so on. They are called blow-ins because they are simply "blown" in between the magazine's pages rather than bound in or affixed with adhesive.

Display ads are the most impressive and, if your product or service has more than specialized appeal, they are the most effective form of print advertising. They generally employ headlines, illustrations, and body copy (the running text that delivers the details of your message), all designed in a way that communicates effectively. The graphic quality of the display ad sets it apart from the news stories that surround it. Naturally, display advertising is the most expensive newspaper or magazine advertising.

A variation on the display ad is the display classified ad. While these employ the same elements as the display ad proper—headlines, illustrations, body copy—they are designed to fit within the classified columns rather than to be integrated into the main sections of the newspaper or magazine. A display classified ad is substantially cheaper than a display ad, and, depending on your product or service, it can be just as effective—maybe even more effective. If what you sell is something people generally seek in the classifieds (real estate, used cars, and so on), a display classified can be highly cost effective, though, of course, it must compete with a welter of other display classified ads.

The least expensive advertising option in most newspapers and magazines is the classified—or line classified—ad. Graphic options are few: usually no pictures, only headlines and body copy, though you may be able to use a corporate logo. Pricing is by the word or by the line rather than the column inch.

Free-standing inserts and blow-in cards are usually quite expensive to produce and almost certainly require the services of professional designers, copywriters, and print production people. However, if you decide to invest in a slick promotional brochure, the FSI is another way to use and distribute it, thereby maximizing its exposure. Conversely, if you decide to invest in an FSI, you might plan, write, and design it so that it can also function as a stand-alone brochure or mailing piece. Think carefully about the publication or publications in which you will insert your FSI. In many Sunday newspapers, these have become so numerous that their impact has been significantly blunted.

WHERE AND WHEN?

If you are placing a display classified or line classified ad, you have little or no choice about where in the newspaper or magazine to insert the ad. In newspapers, display ads can be purchased on a "run of press" (ROP) basis, which means that the ad will be placed wherever the newspaper production person decides to place it, or you can specify a section of the paper. ROP is less costly, but depending on your product or service, it may be more cost-effective to specify the section that will most interest your target customer. If you offer a financial consulting service, you will want your ad in the "money matters" section, not in "entertainment."

You may also find it advantageous to run your ads at specific seasons or on certain days of the week. Some of these choices should be obvious to you. Your big feature on air conditioners probably won't go over well in December—unless you are advertising some spectacular off-season promotion, in which case your ad's visuals can be designed deliberately to work *against* the season: think of an ad placed in midwinter with a headline announcing an inventory clearance accompanied by a photograph of toil in the blazing sun.

Similarly, you may find some days of the week more effective than others for running certain ads. Thursday or Friday are good choices if your business involves leisure activity. Monday may be the best day for ads directed at businesspeople—unless you believe in the Blue Monday syndrome and don't want to catch your target customer in a down mood. In that case, put the ad off until Tuesday. On the other hand, if your product is aimed specifically at rescuing the harried executive from overload and burnout, perhaps Monday *is* the best day, after all.

LAGNIAPPE

Anyone who visits New Orleans soon hears this strange word. "Lagniappe" means a little something extra, an unexpected bonus. Often, it is a small gift a shopkeeper will include with a customer's purchase. Coupons in ads can serve as lagniappe. Now, for many companies, coupons are a major part of advertising; indeed, the entire ad may consist of coupons. But even a non-coupon-oriented business can benefit from including them. They provide incentive to purchase, and they also help you monitor the effectiveness of your advertising. If you don't want to use up valuable ad space to print an actual coupon, just instruct your customer to "mention this ad and receive a $XX discount off your purchase."

DESIGN AND COPY

Display advertising has two major components: design and copy. Which is more important? Designers will tell you that design does most of the selling in an ad, while copywriters will insist that design exists simply to help the copy do the real work, which is selling.

In fact, both elements are important. Now, it is beyond the scope of this book to provide anything approaching a manual of advertising design. Such is the subject of several books, and if the topic interests you, I suggest that you begin by consulting any of the following:

- ❏ John Caples, *How to Make Your Advertising Make Money* (Englewood Cliffs, N.J.: Prentice-Hall, 1983)

- ❏ Dell Dennison and Linda Tobey, *The Advertising Handbook* (North Vancouver, B.C.: Self-Counsel Press, 1991)

- ❏ Levinson, Jay Conrad, *Guerrilla Advertising: Cost-Effective Tactics for Small-Business Success* (Boston and New York: Houghton Mifflin, 1994)

Unless you are artistically inclined, design of display ads is best left up to a professional designer. In some respects, this statement is less true than it was ten years ago, before the advent of desktop publishing. Powerful personal computers capable of processing graphics at high speed, coupled with equally versatile graphics and design software, have put the basics of design and layout within the reach of almost anyone who cares to avail themselves of these tools. Yet it is well to heed in particular one word in the preceding sentence: *basics.* If it is true that, in some respects, design is now properly in the hands of Everyman and Everywoman, it is also true that—in some respects—now, more than ever, design is best left to professional designers. Desktop publishing has allowed a great many nonprofessionals to design ads—many of them very poor ads. Since more people have the tools of design at their disposal, the *professionally* designed ad is probably more powerful than it has ever been, especially where the small budgets of small businesses are concerned. This said, I by no means wish to discourage anyone who, for business or personal reasons, wants to invest the time, effort, and imagination necessary to *learn* how to design effective ads. It should simply be understood at the outset that creating such work does require time, attention, and practice, which you may not be able to afford if you are too busy with other things. And, alas, talent and inclination also help.

While I assume that the reader of this book will be less inclined—or prepared—to take on the major responsibility for designing his ads, I also assume that he is in a better position to write copy for them. To be sure, you can benefit from a professional copywriter just as you can benefit from a professional designer. However, most of us have better verbal mental equipment than graphic mental equipment, and it is quite likely that the small-business owner or manager who hires a designer to lay out his ad is nevertheless capable of writing the copy for that ad himself. He knows the business. He knows what he wants to say about the business. This is not to declare that the small business operator should avoid hiring a professional copywriter—or, for that matter, should avoid turning all his advertising over to an agency. But where budget is a limiting factor—or where you want personal control over a personal message—you should consider writing your own copy. Where funds are limited, invest them in good design help and in getting the best placement of your ad. Draw on your own understanding of your business to create the verbal message of the ad. Accordingly, the remainder of this chapter devotes more specific attention to writing copy than to creating design. This is not to suggest that the one is more important than the other, but only to reflect what is most useful to a small-business operator and what takes greatest advantage of the skills he is most likely to possess.

DESIGN GUIDELINES

For every design guideline there is a good reason to violate it. While good design is rarely "arty," it is an art, and, as such, it is not reducible to a series of rules. That said, the single most useful general guideline is that good design serves the copy. It does not fight the copy. It does not obscure the copy. It does not overshadow the copy. It enhances and helps to convey the copy. This is true of all the design elements, including typography, type size, layout, use of white space, and use of illustration.

HEADLINE DESIGN

The kernel of most display ads is the headline. The picture may pack punch, but it is the headline that delivers the most succinct, focused, and specific message. The typography and size of the type should enhance the message. Designers have a wide variety of type styles from which to choose, each of which conveys a different emotional message.

Smith and Company
presents

A BOLD NEW LOOK

is very different from

Smith & Company
invites you to view

An Elegant New Look

In general, it is best to take a conservative approach, avoiding excessive, extravagant, and clashing combinations of typography. However, type style, type size, and type weight (light, regular, and bold) can be manipulated to emphasize the most important part of your message. You must demand and capture the attention of readers who skim the page. You would think that the most obvious way to accomplish this is to use the biggest possible headline. Sometimes this is indeed the case. Yet it is also possible to keep headlines deliberately small, using the surrounding white space to draw the reader in. Veteran grade-school teachers quickly learn that the most effective way to gain the attention of the class is not necessarily to shout, but suddenly to speak very, very softly. You should also be aware that headlines using all capital letters are harder to read than headlines using capitals and lower case. Short, exclamatory headlines may benefit from all capitals, but anything that approaches sentence length is usually best expressed using both capital and lowercase letters.

BODY TEXT DESIGN

The type size, style, and layout of the body text of your ad also convey important messages. Body type should, above all, be highly legible. Particularly in newspaper ads, which pose special legibility challenges on account of the pulp paper stock used, headlines are often made more effective by using reverse type—that is, printing white letters on a black background. This can work well for headlines, but it should be avoided in body type because it makes smaller-size text hard to read. Obviously, it is also best to set any kind of body copy in a readable type size. Nobody likes straining to read fine print. On the other hand, if you set the body copy too large, you not only reduce the amount of space available for your message, you risk giving your ad a classroom look. Be sensitive to the age of your target audience. If you are appealing primarily to senior citizens, favor larger type sizes.

Common sense tells you that sans serif typefaces—the simple, clean, modern-looking styles such has Helvetica and Optima—should be easier to read than the more traditional serif faces, such as Times Roman. Strangely enough, common sense is wrong. In running text, traditional serif faces are easier to read than sans serif faces.

Layout also affects ease of reading. Generally, you have five choices for laying out the body type of your ad.

1. *Fully justified:* The lines are flush with the left and the right margins.

2. *Ragged right:* The lines are flush with the left margin, but are ragged—or not justified—at the right margin.

3. *Centered:* Each line is centered under the preceding line, as in a formal invitation.

4. *Flush right:* Each line is flush with the right-hand margin, but ragged on the left.

5. *Wrapped:* The lines of type are "wrapped" or contoured around an object, usually an illustration.

Of these, the fully justified style is the most traditional (it is the way most books are printed), but in ad copy, ragged right is actually the most immediately readable. The unevenly ending lines tend to draw the reader's eye from one line to the next. Does this mean you should always insist that your ad copy be set ragged right? Not necessarily. There is often a good design reason to choose the other options. However, if your ad contains a lot of text and there is no pressing design reason to do otherwise, then it is best to set copy ragged right.

PHOTOS AND ILLUSTRATIONS

Contrary to what many of us might believe in a world saturated with images, photos and illustrations are not necessary to make an effective ad. For the very reason that each of us is awash in a sea of media images, a graphically strong type-only ad can be highly effective. However, depending on your product or service—and the space available in the ad—illustrations may be required or at least helpful.

The range of illustrations is, of course, enormous. Spot illustrations—also called clip art—are inexpensive graphic elements, often available as "stock items" from a designer or printer, or as desktop publishing software rather than as custom-designed pieces specially commissioned from an artist. Spot illustrations "dress up" an ad, but they rarely educate the reader about your product or service. More elaborate artwork might include a cartoon, used to make a humorous point; a painting, used to create a mood, evoke an emotion, establish an image, or simply to illustrate the product; or a photograph, which may be used for the same purposes as a painting. In general, photographs make the strongest emotional appeal because they are the most immediately believable visual vehicles. All of us have been taught (quite falsely, of course) that "the camera doesn't lie," so a photo strikes us as practically the same thing as seeing a product or service for ourselves. We accept a photo less as an illustration than as evidence.

Few design elements are more detrimental to an ad than a bad photograph. Unless you are a very good photographer and have access to adequate studio equipment, invest in good professional photography not only to show your product at its best, but to convey a thoroughly professional image. If the photograph of your product is crude, the reader of your ad is apt to assume that the workmanship of the product itself is commensurately crude. And consider a line illustration or other alternative to a photograph in cases where your product is not especially photogenic or where you want to make a particular graphic point. Of course, if you are conveying an abstract concept—which is often the case when you are selling a service rather than a particular item of merchandise—a nonphotographic illustration may be your only viable choice. How would you illustrate a headline like this?

> Look inside the imagination of
> an Acme financial consultant.

You would almost certainly commission a creative drawing or other nonphotographic artwork. Similarly, paintings and other nonphotographic techniques can communicate a wide range of messages:

> Airbrushing conveys a sleek, ultra high-tech look.

> Computer graphics suggest up-to-the-second technology.

> A pastel might evoke a world of nostalgia or romance.

> A quick pen-and-ink sketch may be used to suggest responsiveness and immediate action.

> A childlike crayon illustration suggests innocence and honesty.

Is artwork expensive? It can be. Major ad agencies regularly commission the world's leading artists and photographers to create illustrations, some of which are actually preserved as "legitimate"works of art. For example, during the 1920s, 1930s, 1940s, and 1950s, various companies commissioned Norman Rockwell to create advertising art, and, for years now, the Absolut Vodka company has commissioned a whole range of artists to create works that are museum-quality variations on the starkly contoured Absolut bottle.

Of course, you need not commission a well-known and high-priced artist to create an illustration for you. It is possible to use older, well-recognized, and highly familiar works of art or other symbols to make a point. How many ads have you seen that incorporate an image of the Statue of Liberty? the *Mona Lisa? Whistler's Mother?* In many cases, where the artwork is in the public domain, you do not have to pay any usage or copyright fee for the work of art. In other cases, you will have to contact the copyright holder for permission to use an existing image. Depending on the nature of the image and the needs, desires, and whim of the copyright holder, this can be prohibitively expensive.

Alternatives to expensive artwork include commissioning young artists who are just starting out and who are eager for exposure. Promise to credit their work in the ad. Also, various "stock agencies" have vast catalogs of artwork—in photographic as well as nonphotographic media—which they will rent to you for a fee. In this age of the CD-ROM, software publishers have made large amounts of stock art available in computer-readable and laser-printer-reproducible form. Early twentieth-century or late nineteenth-century books, on which the copyright has lapsed, are also fair game for images. Some of these publications contain gorgeous steel engravings and other examples of strong illustration. If the item was published at least 100 years ago, it has entered the public domain, and you may reproduce from it freely, provided you reproduce it from the original edition. A few book companies, most notably Dover Books, publish entire product lines of reprint illustrations drawn from old volumes. These may be reproduced at will. In using such "found" artwork, just make very certain that you are not treading on somebody's copyright. Using a copyrighted image without permission—especially to sell a product or service—is a violation of civil law and can prove very expensive. If you have any doubts, and the source of the image is from a publication less than a 100 years old, contact the publisher of the material. In some cases, you might need to consult a copyright attorney. Generally, however, if your doubts require such a potentially costly and time-consuming step, you are better off simply finding another piece of artwork or even commissioning something. Of course, you may not use anyone else's logo or trademark in your advertising without explicit, written permission—and all permission, for usage of any image, should be secured in written form.

LAYOUT

How all the elements of the ad—headline, body text, illustrations—relate to one another is called layout. There are no hard-and-fast rules for laying out an ad, except the rule that applies to any other mechanism you might assemble: Put it together so that everything works.

Back when clocks were something you wound up, most children, at one time or another, took a clock apart to see how it worked. They admired the relationship of one gear to another, then tore into the mechanism, only to find that it was quite impossible to reassemble. Similarly, it is not enough to toss the elements of the ad together and hope that they will work.

Layout takes thought and planning, and this is one of the areas in which a good professional designer can help. Not that layout is exclusively a matter of art and an aesthetically pleasing arrangement of elements. An ad should look good. In fact, it should look great. But, even more important, its look—its layout—should *function* to deliver your message and sell your product or service. Generally, the layout should:

1. Increase the impact of the headline
2. Enhance the effect of the illustration or illustrations
3. Invite reading of the body text

Is it best to have a harmonious layout? Usually. But not always. Sometimes a deliberately jarring, even violent or disturbing juxtaposition of elements makes the statement you want.

Is it best to have a simple, clean layout? Often. But sometimes a deliberately busy, even cluttered look suggests the richness and wealth of possibilities you want to convey.

Is it best to allow ample room for the body text? Most of the time. But many effective ads consist of little more than a headline or a headline and an image. (For most small businesses, however, which, by their very nature, lack the recognition factor of national firms, room for substantial explanatory body copy is important.)

Writing Effective Headlines

What a stupid, boring headline for a chapter section! Please, let me try again.

How to Write Headlines

(Close. However, no cigar.)

How to Write Headlines That Make Money

(Yes!)

Create Money-Making Headlines

(Yes again!)

How I Make Money with Great Headlines

(Another good one.)

Designers and art directors may insist that it is the look of the ad—with special emphasis on the illustration—that does the selling. I'm not here to say that they are wrong. But most veteran advertising professionals, while they will give designers their due, say that the single most important element of the print ad is the headline. Here's why:

1. Either it establishes a bond between your product/service and your target customer
2. Or it does not.

In either case, the headline determines your fate—so far as that particular customer is concerned—and, of course, your ultimate fate is the sum total of your fate vis-à-vis each customer, one by one. The headline must grab the reader, not merely interest him. It must make him want to read more of your ad. You can have a great product. You can have an attractive picture to sell it. You can have informative, inviting body copy. But if the headline fails, chances are that none but the most diligent, compulsive, or otherwise unemployed readers will ever know any of this.

Headline Guidelines These are not rules, and no single headline can incorporate all of them. Use them only as a checklist of ideas when you are composing your next headline.

1. Use *you*. Headlines that speak directly to the reader naturally (that is, by the conventions of language) command attention. For example,

   Here's News You Need

   If you use *(type of product)*, you'll want to know more about *(product)*

2. Use the most compelling format of logical discourse: if . . . then. Many advertising mavens tell you to avoid logical argument in favor of emotional appeal. But we have all been trained from a very early age to think in terms of cause and effect. Exploit this *almost* primal urge. Note that the word *then* need not actually be used. Often, in English, it is merely implied. Examples are

   If you love *(something)*, then you need *(product)*

   If you haven't tried *(product)*, you are wasting valuable time *(or other resource)*

3. Assert *need* or necessity.

   You need *(product)*. It's that simple.

   If you love *(something)*, then you need *(product)*

   Drain plugged up? You need Drop Kick.

4. Write a news headline. This is especially appropriate in newspaper advertising. Presumably, your reader has the paper in her hands because she's seeking news. Why not give her some?

   New Discovery Is Medical Breakthrough for People with Hammer Toes

   (Name of company) Introduces Solution to *(Problem)*

5. It's hard to avoid writing headlines without the word *new* in them. Well, don't avoid it. *New* and *free* are two of the most powerful words in advertising. *New* is especially powerful when it is combined with something old and familiar, perhaps even all too familiar:

A New Way to Do Your Laundry

New! A *(service company)* That Doesn't Treat You Like a Number

6. Make your product or service special with words like *presenting* or *announcing* or *introducing:*

   Announcing the only *(product)* you'll ever need

   Presenting the most effective *(product)* in the history of *(field)*

7. Use a date to turn a sales pitch into a special—even newsworthy—event:

   On July 8, 19XX, the way you do *(activity)* will change forever

8. Put a price in the headline—sometimes. When? Include it if the price is a particularly good one, certainly, and is therefore a selling point. But you might also include it if you want to *persuade* your target customers that it is a good price. (The fact that you announce it so boldly implies this.) For traditionally high-ticket items or for products and services where price is sometimes a mystery, being upfront about it can break through resistance.

   $XXX for *(product/service)*?

   Would You Pay $XXX to Learn *(Something)*?

   Enjoy *(product/service)* for only $XXX

9. Take the price issue a step further by breaking it down into "easy payment" terms:

   Peace of Mind Costs $1.00 a Day

   It is even better if you can use a symbol rarely seen these days—the "¢" sign:

   Peace of Mind Costs 25¢ a Day

10. Can you offer anything for free? If you think your target customer is too there's-no-such-thing-as-a-free-lunch sophisticated to read about a free offer, think again. Because you're wrong.

    Free! Buy One *(Product)*, Get Another for Free!

    Here's a free offer you cannot afford—to miss

11. Offer something of value: information—

Bank service fees eat into your bottom line. Here's how to avoid them: . . .

12. Fashion a hook to pull your reader from the headline into the body text.

SHE WAS JUST LIKE YOU, CONVINCED THAT HIRING A "PERSONAL SHOPPER" WAS ONLY FOR THE VERY WEALTHY, BUT THEN SHE PICKED UP THE PHONE, DIALED 555-0000, AND, SUDDENLY . . .

13. Instruct or advise.

How to Save $XXX On Your Next *(Product)* Purchase

Important advice for people who want *(something)*

14. Highlight a testimonial in your headline.

"The only *(product)* I would ever *think* of using is *(Name of product)."*

"I had my doubts. Then I used *(Name of product),* and all my doubts vanished."

"*(Name of product)* saved me $XXX in only *(time period)."*

15. Want a technique that's really powerful? Ask a question. Questions have their own momentum. Ask one, and your reader has a natural tendency to answer it—or to read on for the answer.

Are you tired of *(whatever)*?

Which *(product)* beat every other *(product)* in a national sales test?

16. Point to an answer.

Why 5,000 Chicagoans Moved to Wichita Last Year

Why 245,097 "Their Brand" Users Switched to "My Brand"

17. Give 'em a multiple-choice test.

Which *(type of product/service)* creates the most customer satisfaction—year after year after year?

A. *(Product/service 1)*

B. *(Product/service 2)*

C. *(Your product/service)*

18. Create a sense of urgency.

By the time you read this ad, it may already be TOO LATE to make the right decision.

PRICES THIS LOW WON'T LAST LONG

ORDER *(NAME OF PRODUCT)* TODAY—OR RISK BEING SHUT OUT FOREVER

19. Offer the Zen of a single powerful word.

Free!	Go!
Cheap!	Act!
Value!	Think!
Stop!	

COPYWRITING: HOW TO CREATE THE BODY TEXT

The main reason why the headline is probably the most important part of your ad is that relatively few readers will ever get beyond it. Those who do, however, are your most important target customers. The person interested enough to read beyond the headline is most likely to buy your product or service.

Now, how do you cultivate this prospect?

You educate her through the body copy of your ad. This material can take many forms. It can be long, or it can be short. Our old friend common sense would have us believe that short is always best, since (as we all know) the public has a very short attention span. Yet many advertising professionals believe longer copy is more effective than brief copy. It is not that the prospect will read *all* of the copy—though she might, if she is really interested—but the fact that there is a lot to say about the product or service and that you are willing to say it generates both interest and confidence in the merchandise.

Longer copy is best punctuated by subheads, miniature headlines that act as signposts, pointing the reader, step by step, in the direction the ad copy is taking. Each subhead might underscore a product benefit or raise an issue the product somehow addresses. A reader who skims the ad should be able to learn a good deal about what you are selling just by taking in the subheads.

Three other text features that stand out from the body copy are callouts, sidebars, and captions. Callouts are brief bursts of text, typographically distinct from the body text, that call attention to some product feature or benefit ("Never needs ironing!"). Sidebars, which are found only in lengthy advertisements, highlight particular features or benefits in some detail. Often, a sidebar is a list of special features. Captions accompany photographs, diagrams, or other illustrations and direct the reader's attention to whatever you want her to take note of in the illustration ("Styling is modern throughout").

Finally, the majority of successful ads conclude with a slogan or tag line. Effective slogans plant the product, the service, the company permanently in the mind of the reader, making the product a familiar fixture of his consciousness. The truly great slogans carve out a permanent place in popular culture or even the English language. Think about how many tag lines run through your mind daily.

Things go better with Coke.

Coke. It's the real thing.

You're in good hands with Allstate.

Gas does the big jobs better for less.

99 and 44 one-hundredths percent pure

Snickers satisfies.

Don't leave home without it.

Just do it.

When you care enough to send the very best.

Nobody doesn't like Sara Lee.

And so on. A good tag line plays upon humankind's ancient propensity to generate proverbs, maxims, and rules to live by. What motivates you to take a trip to the K Mart? Maybe it's their slogan running through your head: "Always the right price." Then again, maybe its the tag line you learned when you were four years old: "A penny saved is a penny earned." It hardly matters. The effect is the same. Whatever else a reader derives from your ad, a "catchy" tag line will plant your identity securely in his consciousness.

How do you write a good tag line? Really, it's almost like composing poetry. Indeed, one of the most famous tag lines in advertising history—"Raid kills bugs dead"—was written by Lew Welch, a poet whose day job was as an ad man. Study that simple line, and you will appreciate what a marvel of language a good tag line can be. Each word in this slogan is a single syllable (not an easy feat in the English language), and each one-syllable word is strongly accented (also a rarity in English, which tends naturally to fall into two-syllable rhythms consisting of an unaccented syllable followed by an accented one). Listen to the line. The "d," "k," and "b" sounds all bounce off each other, making the line almost musical. Also the word *Raid*, the first word of the sentence, makes what poets call a "slant rhyme"—sort of a partial rhyme—with the last word: *dead*.

I've always admired this tag line, and I could go on and on, analyzing it some more. Do *you* have to go through an intense poetic process to create a tag line? No. And I doubt Lew Welch did, either. Learn to hone your feel for language, and just start writing. One good way to begin is to take any number of clichés and twist them into something fresh. Let's say your business is performing some service that has the chief benefit of saving your clients time. Here's a cliché: "There's no time like the present." Maybe your tag line should be, "There's no present like time."

Much of this book consists of generic model pieces of writing for you to customize or fill in. Approaching copywriting that way won't work. Fortunately (or unfortunately, depending on your mood), our world is overflowing with examples of advertising ready to be used as models. Pore through newspapers and magazines, as well as the special-interest journals and other publications in your field. Identify the ads that appeal to you, that make you stop, think, and consider the advertiser's product. Then learn from these messages. The following are some features and points to look out for.

SELLING WORDS

Many novice copywriters make the mistake of assuming that persuasive selling copy is a matter of finding the right adjectives: *gorgeous, beautiful, stupendous,* and the like. As in any other form of writing, however, it is actually the nouns and the verbs that make the difference between unconvincing verbiage and compelling prose. By all means, use adjectives—but only after you have exhausted all the possibilities nouns and verb offer.

An important way to emphasize those nouns and verbs is to write in the active voice, not the passive. "You can buy no better hammer than a Bango" is much more effective than "No better hammer than a Bango can be bought by you." Both are acceptable English, but the first sentence, in the active voice, emphasizes human activity and includes the reader in the action. Passive-voice sentences, like the second example, are not only more complex and wordier, they are downright alienating, shifting the focus from *people* performing actions to *things* being acted upon. Active-voice sentences motivate action, convey honesty and strength, and are easy to comprehend at a glance.

The following is a list of words—nouns, verbs, and simple, straightforward adjectives—that pack a punch in any ad:

act	guaranteed	right
advice	happy	safe
advise	healthy	sale
alternative	hear	save
announcing	introducing	secure
benefits	investment	security
cash	love	see
comfortable	money	smart
delight	new	taste
desire	now	test
desired	people	touch
discover	pleasure	trustworthy
distinctive	presenting	value
easy	pride	wanted
enjoy	proof	why
family	proud	win
feel	proven	winnings
free	relax	wise
fun	reliable	you
gain	results	your
good-looking	reward	

Just as there are potent positive words that will power up any copy, there are potent poison words that will kill any sale. *Avoid* the following whenever possible:

bad	death	hard
burden	debt	kill
buy	decision	lawyer
cheap	die	liability
contract	difficult	loss
cost	fail	must
deal	failure	obligation

order	sell	worry
procedure	wait	wrong
process	waiting	

POSITIVE APPROACH

Never use an ad to defend your product or service. Look for positive features and benefits and promote them. This includes the fact that your's is a *small* business. Yeah, sure, personally and among friends and colleagues you moan and groan about cash flow problems, about visibility problems, and about all the advantages the bigger operators enjoy. But don't let this creep into your ads. If anything, promote your smallness as a positive product benefit. Avis rent-a-car took the fact that it was only the *second* biggest car rental company and turned it into a remarkable advertising asset and one of the great tag lines in promotional history: "We try harder." Not only does a potential automobile renter stride past the airport car rental counters with that phrase firmly planted at some level of his consciousness, he also wonders: *Well, maybe they really* do *try harder*.

MAKE EVERY WORD COUNT

Many commission sales reps learn a little acronym that is literally as simple as ABC:

Always

Be

Closing

That is meant to remind them that, with each and every word they exchange with a prospect, they should be working toward closing the sale. The same goes with writing ad copy. Each word you write should point toward the single goal of closing the sale. This will require writing and rewriting, pruning, adding, then pruning some more to get it just right.

ESTABLISH A UNIQUE IDENTITY

The ads you remember are for the companies you remember. That's because, whatever other information a successful ad conveys, it creates a unique identity for the advertiser. If you write ad copy, only to discover that you could very easily substitute your competitor's name for your own in that copy, throw it out and start again.

EMPHASIZE BENEFITS INSTEAD OF FEATURES

Features are attributes of your product or service. Benefits are what those attributes will do for your target customer. If you sell an automobile that *features* body sheet metal of an extra-heavy gauge, sell the *benefit* of protection for "you and your loved ones." If your detergent *features* a special surfactant that really lifts off grease, sell the *benefit* of dining every evening from china that looks brand new. If you *feature* free delivery, sell your target customer the *benefit* of saving time and cash.

AVOID GENERALITIES AND ABSTRACTIONS

I know I've said it elsewhere. Good writers soon learn to *show* rather than to *tell*. If you trumpet "quality" or say that you're "number one" or "the best" or you "can't be beat," your reader will say to himself, "So what else is new?" Actually, he won't say anything to himself, because it is highly unlikely that he will give your ad a second glance, let alone a second thought.

Instead of an abstract assertion of "quality," write copy that *shows,* that *demonstrates,* that gives *examples* of your particular and unique quality: "At Acme, when we build a widget, we don't inspect it—not once. We don't inspect it twice. We inspect it three times, so that your maintenance staff will never have to inspect it—not once."

FINALLY, CONSIDER TELLING A STORY

Traditionally, some of the most effective ads have been stories: the experience of a satisfied customer, for example, or the saga of a dramatic improvement that results from using a certain product or service. If you have trouble homing in on just what benefits your merchandise offers, if you are intimidated by even the thought of trying to come up with witty slogans and powerful headlines, try sitting down to write a story about what you have to sell. It's a good start. It's a great way to get your ideas focused in your own mind. And—just possibly—it may end up as highly effective ad copy.

For Immediate Release: Creating Cost-Free Advertising with Press Releases

How to Do It

Press releases are the closest thing to free advertising you can get. Sure, Uncle Billy sat you on his knee and solemnly pronounced, "There is no such thing as a free lunch." And, in his way, he was right. Creating a press release will cost you time and effort, but it will not require you to purchase the space in which to exhibit the fruits of that time and effort. Moreover, there is one thing advertising cannot buy: the halo of objectivity that comes with a press release printed as news. People know that advertising is bought and paid for and, therefore, must be taken with a grain (or maybe a whole lump) of salt. In contrast, people *think* they know that "the news" is objective truth and cannot be bought. Furthermore, news is by definition useful or valuable information: stuff you *should* know about, information you *want* to have. Advertising—well, that may or may not be valuable. Generally, you buy a newspaper or trade journal for the *news,* not the ads.

To an extent, this popular view of advertising versus the news is accurate. At least, to an extent. But—to an extent—it is also naive. We like to think that news consists of *events* that simply *occur* and then are *reported*. In some cases, this is quite true. An event happens. A reporting team is dispatched. The public gets coverage. But a large proportion of "news" doesn't just happen. It is manufactured—not made up, but created—and then it is *sold* (like any other product) to some element of the media: newspapers, TV, radio, a trade journal, and so on. This doesn't mean that the newspaper pays for the news item, but that the news item is packaged in such a way that the newspaper is persuaded to publish it as news, "spending" its most valuable commodity: space.

The key packaging device is the news release. A news release is not reportage. It is not by its nature objective. It is advertising in the guise of useful information. It doesn't just happen. It is created. If you can convince a newspaper or trade journal that the press release contains information their subscribers will consider valuable and will want to have, then you will succeed in "selling" the news release to the publication.

How difficult is it to "sell" a press release?

How difficult is it to sell into any marketplace? The answer is: it varies.

If you are trying to place a news release in a big-city newspaper on a day or a week or a month jam packed with momentous news, it might be next to impossible to sell your story. If your "news" appeals to a very specialized segment of the population, it will be difficult to sell the release to any general-interest publication. However, many publications depend on press releases for a large proportion of their editorial copy. This is especially true of certain professional and trade journals and of community and neighborhood newspapers, most of which have tight budgets and very limited reporting staffs. If you choose your venues carefully, chances are you will find editors who are actually grateful to have a juicy news item dropped into their laps.

BUILDING A PRESS RELEASE

Your chances of selling any product are greatly increased if the product is perceived as valuable, attractive, trouble-free, and well made. The same is true of "selling" a press release. If an editor has a hole of a certain size to fill, and he has a choice of three or four press releases with which to fill it, she's going to make her decision based on two factors:

1. Her judgment of newsworthiness—that is, the number of readers who are likely to be interested in the item

2. The quality of the release—that is, how ready the release is for publication

If you have to choose between buying two used cars, same model, same price, but one "needs work" while the other can be driven right off the lot, which will you take? Same holds true for a news release. All other things being even approximately equal, an editor will choose to publish the press release that requires the least rewriting.

Here are guidelines for building press releases that are "ready to drive":

1. Construct the time-honored "inverted pyramid." The classic news story (and this includes press releases) is put together to help the editor edit. Newspapers have limited space. Therefore, stories must be constructed for maximum flexibility. The "inverted pyramid" format means that you pack as much essential information in the first sentence and the first paragraph as possible, then get progressively more detailed as you proceed through the article. Theoretically, an editor should be able to prune back from the end everything except the opening sentence and still have a news article that is capable of being understood. Don't make the editor (or the reader) hunt for your meaning. Begin with it. The rest of the article is development.

2. Here is another classic structuring device. Pack into that first sentence and paragraph the standard "Four W's": who, what, when, and where. *John Smith joined Acme Widgets of Omaha, Nebraska, as sales manager on December 15.*

3. Put the information in its best light, but avoid hype. Editors develop acute antennas for language that sounds too much like advertising. Your language should sound like information.

4. Ideally, style your press release to harmonize with the prevailing style of your target publication. A press release for a specialized professional journal will differ in tone and style from one intended for a neighborhood newspaper.

5. Present the press release in a neat form. Always double space the typed copy. Editors will tend to reject single-spaced copy out-of-hand for the simple reason that they cannot easily make necessary corrections between the lines. Typesetters also have difficulty reading single-spaced copy. These days, consider sending a diskette version of your press release *along with* hard copy. Unless a specific editor tells you differently, the diskette version should be in DOS-based ASCII text format.

6. Type the press release on your letterhead stationery or on stationery that has been specially designed for press releases. If you have a good computer printer and word processing software with a variety of available fonts, you can easily prepare press release stationery. Print in large, bold letters the phrase "PRESS RELEASE" across the top of the page or down one side. Alternatively, you might print "FOR IMMEDIATE RELEASE." (If you do this, make certain that the press release you send really is for immediate release and not timed to coincide with some later event.)

7. Include the following information in every press release:

    a. The release date.

    b. The date or date range you would like the story printed. You might specify "Please run before *(date)*" or "Please do NOT run before *(date)*." More often, you will want the release printed as soon as possible, in which case specify "For Immediate Release."

    c. The name and phone number of a person who can be contacted for additional information.

    d. A good headline that describes the event: "Acme Widgets Releases Its New Super Widget"

8. Make sure the story is concise. Although you may encounter how-to books and even editors who will advise you never to let a press release run over a single page, this kind of arbitrary commandment boxes you in unduly. The press release should be as long as necessary to tell the story economically and concisely. If the story is simple, the press release may be a single paragraph. If the story is more complex, the release may run to three or four pages. If your news item requires more extensive coverage than this, you ought to consider a full-scale press kit (discussed briefly in a moment). A lengthy press release should not discourage an editor *if* you have constructed the release as an inverted pyramid, so that he can easily trim from the bottom up to fit available space.

9. Try to include some quotations in your story—even if you are quoting nobody but yourself. The print media loves the immediacy of the horse's mouth.

10. If editors—especially those who manage trade journals and the smaller community papers—are often hungry for copy, they are downright starved for pictures. Whenever possible and appropriate, include one or

more professional-quality black-and-white glossy photographs with newspaper press releases. For releases to magazines that run color photos, include black-and-white glossies as well as one or more color transparencies (35mm or larger "slides," not prints). The standard size for black-and-whites is 8 × 10, although 5 × 7 is also acceptable. The photos should be printed on glossy paper rather than matte or textured paper; a glossy stock enhances reproduction.

11. Finally, determine just who should get your release and try to identify this person by name: "William R. Hearst, Business Editor" rather than "Business Editor" or (ugh!) "Editor" or (ugh! ugh!) "News Department."

12. It is conventional to end press releases (and other news copy) with ### or -30- centered at the bottom of the page. This indicates to the paper-shuffling editor and compositor that the story is ended and that he is not missing any pages.

CONSIDER A PRESS KIT

If the story you have to tell is more complex than can be encompassed within a page or two or three, consider creating a press kit. These can be simple or elaborate or somewhere in between. Buy a 9 × 12 folder, create a press release and any necessary background information (brochure, catalog, etc.), and put these in the right-hand pocket of the folder. Put a variety of black-and-white glossies and any other visual material in the left-hand pocket. Create a neat label and affix it to the cover of the folder. That is a press kit.

If you are launching a major project, you might want to invest in a fancier portfolio-type folder, embossed with your logo or name. You might include a video or an audio tape or a computer diskette along with the usual press release materials.

— WORDS TO USE —

accommodate	announce	benefits
accomplishments	anticipated	breakthrough
achievement	appeal	celebrate
acknowledge	appoint	challenge
advances	appointment	commitment
advise	available	community
affordable	beginning	concerns

convenience
create
created
customers
data
decision
demonstrate
demonstration
develop
discover
effective
efficient
event
excitement
expert
explain
facility
family
features
first
free
fulfilling
genuine
great
groundbreaking
hail
help
important
improve
include
increase

information
insiders
investing
leadership
literature
local
mandate
neighborhood
new
news
offer
opportunities
options
outstanding
personal
plans
please
position
primary
prime
program
promise
promoted
proof
propose
prove
quality
quarter
range
real
realize

record
reduce
relief
reputation
resources
responsibility
responsive
revolutionary
rewarding
sales
satisfaction
satisfy
savvy
serious
service
skill
skills
solution
special
stride
success
successful
talent
test
thrilled
trend
unique
unveil
upgrades
vibrant

— PHRASES TO USE —

allow us to serve
coming onboard

community concerns
consumer affairs

cost-effective solution	no-risk
deeply fulfilling	open its doors
departure from tradition	our community
do it right	range of options
eagerly anticipated	received high marks
earned high praise	recognized expert
family of customers	respond to concerns
first time ever	respond to needs
full range	special event
genuine breakthrough	special expertise
give customers everything they need	special sales event
Grand Opening	special features
high-performance	that's why
highly successful	we feel great about
industrywide reputation	we love
look forward	wide selection
no-anxiety	

New Business

(Letterhead)

DATE: *(Date)*
FOR IMMEDIATE RELEASE
CONTACT: *(Name)*
555-555-0000

(Name of community) **to Get New** *(Type of business)*

For the first time ever, *(Name of community)* will have its own *(type of business)*. *(Name of company/store)* will open its doors at *(address)* on *(date)* with a Grand Opening special sales event that will last until *(date)*.

(Name of company/store) will be located in a *(number)*-square-foot facility and will offer area residents a wide selection of such products as *(list)*.

(Name of company/store) president, *(Name)*, explained why he has chosen *(Name of community)* as a location: "This is a great neighborhood, filled with the kind of savvy consumers our quality and service appeal to. When I discovered that *(Name of community)* didn't have a *(type of business/store)*, I said 'Let's do it—and do it right.'"

(Name of company) was established in *(year)*. The *(Name of community)* facility will be its nth store.

(Letterhead)

DATE: *(Date)*
FOR IMMEDIATE RELEASE
CONTACT: *(Name)*
555-555-0000

Personal Shopper Comes to *(Name of community)*

Beginning *(date)*, busy professionals in *(Name of community)* will get a little more of something they all need: time. *(Name of personal shopper company)* will offer a full range of personal shopping services to those whose daily schedules are simply too crowded to fit in time for everything from basic grocery marketing to searching out a special gift for an important client.

Some people resist the idea of a personal shopper, believing it is a luxury only the "idle rich" can afford.

"Hiring a personal shopper can be a luxurious treat," says company president *(Name)*, "but my customers aren't just people with money to burn. It's folks who want to spend more time with their families—or simply more quality time for themselves—who come to me most often."

(Name of company) offers a wide range of personal shopping programs to fit all needs and budgets. "Just give me a call at 555-0000," advises *(Name of president)*, "and we'll figure out what's right for you."

(Letterhead)

DATE: *(Date)*
FOR IMMEDIATE RELEASE
CONTACT: *(Name)*
555-555-0000

(*Type of consultant*) Offers (*Type of business*) New Outsourcing Options

Responding to the industrywide trend toward outsourcing *(type of operation)*, *(Name of company)* was created on *(date)* to offer *(type of business)* a range of options for taking *(type of operations)* out of house.

(Name of company) was started by *(Name of owner/president)*, a *(number)*-year veteran of the *(type of business)* industry, who has served as vice president of *(Name of former company)* and president of *(Name of another former company)*.

"After managing a lot of in-house *(type of operation)* operations in the companies I ran," *(Name of owner/president)* recently observed, "I became very well aware of just what a strain these operations put on in-house resources. This is one area where it makes serious sense to take the operation out of house."

(Name of company) joins a small but growing cadre of *(type of operation)* outsourcing firms.

"What sets us apart from the others," according to *(Name of company)* vice-president, *(Name)*, "is our experience and the level of service we offer. We've been in this industry for over *(number)* years. We know the problems—and we know the potential. Sure, it's getting to be a highly competitive field. That's what makes us so good."

Companies interested in learning more about the advantages of outsourcing *(type of operation)* should contact *(Name of owner/president)* at 555-555-0000.

New Facility

(Name of company) Moves to Expanded Facility After *(Number Years)*

"Like everybody else in *(Name of community)*, we love the old building, but it's just not big enough for us anymore."

This is how *(Name of company)* president *(Name)* explained his firm's decision to leave the landmark *(Name of building)* at *(location)*.

"Our business has increased *(% amount)* percent over the past *(time period)*—*(% amount)* percent since *(year)*, when we first moved into *(Name of building)*," *(Name of president)* said. "We realized that our customers needed a facility twice as large as what we could offer, and that's why we're moving to *(new location)*."

The move is slated for *(date)*. As to the old and much-beloved *(Name of building)*, it has been sold to *(Name of realtor)*, who intends to develop it as professional office space.

"We feel great about a move that will allow us to serve our customers better than ever," says *(Name of president)*, "and we're delighted that our wonderful old landmark building will be in loving hands after we leave it."

————

(Letterhead)

DATE: *(Date)*
FOR IMMEDIATE RELEASE
CONTACT: *(Name)*
555-555-0000

(Name of store) to Provide Free Parking

(Name of store) shoppers who loved the convenience of a downtown location, but hated looking for a place to park will have rea-

son to celebrate, beginning *(date)*. That's when *(Name of store)* will open its free parking lot alongside the store.

"We love being downtown," says store owner *(Name)*, "and we know that our customers love the excitement of shopping in this vibrant atmosphere. But we also know what a pain it is to hunt for parking spot and have to punctuate every hour of your day by feeding a meter. That's why we acquired the property next door."

The parking facility, which will accommodate *(number)* cars, will open on *(date)*.

Says *(Name of owner)*: "We want our customers to enjoy shopping at *(Name of store)*, even before they walk in the door."

New Personnel

(Letterhead)

DATE: *(Date)*
FOR IMMEDIATE RELEASE
CONTACT: *(Name)*
555-555-0000

(Name) Joins _(Name of company)_ as _(Title)_

(Name of company) announced the appointment of *(Name)* as *(title)*, effective *(date)*.

(Name), who has worked in the *(type of industry)* for *(number)* years, was most recently *(title)* at *(Name of former company)*. He brings to his new post with *(Name of company)* special expertise and leadership in *(field)* and a record of achievement well known to industry insiders.

"I am thrilled to be joining *(Name of company)*, a dynamic firm that offers the kind of leadership opportunities I have always sought," said *(Name)*. "I look forward in particular to developing the company's *(type of program)* program."

(Name), a native of *(Place 1)*, grew up in *(Place 2)* and attended local schools there. After serving in the army for two years, he attended *(Name)* University on a full scholarship and received a master's

degree in *(field)*. After taking his advanced degree, he went to work for *(Name of former company)*, rising rapidly in that organization and doing much to develop the field of *(field)*. *(Name)* is married to *(Name of spouse)*, a *(name of occupation/title)*, and the couple has *(number)* children.

(Letterhead)

DATE: *(Date)*
FOR IMMEDIATE RELEASE
CONTACT: *(Name)*
555-555-0000

PUBLISHING EXECUTIVE JOINS *(NAME)* CONSULTING FIRM

(Name), formerly executive editor for *(Name)* Press, has left that position to become a senior partner in *(Name of company)*, a research, writing, and planning firm serving cultural organizations.

(Name), *(age)*, holds a *(degree)* in *(subject)* from *(Name)* University. At *(Name of former company)*, he acquired numerous highly successful books, including *(list)*.

A widely published author himself, *(Name)* has written *(list)*.

"We are delighted to have *(Name)* as a senior partner," said *(Name of company)* president *(Name)*. "With his track record of successful publishing ventures, he brings added depth and expertise to the publications consulting and services we offer."

(Name) lives in *(city)* with his wife, *(Name)*, and *(number)* children.

(Letterhead)

DATE: *(Date)*
FOR IMMEDIATE RELEASE
CONTACT: *(Name)*
555-555-0000

(Name of company) Creates Position of Customer Ombudsman

In a departure from tradition, *(Name of company)* has replaced its "customer service" desk with the position of Customer Ombudsman and has hired noted local consumer advocate *(Name)* to fill the post. The new position and appointment were announced simultaneously on *(date)*.

(Name of company) president *(Name of president)* explained: "Too often, customers get the impression that 'customer service' serves the company first and them second. We want to make it perfectly clear that our customers' needs and issues are our number-one priority. For that reason, we have created a new position to ensure that our customers will have a genuine full-time advocate, somebody they can turn to at all times. It is a unique position."

To fill the position, *(Name of company)* hired *(Name)*, a well-known consumer advocate, who left the post of Consumer Ombudsman with the city of *(Name of city)* to take the position at *(Name of company)*. *(Name)*, a recognized expert in consumer affairs, was born and raised here in *(Name of place)* and educated at *(Name)* University. He is the author of *Consumer Handbook*. *(Name)* is married and has *(number)* children. Her husband, *(Name)*, is a noted *(occupation)*.

Staff Promotion

(Letterhead)

DATE: *(Date)*
FOR IMMEDIATE RELEASE
CONTACT: *(Name)*
555-555-0000

(Name) Becomes *(New title)* at *(Name of company)*

(Name) will be promoted to *(new title)* at *(Name of company)* effective *(date)*. He was *(old title)*.

(Name) joined *(Name of company)* in *(year)*, after graduating from *(Name)* University. While serving in *(old position)*, he earned an industrywide reputation for *(describe chief accomplishment[s])*, and *(Name of company)* president *(Name of president)* announced that his primary mandate in the position of *(new title)* will be *(describe)*.

"We were looking for somebody who could *(describe)*, and we realized that we didn't have to look any further than our own staff. *(Name)* will do an outstanding job as *(new title)*," said *(Name of president)*.

———————

(Letterhead)

DATE: *(Date)*
FOR IMMEDIATE RELEASE
CONTACT: *(Name)*
555-555-0000

(Name of company) Announces Promotion of *(Name)* to *(New Position)*

After serving as *(old title)* for *(number)* years, *(Name)* will be promoted to *(new title)*, *(Name of company)* announced today. *(Name's)* new responsibilities will include *(list)*.

"Needless to say, I am thrilled to accept the challenges of the new position, and I will serve the customers of *(Name of company)* by *(list goals)*," *(Name)* said.

(Name), who was born and raised in *(Name of place)*, was educated at *(Name)* University and holds a *(graduate degree)* in *(subject)* from *(Name)* University. She worked for *(number)* years at *(Name of former company)* before coming onboard *(Name of present company)* as *(former title)* in *(year)*. *(Name)* is married and has *(number)* children.

Retirement

(Letterhead)

DATE: *(Date)*
FOR IMMEDIATE RELEASE
CONTACT: *(Name)*
555-555-0000

(Name) Steps Down as *(Title)* at *(Name of company)*

After serving as *(title)* with *(Name of company)* for *(number)* years, *(Name)* announced his retirement, effective on *(date)*.

"I cannot express how deeply fulfilling and rewarding these *(number)* years have been, serving a great family of customers and working with the staff of *(Name of company)*," *(Name)* said.

"While I have to admit that I have some sadness at leaving, I also look forward to two things: fishing at Big Bear Lake with my grandson and watching *(Name of company)* continue to grow under the leadership of *(Name of replacement)*," *(Name)* said.

(Name of replacement), who is leaving *(Name of former company)* to join *(Name of company)*, was handpicked by *(Name of retiree)*. *(Name of replacement)* has announced that he will continue the company's major programs and that she will add programs in *(areas)*.

"It is customary to say that the person you're replacing is 'tough act to follow.' Actually, *(Name of retiree)* has made it easy to pick up where he has left off," *(Name of replacement)* said. "He has left *(Name of company)* in a very strong position, poised for further growth. We all owe him our thanks."

(Name of retiree) plans to move to *(Name of place)* and "get to know my grandson before he grows up and forgets who I am."

New Product/Service

(Letterhead)

DATE: *(Date)*
FOR IMMEDIATE RELEASE
CONTACT: *(Name)*
555-555-0000

(Name of company) Unveils New (Product)

On *(date)*, *(Name of company)* will unveil its revolutionary new *(product)*, which will be marketed under the brand name *(Brand name)*.

The *(product)*—*(describe)*—represents a revolutionary approach to *(task/operation)* because *(describe revolutionary aspects)*. *(Name)*, of the American Association of *(Professionals)*, hailed *(product)* as a "genuine breakthrough, which will save time and money."

(Name of company) will conduct a demonstration of *(product)* for all *(type of professionals)* at the *(Name of convention)* on *(date)* at *(time)*, *(time)*, and *(time)*.

———

(Letterhead)

DATE: *(Date)*
FOR IMMEDIATE RELEASE
CONTACT: *(Name)*
555-555-0000

Breakthrough (Product) Introduced by (Name of company)

Responding to demand for an efficient and cost-effective *(product)*, *(Name of company)* today officially announced *(Name of product)*, which will be available in stores beginning *(date)*.

(Name of product), which has been eagerly anticipated, was *(number)* years in development. It *(list special features/benefits)* and is priced under *($ amount)*.

"Our goal was to make available a high-performance *(product)* at an affordable price. And that is just what we've done," *(Name of company)* owner *(Name)* said.

Industry insiders, who had been given the opportunity to test *(Name of product)*, agree. The unit received high marks for *(list features/benefits)*.

Complete literature on *(Name of product)* is available directly from *(Name of company)* at 555-555-0000.

(Letterhead)

DATE: *(Date)*
FOR IMMEDIATE RELEASE
CONTACT: *(Name)*
555-555-0000

(Name of company) Offers New Solution to an Old Problem: _(Problem)_

Those plagued by *(problem)* will be happy to hear that relief will be available on *(date)*. By that time, *(product)* is expected to be generally available. It is a new solution to an old and troublesome problem: *(problem)*.

"*(Product)* is simple, really," says inventor and owner of *(Name of company)*. "It works by *(describe)*. It is the first product to use *(material/technology)*, and it is therefore the first efficient and cost-effective solution to *(problem)*."

(Name of company) plans to produce *(number)* units by *(date)* and has taken steps to ensure that anticipated customer demand will be met. For more information on *(product)*, call the company at 555-555-0000.

New Program

(Letterhead)

DATE: *(Date)*
FOR IMMEDIATE RELEASE
CONTACT: *(Name)*
555-555-0000

Rent-to-Own: *(Name of company)* Announces New Program

(Name of company) today announced a unique new program aimed at customer who are undecided whether to purchase or rent *(product)* and who do not want to commit to a long-term lease. The new rent-to-buy program allows open-ended rental of *(product)*, with *(% amount)* percent of the rental fee applied toward purchase, if the customer chooses.

"We were looking for a low-risk way to allow our customers to assess their *(product)* needs. The rent-to-own program is a win-win program, which give customers everything they need to evaluate their requirements in this area," company chairman *(Name)* said. "The only way to find out whether a *(product)* is right for your business or not is to try it. Up until now, this required a purchase or a long-term lease commitment. Understandably, that scared off many potential customers. It doesn't do anybody any good to frighten away someone who can benefit from *(product)*. So we came up with this rent-to-own program as a no-risk, no-anxiety alternative."

(Name of company) has been a *(product)* dealer in the *(Name of community)* area for *(number)* years.

Those interested in getting more information on *(product)* or the rent-to-own program should call 555-555-0000.

(Letterhead)

DATE: *(Date)*
FOR IMMEDIATE RELEASE
CONTACT: *(Name)*
555-555-0000

(Brand name) Office Copier Self-maintenance Seminars Announced

When the copy machine breaks down, who ya gonna call?

According to *(Brand name)* Customer Service, maybe you should call yourself.

"No item of office equipment is more heavily used—and more abused—than the copy machine. That's why no item of office equipment requires servicing more often than the copy machine. And that includes ours as well as our competitors'," *(Brand name)* customer service manager *(Name)* said. "Yet *(% amount)* percent of service calls are routine and simple, well within the capability of the customer."

The new seminar program for self-maintaining *(Brand name)* copiers will give customers the information and confidence they need to save time and money by performing routine service tasks themselves.

(Name of company) announced that the introductory seminar session will be given free of charge to registered owners of *(Brand name)* equipment. To obtain a seminar schedule or to enroll in the introductory session, customers may call 555-555-0000.

Community Action/Charity

(Letterhead)

DATE: *(Date)*
FOR IMMEDIATE RELEASE
CONTACT: *(Name)*
555-555-0000

(Name of restaurant) Announces Community Food Drive

(Name of restaurant), in cooperation with *(Name of charity organization)*, today announced a program to collect food for needy residents of *(Name of community)* and to make available to them surplus food from the restaurant. The program is expected to feed some *(number)* individuals and families each week.

"We are in the service business," *(Name of restaurant)* owner *(Name)* said at a conference held today. "Sometimes 'service' means providing an attentive staff and a knowledgeable wine steward. Sometimes it means seeing to it that no one in your neighborhood goes hungry."

(Name of restaurant) plans to distribute some *($ amount)* in food each week. The restaurant is also acting as a collection and distribution point for food donated by other members of the community. Please bring the following items to *(Name of restaurant)*, any day of the week, between *(time)* and *(time)*: *(list)*.

(Name of restaurant) and *(Name of charity organization)* ask that you help them help our community. For further information, call 555-0000.

New Program

(Letterhead)

DATE: *(Date)*
FOR IMMEDIATE RELEASE
CONTACT: *(Name)*
555-555-0000

(Name of company) Introduces *(Product)* Upgrade Program

Purchasers and current owners of the *(Name of company)* line of *(type of product)* will now be able to keep up with cutting-edge technology through an upgrade program announced today. *(Product line)* users may now trade up to the latest releases at a fraction of the cost of buying the *(products)* for the first time.

Company owner-president *(Name)* observed: "When a customer buys *(product)*, he or she is investing in technology, not just materials. One of the properties of technology is that it advances, and we owe our customers the benefits of those advances."

Typically, the upgrade price of a *(Name of company)* product will be *(% amount)* percent below the full price of that product. Upgraders will need to present proof of current ownership of the product, including *(types of proof required)*. By calling 555-555-0000, customers may enroll, free of charge, in a special Upgrade Hotline, so that they will receive information on upgrades as they become available.

For more information on *(Name of company's)* new upgrade program, call 555-555-0000.

Record Earnings

(Letterhead)

DATE: *(Date)*
FOR IMMEDIATE RELEASE
CONTACT: *(Name)*
555-555-0000

Banner Quarter for *(Name of company)*

(Name of company), which opened its doors on *(date)*, announced its best quarter yet. Earnings for this new *(type of business)* firm were *($ amount)* for the quarter just ended, *(% amount)* percent higher than the previous quarter.

Asked to explain this growth, company president *(Name)* attributed the increased earnings to *(number)* new products, *(list)*, and "plain old word-of-mouth advertising." *(Name)* said: "Customers know a good thing when they find one, and they tell each other about it. Much of our growth is due to referrals. It is due to our quality and service edge."

How will *(Name of company)* cope with its growing roster of customers?

The firm plans to hire a new customer service coordinator "to ensure that we live up to our growing reputation for service," *(Name)* said. "We like the growth trend, but we don't want to lose the small-company personal service edge."

Problems and Handling Negative Publicity

(Letterhead)

DATE: *(Date)*
FOR IMMEDIATE RELEASE
CONTACT: *(Name)*
555-555-0000

(Name of company) Responds to Community Concerns over New Parking Lot

Responding to concerns expressed on *(date)* by members of the *(Name of community)* Council, *(Name)*, owner of *(Name of company)*, reported that the new parking lot proposed for the *(Name of street)* Street store would enhance the life of the neighborhood, not impact negatively on it.

"Anybody who has driven around block after block between *(time)* o'clock and *(time)* o'clock on a weekday or a Saturday desperately searching for a place to park knows what it is like to try to shop in a community where parking is tight and, at times, nonexistent," *(Name of store owner)* said. "The parking lot we propose will help to alleviate that situation. Far from blighting *(Name of street)* Street, it will enhance life in our neighborhood by reducing frustration and increasing business."

(Name of owner) announced an "open house" at his store on *(date)*, between *(time)* o'clock and *(time)* o'clock, to meet with concerned residents.

"I'm a neighbor first and a businessperson second. If my neighbors aren't happy with me as a neighbor, they won't patronize me as a businessperson. I want to do what's best for us all," *(Name of owner)* said.

(Letterhead)

DATE: *(Date)*
FOR IMMEDIATE RELEASE
CONTACT: *(Name)*
555-555-0000

Noise Abatement Program Announced at *(Name of company)*

Responding to community concerns about noise levels associated with its *(type of operation)* operations, *(Name of company)* announced a three-point noise abatement program today.

In presenting the measures, company owner *(Name)* observed that *(Name of company)* is presently in full compliance with noise-level regulations governing its commercially zoned location. "But that," *(Name)* said, "is not good enough for us. We intend to do better than what the city says we have to do. We intend to be more than a compliant citizen. We intend to be a good neighbor."

The program, which will go into operation by *(date)*, consists of three phases:

1. *(explain)*

2. *(explain)*

3. *(explain)*

The cost of the program is estimated at *($ amount)*.

"I've never been more pleased to spend money," *(Name of company)* owner *(Name)* remarked.

(Letterhead)

DATE: *(Date)*
FOR IMMEDIATE RELEASE
CONTACT: *(Name)*
555-555-0000

(Name of company) to Hire More Local Residents

(Name), owner of *(Name of company)*, announced today that the company is actively seeking residents of *(Name of community)* to apply for the following positions:

(list)

"Recently, a number of members of our community have expressed their concern that we do not hire locally. We are a small company, but, of our *(number)* employees, *(number)* live within *(number)* miles of our facility. However, we would like to increase that number by hiring local talent for the new positions we have to fill."

(Name of company) is advertising the new positions in *(Name of neighborhood newspaper)* and has posted them at *(locations)*. Applicants should report to *(address)* and ask for *(Name)*.

PART IV

On the Air

Drumming Up a One-Person Band

Have you ever been tempted to buy a product because it bore a sticker proclaiming "AS ADVERTISED ON TV"? I know I have. It's not a particularly rational urge—but, so what? There is something about broadcast advertising—in contrast to newspaper or trade-journal advertising—that seems to set a special "seal of approval" on a product or service.

Why?

Maybe it's because the broadcast media more immediately reflect and influence our day-to-day culture than the print media do. Or maybe it's because most people believe broadcast advertising is extremely expensive and therefore inaccessible to all but the U.S. government and the most successful big businesses.

Is broadcast advertising beyond the reach of a small business?

Not at all—but the public *perception* that the broadcast media are reserved for the "big guys" can work to your advantage by enhancing the prestige of your product or service.

Radio

Radio can be downright cheap. In small markets, air time can run as low as $5 per thirty-second spot. *That's $5.* In larger markets, you can expect to pay anywhere from $35 to $250 per spot, depending on the "daypart" division you choose. Usually, the "A.M. drive" (morning drive time), from 6 A.M. to 10 A.M., draws the most listeners and is therefore the most expensive daypart. The P.M. drive (3 to 7 P.M.) draws fewer listeners, but they tend to be in a more receptive buying mood and, therefore, the P.M. drive costs the same as the A.M. drive. In between is "midday" (10 A.M. to 3 P.M.), with an audience lower than that for the drive times, followed by "evening" (7 P.M. to midnight), and "late night" (midnight to 6 A.M.). Late night obviously offers the cheapest air time, also offering the fewest listeners, but it may actually command the most loyal audience and, depending on your product or service, can be a very cost-effective bargain.

Buying the time is one thing, of course, but producing the radio spot is another. Isn't this expensive, involving writers, announcers, sound effects, even actors?

You can, if you wish, lavish a considerable sum on producing the radio commercial, but there are low-cost options, which will produce effective ads. Chapter Seventeen outlines strategies for using inexpensive "voice talent," relatively inexpensive celebrity voice talent, finding cheap music and sound effects, and creating an effective script.

Television

Television, which many advertisers believe is the single most powerful advertising medium, is, with one exception, more expensive than radio. The exception is the special announcement channel many cable TV operators offer: this is a channel that functions as a visual bulletin board, running still-image announcements continuously over a background of music. The cable operator offers all production services, which include designing and laying out your ad, including a digitized image (you supply the original photograph). Costs vary with market, and you will have to ask yourself whether this kind of bulletin-board advertising is cost-effective and whether or not it conveys the image of your business you want to create.

Most advertisers are more interested in mainstream ads, with actors and a full visual presentation of a product or service. Do you really need to invest in this? Without doubt, television is a culturally powerful and influential tool. It is also the only medium that allows you to sell verbally, visually, and musically—all at the same time. If your product or service requires creating in potential buyers the closest thing to the experience of actually owning the product or using the service, then television advertising is worth investigating.

Costs of producing a thirty-second television spot vary widely. If you are looking for the kind of production values Coca-Cola gets from its spots, you will need to spend hundreds of thousands of dollars. If, however, you are willing to negotiate with a local television production crew, you can produce a full-scale thirty-second ad for $500 to $5,000. Costs of buying the air time are even more variable than for radio time and are highly dependent on the time of day into which you are buying. As a small-business operator, you will almost certainly be buying local time only. In a small market and at an off-hour, this can be as low as $30 for thirty seconds. In larger markets, thirty seconds will cost anywhere from a few hundred to $1,000—for local coverage.

It used to be that television advertising was only for products and services that have broad markets and that, even when the advertiser is local, are available over a large local area—the area reached by the broadcast—rather than in a particular neighborhood. This was true in the days when all television was broadcast over the airwaves. Today, however, many households (the national average is now more than 50 percent) are served by cable television. This has impacted smaller advertisers in three ways:

1. It has made television advertising generally less expensive.

2. It has created special-interest venues for more specialized advertising of special-market products.

3. It has made advertising local, even neighborhood businesses feasible and effective.

Radio and television have always been paradoxical media: capable of worldwide coverage, yet also capable of reaching into the home in a most intimate and individual way. *Intimate* and *individual* are words small businesses should be very comfortable with. And that makes radio and television worth exploring as vehicles for advertising.

Chapter 17

Drive Time and Off Time: Creating and Buying Inexpensive Radio Spots

How to Do It

When Louis Jacques Mandé Daguerre invented the first practical camera and photographic process in 1837, the French painter Eugène Delacroix declared: "Painting is dead."

He was mistaken.

Similarly mistaken were those who counted out radio when television began to take the nation and the world by storm during the 1950s. While photography did not kill painting, it did encourage the art to change—and such "nonrealistic" movements as Impressionism and Abstraction were born. Likewise, television steered radio away from the dramatic and comedy shows it had carried in the 1930s and 1940s, and made it a medium for music, news, and talk. Furthermore, while television stations tried to be all things to all people, individual radio stations began to specialize, cultivating loyal audiences interested in a particular kind of music (classical, country, rock—various varieties of rock, at that—easy listening, and so on), those interested in continuous news reports, and those interested in talk. Far from being an old-fashioned or outmoded medium, radio was a forerunner of the individualized "interactive" electronic information media just emerging today. Whereas *broad*casters traditionally tried to appeal to the *broadest* possible market, radio (in the post-television age) anticipated what has been called *narrow*casting, appealing to more precisely defined and specialized markets. In many cases, listeners are invited to call in while the show is in progress, making the broadcast experience genuinely interactive, rather than one-way and passive.

What does this mean for the small-business advertiser?

It means that target customers can be more precisely targeted. If you sell a product that appeals to teenagers, you will want to advertise on the rock station that offers the music that group listens to most. If you are selling, say, a monthly investment guide, you will want to advertise on the continuous news station—and most specifically during the financial segment of the news. If you want to personalize your product or service to build customer loyalty (let's say you operate a hi-fi store pledging to set your customers up with the best equipment at the best prices), you will want to advertise on a show that has a popular, personable, and credible DJ.

Even more than in most print-media situations, radio advertising requires careful thought devoted to just *where* you should place your spots. Begin by identifying your target customer. Then determine:

1. What kind of station appeals to my target customer

2. What particular shows (if any) my target customer listen to

3. What time ("daypart") my target customer tunes in: A.M. drive (6 to 10 A.M.)? Midday (10 A.M. to 3 P.M.)? P.M. drive (3 to 7 P.M.)? Evening? (7 P.M. to midnight)? Late night? (midnight to 6 A.M.)? Or primarily weekends (all day Saturday and Sunday)?

4. Radio personalities with whom my target customer identifies

WHAT IS A RADIO SPOT?

Let's define just what it is we are talking about when we speak of a radio commercial or "spot."

First, spots are generally thirty or sixty seconds long. A minute, let alone half a minute, may seem like an impossibly short time in which to say anything meaningful about your product or service, and, indeed, if you were in a one-on-one, face-to-face conversational selling situation with a client, such a time constraint would be daunting. But, on radio, you will find that thirty seconds—let alone sixty—are not easy to fill *creatively* and *effectively*. What is the criterion for "creatively" and "effectively"? Filling the time in a way that captures and holds the attention of your target customer.

For most advertisers, thirty seconds, which costs 60 to 75 percent as much as sixty seconds, is sufficient time to get the message across. However, you need more time if you want to introduce a product or service that genuinely requires explanation (as in enumerating the benefits of a radically new and unfamiliar product), if you need to express a point of view (as in a political or professional advertisement), if you plan to include more or less elaborate music and sound effects, or if you believe that the most effective advertisement for your product or service is dramatic, in effect a miniature story.

Some stations offer even briefer spots than thirty seconds: twenty, fifteen, even ten. For general purposes, it is pretty difficult to do much with these, unless they used to carry reminders or "teasers" that are part of a larger ad campaign consisting of a series of related messages. You may also work with stations that charge "unit rates" rather than different rates for thirty-second or sixty-second spots. In this case, it's hard to settle for thirty seconds when you can get sixty for the same unit price.

Unlike print ads or television ads, which usually have a strong visual component, radio ads are always heavily verbal and script dependent. So it is useful to think of the length of the spot in terms of the number of words that can effectively be presented within thirty or sixty seconds. Thirty-second spots are typically 60 to 90 words long. Sixty-second spots average 150 to 170 words. Add sound effects and music, and you may have time for even fewer words.

WHEN TO RUN YOUR SPOTS

Once you determine who your target customers are and you decide what stations they are most likely to listen to and at what times, you need to figure out, first, whether you can afford your first choice of station and daypart and, if so, how much exposure you need. The rate you pay is determined by:

1. Size of market

2. Daypart

3. Length of the spot

4. The number of spots you buy. There is usually a discount for volume buys; you'll pay less per spot for thirty—as opposed to ten—purchased in a month

5. Whether you pay national or local rates. National rates are what stations charge ad agencies. Local rates are reserved for time you buy directly from the station. In many cases, however, if you use a local (as opposed to a national) ad agency, the station will also quote local rates.

These are the basic cost factors. But cost ultimately also depends on your buying *strategy*. Generally, you may adopt one of four strategies to pinpoint the placement of your spots. Buying specific dayparts guarantees the spot or spots will be aired during a certain time range. Since stations want your business, especially in competitive markets, you can also often persuade the advertising manager to run your spots at fairly specific times *within* the daypart. If you happen to know that most of your target customers commute late in the morning, you will want to get your spots put into the later part of the "A.M. drive."

One way to cut costs is to place all your spots in the least listened-to daypart, late night. Unless you are selling products or services that appeal to insomniacs, however, this daypart, while cheap, may not be cost-effective. An economical alternative to putting all your spots into a cheap daypart is to buy a "package." This is much like buying run-of-press (ROP) ads in a newspaper as opposed to paying extra for the privilege of placing your ads exactly where you want them. Radio packages are sometimes called run of station—ROS— because the station decides when to run them. (Some stations call package buys "total audience plan"—TAP—or "best time available"—BTA). Remember, in most cases, it is in the station's interest to see to it that your ads get results, so that you will continue to buy time from the station. Therefore, most stations will attempt to distribute your package of spots fairly across the range of dayparts. Depending on the station, you may also be able to express some preferences and restrictions: no late-night spots, no weekend spots, and so on.

In the earlier days of radio and television broadcasting, most ad time was sold on the basis of sponsorships. You had the "Brand X Coffee Comedy Hour" or the "Brand Z Soap Flakes Theater" and so on. Today it is still possible to buy sponsorship of certain programs, so that your company's name becomes associated with that program: "'Morning Talk' is brought to you by Wibble Widgets." Depending on the show, sponsorship can be expensive—or simply impossible to get at any price. However, you can arrange to have spots run *adjacent* to a particular program with which you want to be associated. If you know that your target customers love to listen to "Such-and-Such a Program" (and who *doesn't* love Such-and-Such?), then it is probably worth paying a premium to ensure that your spots are run just before or after the show. It is also usually possible—again, for a premium charge—to specify a specific time for running your spot. This is called buying a fixed position.

The problem with sponsorships, adjacencies, and fixed positions is that they can be expensive, but, even more daunting, they can simply be impossible to get. If a show is popular, you may find yourself at the tail end of a very long line of advertisers who want association with the program.

How Often to Run Your Spots

A well-placed print ad, run once or twice, is likely to produce tangible results. Run a radio ad once or twice, and nobody will hear you. Advertising in the broadcast media thrives on repetition, so that your message becomes (for a time) part of the electronic environment in which we all live.

As you may have already guessed, the "right" number of ads to run is extremely variable. A good rule of thumb, however, is to air no fewer than twenty spots per week during a campaign. It is a highly effective strategy to cluster your spots rather than spread them out, so that they have greater impact on a particular group of listeners—presumably the group you perceive as your target customers. If you've budgeted twenty spots per week, don't run them every day, but cluster them during, say, a four-day period. Or omit one week during a month, so that, say, eighty spots are clustered into three weeks rather than four.

Depending on the size of the market and the makeup of your target customers, you should try to run your spots on more than one station. This is especially true, say, if your target customers are teenagers whose loyalty is generally divided among two youth rock stations in town or if your product appeals to divergent target groups: the typical fan of country and the person who keeps his dial tuned to talk radio.

How'm I Doin'?

As in television broadcasting, the radio industry is served by a number of rating services that measure audience size. A station's advertising rep should be able to furnish you with copies of ARBitron and Nielsen surveys of the local market (in Canada, the rating service is the Bureau of Broadcast Measurement). These should help you make intelligent buying decisions. Even more relevant, however, are the surveys *you* should do yourself. Develop quick, painless point-of-purchase questionnaires for your customers, which include the question "How did you hear about us?"

PRODUCTION

As with creating print ads, you have a range of options for producing radio spots.

1. You can leave everything to an ad agency.

2. You can hire a professional script writer.

3. You can take advantage of production talent the radio station may offer.

4. You can work with the radio station or an independent sound-recording studio to create the spot yourself.

Whichever route you take, the two prime considerations are the script and the voice. The script is the subject of the entire final section of this chapter. Let's consider the voice first. Whose voice should it be?

You could use your own. In recent years, even large companies have pressed their CEOs into service as spokespeople—often with considerable success. Think of Chrysler's Lee Iacocca, for example, or the long-running series of television ads for Remington electric razors in which Victor Kiam told viewers that he was so impressed by the razor that he "bought the company." In the case of a small business, it may be even more appropriate for the owner or principal partner to speak directly to potential customers, especially if you are selling the personal service advantage inherent in a small company. Of course, it helps if you have a good voice and are comfortable speaking (via recording) on radio. It is even possible to use the nonprofessional, untrained qualities of your voice to your advantage. Radio listeners are accustomed to hearing the polished tones of the professional announcer. They may become so accustomed to this, that they are easily lulled into indifference, and the announcer's highly trained voice readily recedes into the background. The sound of your John or Jane Q. Public voice, in contrast, may actually capture more attention because it's not what the audience expects to hear.

On the other hand—and there is always another hand—an amateur voice, including your own, may be unpleasant, hard to understand, or stiff and stilted. If you cannot get beyond a monotone I-am-reading-every-word-of-this-incredibly-tedious-message-and-you-have-stopped-listening-to-me-long-before-I-am-finished approach, don't torture yourself, your listeners, and your bottom line. Hire professional voice talent.

Sound expensive? Not necessarily.

If you get a local station to produce your spot, chances are they will throw in the services of the DJ or another on-air personality as part of the deal. If not, or if you produce the spot yourself, such services are usually relatively inexpensive. Using a show's regular DJ, announcer, or host has advantages as well as disadvantages. If the personality is popular, his or her voice and presentation may well be a great asset to the image of your product or service. A good radio personality may ad lib a little extra "personal" message to enhance the impact of your script. (After presenting your message, she may add: "You know, I started using Brand X, and it *really* worked.") But it is also possible that listeners will tend mentally to tune out a message delivered by the same voice responsible for the rest of the program. In print ads, advertising is designed deliberately to contrast with the surrounding "editorial" content. The same principle can also be useful for radio spots.

How do you obtain a voice to contrast with that of the regular announcer or DJ? One low-cost alternative is to ask the station to use, say, the late-night DJ to do the spot you've placed during the A.M. drive daypart. He still works for the station, but his voice will be new to drive time listeners. Another obvious choice for contrast is to use a woman to deliver your message. Women are in the minority among radio personalities and announcers. Using a woman's voice may in and of itself set your message apart from the crowd.

Finally, you have two higher-cost voice alternatives. You can hire professional voice talent outside of the radio station. You may do this through an ad agency or through an agent that specializes in voice talent. The advantage of going this route is that you get to audition the voice that you feel is perfectly suited to the image you wish to create and convey. Maybe you want a folksy sound. Maybe you want an innocent effect. Maybe a hip young sound. Maybe you want a range of voices for a range of spots. If so, professional talent is the way to go.

An inexpensive alternative to auditioning established professional voice talent is calling on a local drama school or a local little theater group. Here you may find aspiring actors and actresses who are eager for exposure and who are, therefore, receptive to an economical offer.

Finally, there is celebrity voice talent. As you may imagine, this is the highest-priced alternative, but, depending on the magnitude of the star you aim for, it may not be out of reach. Those who have attained the heights of popularity generally market their names and voices dearly, but others, still familiar and recognizable—members of supporting casts rather than stars—may charge nothing more than twice basic union scale. If you believe that an implied celebrity (or semicelebrity) endorsement will significantly enhance the image of your product or service, or if you feel that such a voice will command attention, using celebrity voice talent may be worth the added expense.

OTHER PRODUCTION ELEMENTS

Your radio message may consist of nothing more than a voice reading a script, and, depending on what you are selling, this can be perfectly adequate. However, your script may also be more elaborate. Perhaps you've decided to create a dialogue or a minidrama. Or perhaps you've decided to enhance the spoken message with music and sound effects.

Music *can* be obtained cheaply. Most stations maintain a library of free music, available for use in spots. You can purchase, again inexpensively, so-called "canned music," tunes that *sound like* the work of popular performers and composers. This music is not subject to costly royalties, but may be used for a reasonable "drop-needle fee." Most expensive is obtaining the rights to use the real thing: a tune and/or performance by a name artist. This can be prohibitive. Speaking of prohibitive, the one thing you should *not* do is attempt to use a commercial recording (or an unauthorized private recording of a live performance) without full written permission. Unauthorized use of such material is a violation of copyright law and lays you open to severe civil and even criminal penalties. Even commercial recordings of works that are clearly in the public domain—a Mozart piano concerto, say—are protected because the particular *performance* is copyrighted.

For most small-business advertisers, the final frontier, musically speaking, is commissioning an original jingle. Costs vary widely, from a minimum of $500 to more than $1,000, and a jingle is not always appropriate. If you're in the funeral business, for example, you're better off without one. But for many products and services, a short, catchy jingle does a great deal to plant—or *implant*—a name in the collective consciousness of an audience. How many of us, perhaps even to our embarrassment, find ourselves humming or singing an all-too-familiar jingle?

A word of caution: A catchy jingle will give you visibility. An obnoxious or dumb-sounding jingle will create negative associations that may be difficult to live down. Proceed thoughtfully and cautiously.

Sound effects are also low-cost, even no-cost embellishments for your message. Use them sparingly, but do use them when you think they will help sell your product. Do you want a dialogue spoken over a backyard barbecue?

Record it in the studio, and let the station add the sound of sizzling steaks and children's shouts in the distance. Want to create a feeling of tranquility for your peace-of-mind message about your investment counseling service? Provide a background that evokes the countryside: a babbling brook, the sound of birdcalls. Remember that, as an entirely aural medium, radio must appeal to the imagination through sound.

The Script

Scripts for radio spots may be divided into two broad categories:

1. Straightforward announcements
2. Monologues, dialogues, and minidramas

Whichever option you choose, remember that you have room for about eighty words in a thirty-second spot. Those aspiring to be public speakers are generally admonished to "speak more slowly." In the case of radio spots, however, speech should be slightly more *rapid* than normal. Of course, you should avoid creating the impression of the proverbial "fast-talking salesman," but a crisp script delivered at a lively clip, yet with each word clear and accurately pronounced, not only allows you to pack in the maximum amount of information into a short span of time, it is most likely to grab and hold the listener's attention. On radio, listeners tend to tune out a slow speaker.

Whatever format you choose for your script—straightforward message or something more dramatic—and at whatever speed you deliver the message, your goals are always the same. The effective radio spot must:

1. Command attention within two to three seconds.
2. Make a clear offer.
3. Enable the listener to *act* on the offer.

Commanding Attention

The function of the opening line of your spot's script is to make your target customer stop what he or she is doing and listen. Stop 'em in their tracks. The way to do this is to identify the target customer and offer (or imply) a benefit to them—all *within the opening sentence*. If that seems hard, well, it sounds more complicated in theory than in practice. Look:

Word processor users, would you like a free book of time-saving tips?

The sentence calls out to a specific group, getting their attention. Then it offers a benefit: *time-saving* tips, which, moreover, will cost nothing. Note, too, that the word *free,* as in any other ad, is pretty hard to resist in a radio spot. Also, the question format in and of itself commands attention by demanding the listener's involvement. Beginning with a question is almost always an effective way to build an attention-grabbing opening sentence:

Do you suffer from *(whatever)*?

Are you a frustrated *(whatever)*?

Do you have enough money?

Would you like to make more money?

Do you want to lose weight?

Need to lose weight?

Are you happy?

Are you happy with *(whatever)*?

Need a better job?

Are you paying to much for *(whatever)*?

What will you do when *(whatever)* happens to you?

A variation on the question opener is the quiz or test:

Here's a quick test for anyone who loves good music.

Are you getting enough vitamin A? Take this quiz.

The question and quiz formats automatically engage the listener, but they are hardly your only options for an opener. Offer advice:

Here's a money-saving tip for taxpayers from the area's number-one tax expert.

Let me offer a word of valuable advice—

Here's the most valuable free advice you'll ever get.

Or offer news:

Let me give you news about a remarkable breakthrough . . .

Here's news of an offer you can't afford to miss.

Or assert need:

> I'm here to tell you three things you need to know.
>
> There are three things every homeowner in *(Name of community)* must know.

Notice also the power of quantifying your opening statement. "There are three things no business traveler can afford to be without" commands far more attention than "Here are a few things the business traveler needs."

Another naturally powerful opening is the "if . . . then" statement:

> If you need cash now, then you cannot afford to miss this opportunity from *(Name of company)*.
>
> If you are saving to buy your first house, we can help.
>
> If you long for a vacation in the sun, then you'll want to hear about these fabulous offers from *(Name of company)*.

Note that the "then" is not always stated as a word, but it is implied. If . . . then statements have their own internal momentum: the proverbial drop-the-other-shoe effect.

CREATING DESIRE

Once your spot has commanded attention, it must develop the target customer's desire to own the product or purchase the service you offer. Emphasize benefits—what the product or service will do *for* the target customer—rather than features—the mere attributes of the product or service. Build credibility by highlighting a few specific details. Consider the benefits in what follows. First, the beginning, to command attention:

> If you own a telephone and want to make money using it, then take the advice of more than 25,000 men and women who now earn more than $500 a week *on the phone, in their spare time.*

Now the development of desire:

> These folks will tell you that a new book made it possible for them to earn real money in their spare time. *Dialing for Dollars* showed them three ways to turn the telephone into a money machine. It told them about more than 2,000 businesses that pay real money for telephone sales peo-

ple. It told them who to call. And *Dialing for Dollars* gave them the proven, surefire, and unique techniques for making successful sales calls.

These 25,000 men and women will tell you something else: *Dialing for Dollars* makes it all fun and easy. It's been written by Jane Doe, one of the nation's top authorities on telephone sales.

PROMPTING ACTION

Once you have commanded attention and created desire, you need to conclude by prompting action and making it easy for the target customer to act. Let's conclude the *Dialing for Dollars* spot:

> Jane Doe offers high-powered telephone sales seminars for $250 per person. And people stand in line to enroll. *You?* You can get your very own copy of *Dialing for Dollars,* which contains all the secrets of the $250 Jane Doe seminars, for only $29.95. That's right: $29.95 will buy you the secrets of a highly rewarding way to turn your spare time into major income.
>
> Now, *Dialing for Dollars* is not available in any store. You must call 1-800-555-0000 now to place your order. Call 1-800-555-0000 now, and we will include a bonus book on *500 Surefire Follow-up Calls* at no extra cost. This fact-packed volume tells you how to make your telephone sales calls even more productive. It's yours—absolutely free—when you call 1-800-555-0000 now to order *Dialing for Dollars.* The call is free, *500 Surefire Follow-up Calls* is free, and the $29.95 you spend on *Dialing for Dollars* may be the best investment you ever make. Toll-free ordering: 1-800-555-0000.

Prompting action requires a statement of value, a bargain appeal. It implies urgency, even if the offer is not strictly for a limited time only. It tells the target customer how much the product will cost. Some ad experts believe that the object of the ad is to get the target customer to make the phone call. Giving them the pricing details, they believe, may scare off the prospect. In fact, the target customer is less likely to make a call if he is unsure of the price. He does not want to be embarrassed by talking to the voice at the other end of the phone only to find out that the product costs more than he wants—or has—to spend. It is always best to spell out the price if your object is to solicit an order. Finally—and this is most important—provoke action by *telling* the target customer what to do next. In this case, the instructions are: Don't go to a store. Pick up the phone. Dial 1-800-555-0000. That set of digits is your customer's passport to the product and your passport to the customer. Repeat it. Repeat it again. And then, for good measure, repeat it. End the message by repeating it.

— Words to Use —

absolutely
amazing
announcing
approval free
approved
bargain
best
certified
challenge
compare
customized
dependable
discount
durable
easy
endorsed
exclusive
fascinating
fast
forever
guaranteed

handy
honored
hurry
immediately
improvement
improved
indispensable
introducing
latest
lifetime
magic
miracle
modern
now
offer
personalized
prestigious
proven
quick
quickly
recommended

reduced
remarkable
revolutionary
rich
rugged
sensational
startling
suddenly
superior
tested
today
top
unconditional
unconditionally
unique
upgrade
valuable
versatile
wanted
washable
wealthy

— Phrases to Use —

ask for it by name
ask for this free offer
at last just published
begin to enjoy
booklet free
brand new
breakthrough offer
cannot fail
clinical breakthrough
common sense
cutting edge

develop your potential
don't delay
don't be shut out
Don't you deserve . . .?
dramatic improvement
exclusive offer
fantastic bargain
for a limited time only
for the first time ever
free guide to
free introductory *(whatever)*

free to new members

free trial

full customer support

how to

how to begin

how to create

how to generate

how to get

how to have

how to improve

how to start

important discovery

important upgrade offer

just arrived

just out

last chance

latest figures from *(source)*

latest technology

learn to enjoy

limited time only

literature free

members receive this bonus

money-making facts free to you

money-saving offer

new and improved

new in this area

new method of

no money down

no obligation

now you can

order before the price goes up

order now

order today

orders shipped within twenty-four hours

profitable tips for

sale priced special price

scientific discovery

send no money

special offer

superfast delivery

supplies are limited

sure way to

tell you how

the key to

these prices won't last forever

try it for ten days free

unbelievable savings

valuable information

vastly improved

Why put it off?

Why not treat yourself?

without obligation

you deserve

you must be satisfied

you will be delighted

you will be glad

you will be glad you ordered

you will be pleased

you will be satisfied

yours absolutely free

yours free

Because the possibilities are virtually limitless, as with print ads, the best way to learn about radio advertising is to start paying attention to some of the hundreds of spots that air every day. Listen to them in a new way, asking yourself what works and why, and what doesn't work and why. Here are a few all-purpose ideas:

Three Retail Spots

SPOT 1

This Saturday and Sunday are great times for shopping at *(Name of store)* in *(Community)*.

(Name of store) will be open from *(time)* to *(time)* on *both* days, so that you can take advantage of incredible savings on items you need for your home.

You'll find drastic reductions of our already low prices on *(types of merchandise)*, and that includes *(item)*, which your kids have been pestering about for so long. Regularly *($ amount)*, it's selling—this Saturday and Sunday only—for just *($ amount)*. That's right: *($ amount)*. This Saturday. This Sunday. Only.

Don't forget, that's this weekend. Special prices, very special prices, at *(Name of store)* at *(address)* in *(Community)*. At *(Name of store)*, we work hard to make your money work hard for you.

SPOT 2

Here's an insider tip for anyone who wants exceptional prices on *(type of merchandise)*. Don't tell anyone, but *(Name of store)* is vastly overstocked on *(type of merchandise)*, and, from *(time)* o'clock to *(time)* o'clock on *(day)*, *(day)*, and *(day)*, they will be offering very, very special prices to move that merchandise.

I'm talking reductions of *(percent amount)* to *(percent amount)*. Not just on certain brands, but on every make and model of *(type of merchandise)* in the store. This means *(Brand name 1)* for *($ amount)*, *(Brand name 2)* for *($ amount)*, and *(Brand name 3)* for *($ amount)*. That's *($ amount)* for a *(Brand name product)* that regularly sells for *($ amount)*.

Better not tell anybody about prices like this. We'll keep it between us.

Now, *(Name of store)* is at *(address)* in *(Community)*, and the special prices are good only on *(day)*, *(day)*, and *(day)*. Store hours ar *(time)* o'clock to *(time)* *(o'clock)*, all three days.

Spot 3

Anytime's a great time for buying at *(Name of store)*. Why? Because nobody delivers the value, service, variety, and prices we give you.

But right now is an especially great time for doing business with us. Why? Because when you buy *(types of merchandise)*, we'll give you a very special bonus. For a limited time only—while supplies last— you get a free *(item)* with any purchase of *(types of merchandise)*.

You heard me correctly. A free *(item)* with any *(types of merchandise)* purchase.

What's the catch?

The offer is good only while supplies last. And, quite frankly, we don't expect them to last long. Look, just imagine getting a *($ amount)* value *(item)* for free when you purchase *(types of merchandise)* at prices nobody else can match. How low are our prices? Look: *(list specific items and prices)*.

Anytime's a great time to do business with *(Name of store)*. But if you come in now—and I mean *right* now, because supplies *are* limited—you'll get a *(item)* free with every *(types of merchandise)* purchase you make.

Self-help Program Spot

(A testimonial-style spot written for a popular announcer/host/DJ)

I bet most of you listening to me think I'm Mr. Glad Hand—speak right up, get along with everybody, great fun at parties. After all, I'm on the air forty hours a week, talking to thousands of strangers. Right?

I'll let you in on a secret.

I have a very hard time meeting people, and I'm shy around strangers. And let me tell you something else: I bet a lot of you are just like me.

Now, if you are shy—if you have trouble meeting new people, if you don't handle business and social contacts as well as you'd like—I've got some news you need to hear.

The Shyness Clinic can help. Really help.

I'd like you to do what I did recently. I attended a free, no-obligation introductory seminar at the Clinic. The next seminar will be offered on *(day)*, *(day)*, and *(day)*. To sign up for one of these free sessions, just call 555-0000. Here's what you'll get: You'll get a free introduction to the special, unique, and proven techniques anyone can learn to overcome shyness, to meet more people, to create more satisfying relationships—and to create more profitable business connections. You'll also get—absolutely free—a thirty-minute audio tape you can take home and begin to practice the techniques that will give you social strength.

I can tell you, the Shyness Clinic helped me. And I can tell you what some other people have said. A women who took the Clinic's full course said, "I used to spend most of my days watching soap operas. Now I'm office manager for a law firm." Or a salesman: "It used to be that I actually dreaded each sales call I made. Now I look forward to them—and it shows. I sell more, and I've learned to love my job."

These are real people. With real problems. And they found real solutions.

You can, too.

You owe it to yourself to call 555-0000—now—right now—and enroll in a free, no-obligation introductory seminar. Don't be shy. Call 555-0000.

A Spot for a Bank

(Note: "SFX" in a script stands for "sound effects.")

SFX: Bank lobby background noise.

Customer 1:	This is the longest line I've ever been in.
Customer 2:	You don't come to this bank often, then?
Customer 1:	You mean it's always like this?
Customer 2:	No. I mean this is a *good* day.
Customer 1:	At *(Name of advertising bank)* it's never like this. There are a lot more tellers, for one thing. There are also a lot

more ATMs—right *inside* the lobby. You almost never have to go to customer service. The teller takes care of everything—or brings customer service to you. You don't get into another line. And they're so friendly . . .

Teller
(from afar, barks):   Next! Next in line! Come on! Next!

Customer 1:   . . . and accommodating . . .

Teller
(from afar,
laughing):   You want *what* . . .?

Customer 1:   I mean it's real service . . . I should never have left *(Name of advertising bank).*

Customer 2:   I'll say. It sounds great! What made you come *here* instead?

Customer 1:   Well, this bank's much closer to my psychiatrist. I'm being treated for acute masochism. Here . . . please . . . would you mind taking this hammer and hitting me . . . right here?

Announcer: For *most* people, there is absolutely no question. *(Name of bank)*, at *(location)*, is your best banking choice. Why not drop by and see for yourself?

CHAPTER 18

Cable Grams and Shoe Strings: Creating Affordable Television Advertising

How to Do It

When it originated in 1949, cable television was not meant to compete with the "over-the-air" broadcast networks that were just then emerging. Cable was nothing more than a technological alternative for transmitting available broadcasts to areas where over-the-air television signals were weak. Cable therefore spread quickly in relatively isolated rural municipalities. It was not until the mid-1970s that cable operators began to see their product as an alternative to the fare offered by the three almighty networks, CBS, NBC, and ABC, as well as local broadcast stations. By late 1975, a growing system of privately financed earth communications satellites made it technologically feasible to increase the range of cable offerings. Centralized production and broadcast facilities originated a program, sending its signal to a satellite, which retransmitted it back to earth, where it was picked up by cable receiving stations and sent, via cable, to local viewers.

Home Box Office (HBO) was the first cable programmer to contract for domestic satellite delivery, and, by the end of the decade, entrepreneurs such as Ted Turner began providing even more programming, including, on June 1, 1980, Turner's Cable News Network (CNN), which soon offered network news intense competition.

Throughout the 1980s, an extensive menu of specialized cable "networks" appeared, including Arts and Entertainment, Black Entertainment TV, Christian Broadcast Network, the ESPN sports network, Financial News Network, Nickelodeon (a children-oriented network), the Weather Channel, and many others, mostly special-interest "narrowcasters" offering programming tailor-made to suit the needs of a particular audience. Of all these emerging cable networks, MTV, introduced in 1981, provided the most dramatic proof of "narrowcasting" as a powerful way for advertisers to reach a specific set of target customers. Conventional broadcast television offered advertisers a very broad market—but at very great expense—whereas cable, by focusing on highly defined markets, offered lower-cost advertising that could be directed cost effectively at the advertiser's desired market. Today, cable subscribers account for more than half of all U.S. television viewers; in some localities, the figure is 80 percent.

Without doubt, then, television is a powerful advertising tool, and cable has made it a precision tool—for many businesses a more cost-effective tool, and for small businesses in particular an affordable tool.

The topic of affordability, however, is a highly relative one. Simply to produce a sophisticated thirty-second commercial can cost upwards of $100,000—and that does not include buying the time to air it, which, in a large *local* (not national) market can cost more than $1,000 per spot. At the other extreme, it is possible to use a local television crew—either at the station or a group of independents—and produce a simple but effective spot for under $1,000 and buy nonprime air time in smaller markets for little more than the cost of a prime radio spot. On many cable channels, the cost of *prime-time* spots is about $20 for thirty seconds—remarkably cheap. Moreover, if your object is just to get on television—*some*how, *any*how—you can take out a "cable classified" ad, a video still-image "slide" prepared by the cable station using an image and text you supply and run on a special message-only station. Such ads are cheap, but probably not very cost-effective, since few cable viewers tune to a channel featuring nothing but advertising "slides." However, some cable operators are beginning to segment these "classified" channels, running ads for certain kinds of services and products at specific times, so that viewers can use the channel just as they would use the classified section in a newspaper, perusing ads for specific items. If you have a product or service that lends itself to classified print advertising, inexpensive cable classifieds may prove effective.

Buying Time

For a great many small businesses, the more specialized cable networks and programs represent the most cost-effective vehicles for advertising. If, for example, you sell a computer software product, you will want to buy time on one of the cable networks that offer programming aimed at users of personal computers. Or, perhaps, you will want to advertise on a network aimed at business viewers. If your software is meant, say, to store and sort recipes, then you'll want to be associated with a food network or some specific cooking shows. Unless you have a large budget, you will probably not be making your buys directly from the network programming supplier, but locally, from the operator of your area's cable franchise.

If you are buying advertising on cable, then, the decision of when to air your message is often driven by what special-interest program is being aired at a particular time. When you are buying conventional broadcast time (or buying from a cable operator irrespective of specific programming), considerations of cost and your target audience are largely—as with radio—a function of daypart. Usually, television broadcasters divide their weekday programming into seven parts:

1. Morning (6 to 9 A.M.). This daypart is heavy on news and weather as well as talk shows. Some stations offer cartoons and other children's programming. The typical audience consists of people getting ready to go to work and, for some stations, children getting ready to go to school. Homemakers are also likely to watch, especially toward the end of this daypart.

2. Midday (9 A.M. to 4 P.M.). This is the heart of daytime television and is heavy on soap operas, game shows, older movies, and an apparently endless flood of syndicated talk shows. The typical audience is the homemaker. However, you will also reach people who work nights, shut-ins, people who work at home, people who take their lunch hour at home, and the unemployed. Depending on your product or service, the latter category may be an important target customer—especially if you offer, say, a resume writing service or job training.

3. Early fringe (4 to 7 P.M.). This daypart schedules children's programming, local and national news, game shows, syndicated talk shows, and syndi-

cated tabloid news shows (especially toward the end of the daypart). Audiences vary, including children returning from school, adults return- ing from work, families watching together—maybe over dinner.

4. Prime access (7 to 8 P.M.). Game shows and general entertainment dom- inate this daypart, appealing to a general audience.

5. Prime (8 to 11 P.M.). This is the richest daypart, offering the most elabo- rate and original programming, drawing the largest audiences, and com- manding the highest fees from advertisers. The audience is general, and most advertisers carefully select the specific programs during which to run their ads.

6. Late fringe (11 P.M. to 1 A.M.). Local news, network and syndicated talk shows, and movies dominate. Typical viewers include adults and teenagers.

7. Late night (1 A.M. to sign-off or morning). Older movies—including so- called cult classics—dominate this daypart. The audience includes adults and teens. While the audience is comparatively small, advertising during this daypart is correspondingly cheap, and you will probably command the full attention of your relatively small audience.

While the daypart is important in determining the target customer and cost of advertising, program ratings also play an important part, especially in prime time. Buying advertising time during a highly rated show's time slot is more expensive than buying the same time on a lower-rated show. Stations may also set prices in part depending on a program's demographics. Shows that appeal to those in the twenty-five- to forty-nine-year-old age group command higher rates than those aimed at senior citizens, for example. If your product or service appeals to those over fifty, you're likely to get a price break. If, like most other businesses, you are aiming at the younger audience, you'll have to pay a premium.

Finally, television ad rates are also linked to season. Summer rates are lower; fall and winter rates are higher, because the number of viewers is greater.

How Long?

Not too many seasons ago, the typical television commercial was 60 seconds long. As prices have generally risen, however, the standard spot has fixed at

30 seconds. Most stations also sell spots as short as 10 seconds and 15 seconds. Forty-five-second spots as well as 90- and 120-second spots may also be available. Two trends have come to the fore of late: the use of fifteen-second spots and the use of half-hour "infomercials." The latter are full-scale productions, actual television programming devoted to discussing and demonstrating a product or a service. Because they are complex productions, they require the services of professionals and are well beyond the scope of this book. However, infomercials may be cheaper than you think. Most of them are run during the late night daypart and/or on cable stations at an off hour. Even a half hour of such time may command, locally, no more than a few hundred dollars. Production costs can be high, but they are probably lower than the cost of a slick, national-broadcast-quality thirty-second commercial because an infomercial is usually little more than a videotaped (and edited) demonstration, discussion, and/or promotional event. It is not an elaborately filmed movie-style production.

In discussing radio spots in the preceding chapter, we mentioned that ads running shorter than thirty seconds are not cost-effective (in most cases and unless they are part of an integrated series of spots). This is less true in television. Because the visual element is added to the audio, you can convey more "information" in fifteen television seconds than with fifteen radio seconds. If your product is visually appealing—or your service can be associated with a high-impact image—a fifteen-second spot may save you money. Buy carefully, however. In many instances, a fifteen-second spot does not cost much less than a thirty-second spot.

How Often?

Determining just how often to run your spot is one of the black arts of television advertising. If you create a great spot and run it during a highly rated show, you will not have to air it very often. Which is a good thing, since you won't have enough money to run it very often, anyway. The safest course is to start with the rule of thumb most professional advertising agencies use. During any month that you advertise, you should buy a minimum of 150 gross rating points (GRPs), which represent the sum of all the ratings delivered by a given list of "vehicles" (that is, television programs). Buying 150 GRP means that your spot will air during the month on 150 percent of the television households in the market. This can translate as airing three times during the month on 50 percent of the TV households or six times on 25 percent or some other combination totaling 150 GRP.

Taking into account the GRP will also help you derive a meaningful cost figure for your spot. In very small markets, stations may charge as little as $5 per GRP. Larger markets—still at the local level—may charge as much as *one hundred times* that amount, or $500 per GRP. This means that your minimum television advertising budget for a single month may vary anywhere from $750 to $75,000!

I hope that helps you.

And do bear in mind that the GRP method is truly a "gross" method, intended for advertisers using general-interest broadcast television and trying to appeal to the widest possible audience. GRP means little when you are targeting a specialized cable audience, for example.

As with radio, you can maximize the bang for your buck by clustering your spots rather than spreading them out over the entire month. If you've got a major sales event planned for, say, the last week in March, cluster your spots during the third and fourth weeks of the month, with 75 percent of them running during that fourth week. For ongoing ad campaigns, consider a strategy of alternate weeks: week 1 in any given month filled with your spots, week 2 empty, week 3 filled, week 4 empty.

Volume buying and package buying will also lower your costs, though with packaged buys, you run the risk of having your spot bumped to a less favorable time slot if a full-priced ad muscles in. (The station must make up for this by running the ad later at an equally desirable time; this is known as a "make-good.")

Buying Strategy: Last Word for the Small Business

I have attempted to outline the mainstream guidelines for planning and buying television advertising exposure. But yours is a small business, and one thing you've learned is that the mainstream is not always the best stream for you. Your best guide to determining where to place your spot and how often to run it is your understanding of the needs and interests of your target customer.

If you offer a specialized product or service, think: Is *any* form of television advertising appropriate? Or am I better off devoting my budget to trade newsletters, journals, and direct mail appeals? If television will allow me to reach more target customers, am I better off with a conventional broadcast vehicle or a specialized cable show?

When do *my* customers watch television?

When—weekdays, weekends, early morning, late at night?—are *my* customers likely to be most receptive to *my* message?

Here's another money-saving tip. Ask yourself whether or not your customers like to record old movies on their VCRs. If so, consider buying a good chunk of cheap advertising during the smallest of the wee morning hours. Chances are, you'll get a lot more exposure than you bargained for when the VCR gets played back. (Of course, many avid VCR fans "zap" commercials with the fast-forward button.) You should also be aware that the late-late day-part commands a small, but often intensely loyal, audience. These folks are likely to see your spot repeatedly.

PRODUCTION

Producing a television spot can be virtually as elaborate as producing a Hollywood film. Or it can be almost as simple as producing a quick radio spot. It can involve an advertising agency, a full production crew, and professional actors, or it can involve a local production crew (perhaps supplied by the local television station), consisting of a camera operator and a combination engineer/sound person, and you—you as writer, director, and principal (perhaps only) actor. Since this book is directed at the owners and operators of small businesses, the balance of this chapter will be devoted to discussing the most economical approaches to creating effective television advertising. You should be aware, however, that there are much more elaborate—and costly—alternatives, and you should also be aware that, depending on your product or service, the cost of professional ad agencies and full-scale production crews and actors may well be justified.

THE CONCEPT

Now, the idea is to produce an inexpensive television commercial, not a sleazy one. And, truth to tell, the vast majority of television commercials produced on a shoestring look like they were produced on a shoestring. Audiences notice the poor production values: video that is below the level established by the surrounding programming, poor sound, dumb salesman talk, and a stiff spokesperson for the product or service or some hokey exchange between two amateur actor types. Viewers pick up on these outward expressions of cheapness, but the real trouble with bad commercials, whence this outward evidence flows, is the lack of a well-thought-out concept.

Creating an effective television advertising concept usually begins with two elements: a striking visual aspect (TV, after all, is primarily a visual medium) and the effective embodiment of the same basic selling principles that motivate good print ads (see the introduction to Part III, In Print, in this book):

1. Emphasize benefits rather than features.

2. Establish and/or underscore your positioning.

3. Focus on one or two ideas at most.

4. Speak directly to your target customer.

Rather cynically, sales, marketing, and advertising "experts" like to trot out the following acronym—KISS—which stands for Keep It Simple, Stupid. Cynical or not, it's a useful concept to keep in mind. Especially on television. In contrast to print ads—and, even more, direct mail copywriting—it is a mistake to try to pack a lot into a television spot. A well-constructed print ad conveys a wealth of information at a glance, inviting the target customer, at his option and leisure, to skim or study the rest of the copy. By its very nature, reading is a contemplative activity. The reader absorbs information at his own pace, when and where he can. Television, in contrast, bombards the viewer with information, sets the pace for the viewer, and tends to defeat any tendency toward contemplation. Therefore, KISS—or risk being ignored.

How do you KISS? Emphasize the visual, keeping words to a minimum. On television, the more you can sell with images, the better. Then keep the images simple, too. Don't neglect words, of course. But just remember that the television audience is referred to collectively as "viewers," not "listeners." We speak of somebody's *eyes* being glued to the television set, not their *ears*. In a print ad, it may be a good picture that will grab the reader—or it may be a good headline. On television, it is the image that commands attention, opening the door for your verbal message.

Of course, the concept should be entertaining. Right?

Wrong.

And again, wrong.

We all love entertaining, especially humorous, commercials. In fact, from time to time, television programmers even put together special shows consisting of viewers' favorite commercials. But your object is not to create television programming. Your object is to sell your product or service. Common sense may suggest to you that, to be an effective selling tool, a commercial must be entertaining. That may be true if your product or service is inherently of little value to your target customers. In that case, the only reason they have for watching your commercial is for entertainment—because they won't be interested in the product or service. However, if you have reason to believe that your target customer will be interested in your product or service, create a concept that develops, piques, exploits, addresses, and satisfies that interest *in the product or service* and not a concept that sidesteps the task of selling by trying to be entertaining. Jay Conrad Levinson, author of *Guerrilla Advertising* (Houghton Mifflin, 1994), put it bluntly: "If anyone ever tells you they loved your TV commercial, hang your head in shame. If they say they saw your TV spot, then went out and bought your product, glow inside because you succeeded at your job."

To Storyboard or Not to Storyboard?

Traditionally, creators of television advertising write a script and produce a storyboard, a kind of comic strip featuring sketches of the visual action with dialogue and/or sound effect notations penciled in below. Usually, each comic strip "frame" is in the shape of a TV screen. Virtually all television advertising created by professional agencies employs storyboards.

Well, we've just said that, in creating the television commercial concept, it is important to think visually. And storyboards certainly are visual. And, moreover, the storyboard is the way of the pros. So you should always start out with a storyboard, right?

Not necessarily.

Unless you yourself sketch the storyboard, it will add several hundred dollars to the cost of producing an ad. (You are, however, left with something you can hang on your office wall.) Worse, storyboards can actually hamper visual creativity. Especially for a low-cost commercial, where studio time is at a premium, encourage spontaneity by working directly from a script and bypassing the storyboard.

You Said the Image Comes First

Well, yes, it does. In your concept. But here's another article of professional advertising heresy that can simplify the production of a television spot:

Before you begin to shoot the commercial, record the soundtrack. The classic composer-lyricist teams like Rodgers and Hammerstein and Lerner and Lowe knew that the words come first and the tune second. This does not mean that the lyricist doesn't have a musical mood—or concept—in mind before he begins to write the words, but it is almost always easier for a composer to write music around a particular set of words than for a poet to find words to set to an existing piece of music. Similarly, where television advertising is concerned, start with a visual concept, but begin the actual production process by laying down a soundtrack. Then shoot the visuals to match the existing soundtrack.

This assumes, of course, that your commercial does not feature an on-camera talking head or close-ups of actors acting. If you are using mostly on-camera dialogue, then it is usually simpler and more convincing to record video and audio simultaneously. But the point is this: most effective low-cost commercials feature the product or visual evidence of the benefits of a product or service rather than live-action talking heads.

LIVE ACTION OR STILL LIFE?

That brings us to another selling (and cash-conserving) point. An effective television commercial need not be a miniature TV show. It can be something closer to a print ad, using slides or other artwork—including effective shots of your product (think of the almost pornographic way the camera caresses sheet metal in commercials for new cars)—over a soundtrack instead of a minidrama played out by actors or a static shot of an announcer delivering a spiel.

The absence of actors does not mean the absence of life. If your central image consists of your product, figure out ways to move the camera. If your commercial consists of still photographs, figure out creative ways to cut or fade from still to still. Either way, using still images creatively is a viable and cost-effective alternative to live action.

However . . .

In advertising, the 1980s were the decade of the nonprofessional star. Instead of hiring an actor to promote their products, corporate CEOs went on air themselves. Often, the effect was quite successful. Lee Iacocca was a very good spokesman for Chrysler. Victor Kiam did a great job for his company, the maker of Remington electric razors. Certainly, the strategy was appealing enough to have endured into the 1990s. Viewers have become accustomed to seeing real lawyers talk about their law firms, real plastic surgeons talk about what their practice can do for one's self-image, real CEOs talk about their firm's commitment to . . . whatever.

If you're comfortable with it, consider appearing in your own television commercial. After all, nobody has more riding on the success of the commercial than you the owner of your business do. Therefore, nobody is better motivated—or better prepared—to represent your company onscreen.

THE HELP YOU NEED

I don't want to give the impression that all you really have to do is buy, borrow, or rent a video camera, put it on a tripod, press the button, then run around in front of the lens and make your commercial. Even if you want to do the concept creation, writing, producing, and directing yourself, creating a TV spot is not a 100 percent do-it-yourself operation. You do need help.

There are two ways to go. The local television station can produce your commercial, or you can hire an independent production company—which may consist of no more than a single person, though (more often) the field crew will include at least one camera operator, who may also act as director, and an engineer, who operates the video and sound recording equipment. So-called "postproduction" activity includes editing, mixing in the soundtrack, sound effects, and music and superimposing any graphic effects (such as a phone number or company name). Often, a video production company will rent time at a studio to accomplish the postproduction tasks. This is not necessarily a negative reflection on the production company's resources. The fact is that much state-of-the-art postproduction equipment is extremely expensive and, therefore, beyond the financial reach of most independent companies. Renting postproduction facilities—even the services of postproduction personnel—greatly enhances the professionalism of an independent production company's product. Why should the look and style of your commercial be dictated by what your independent producer owns or does not own?

While we're on the subject of postproduction facilities, you will note that I have been assuming that you are using videotape rather than film to make the commercial. Videotape production is much cheaper than film. It is true that film, shot well, gives your commercial more of the quality of an expensively produced movie, but, for the small business operator, this enhancement almost certainly does not justify the extra expense. I should add, too, that a cheaply produced *filmed* commercial looks just as bad as a poorly produced videotaped commercial.

Script Examples: Low-Cost Television Spots

As with print ads and radio spots, the potential variety of television advertising is virtually limitless, and the best way to start thinking about your own ads is to start paying careful attention to what's on TV. Here are some examples of very-low-cost scripts,

SCRIPT 1

Close-up of newspapers, with headlines prominent:
PRIME INTEREST RATE RISES
HOMES HARDER TO BUY
MONEY TIGHT
etc.

Announcer
(voice over):   Are you tired of reading about what you *can't* afford? About the money you *can't* earn? About the savings you *can't* save? Ready for a big change?

Close-up of SMALL INVESTOR *magazine cover.*

Announcer
(voice over):   Then try the good news in *Small Investor.*

Pull back to fuller shot of cover.

Announcer
(voice over):   It's the new investment magazine for people who— quite frankly—don't have a lot to invest. And can't afford to take chances with what they do have.

Announcer's hand reaches for the magazine. Camera pulls back to him holding the magazine.

Announcer
(voice over):   Started by an independent investor like you, *Small Investor* magazine now attracts more than 10,000 readers.

Shots of Announcer seated at desk with magazine.

Learn how to make wise, safe, and profitable investments with as little as $100. Get the inside story on bank charges—and how to avoid them. Find out why diversification is so important—and how you can do it. Discover the secrets of beating the "load fees" that sap the return on your investments. Explore the potential of limited partnerships. Find out about more than 100 investments the U.S. government CANNOT TAX.

Announcer picks up magazine again.

Announcer: So why not make a very modest—and very shrewd—investment right now? Call toll free 1-800-555-0000—

Onscreen: Phone number superimposed beneath Announcer.

—for a money-saving trial subscription to *Small Investor.* Get twelve issues for just $19.95. That's one-half off the regular subscription price and 75 percent off the cover price.

Shot of brochure: "Building Cash Flow Now"

Announcer
(voice over): Call now and also receive this valuable brochure, with 75 strategies for building cash flow—immediately—the kind of cash flow that will give you what you need to start investing.

Shots of Announcer holding brochure and magazine.

Announcer: If your first issue of *Small Investor* is not absolutely everything you want it to be—and more—just cancel your subscription. We'll not only refund your subscription payment in full, we'll let you keep "Building Cash Flow Now" as our gift—just for trying *Small Investor.*

Cut to shot of brochure and magazine, with phone number.

Announcer
(voice over): Call right now. Our operators are standing by. The number is 1-800-555-0000. That's 1-800-555-0000. Stop "saving." Start *investing.* Stop "surviving." Start *living.* Call 1-800-555-0000.

SCRIPT 2

Medium shot, head on, of woman bracing herself at a podium, looking terrified.

Announcer
voice over): Is this you?

Shot of man seated at conference table, looking down at the table. Voice heard in the background: "Any ideas? Anybody got *anything* to say?"

Announcer
(voice over):   Is this you?

Shot of man confronted by woman (his boss). Man dumbfounded.

Announcer
(voice over):   Is this you?

Announcer
(on camera):   If you have trouble speaking up, well, you're not alone. But you're not going to get very far, either. Unless—

Shot of man talking to small group in Speech Counselors classroom.

                      —you enroll now in the unique Speech Counselors seminar series.

Continue shots of activity in classroom. No live audio.

Announcer
(voice over):   In just ten sessions, you will learn the basics of speaking up for yourself, expressing yourself, overcoming fear of public speaking, and establishing rapport. You will learn the art of persuasion and of negotiation.

Shot of Announcer, holding up video and brochure.

Announcer
(on camera):   Send no money. But you do have to pick up the phone and—just this once—*speak up.* Attend our free, no-obligation introductory session—and receive, also absolutely free, this brochure and this video, which will introduce you to the unique Speech Counselors method.

Shot of brochure and video, with phone number in large print.

Announcer
(voice over):   Pick up the phone and call 1-800-555-0000. 1-800-555-0000, for the convenient times and locations of a free, no-obligation introductory seminar session, complete with a free video and brochure. Speak up— and start changing your life. Do it now. That's 1-800-555-0000.

SCRIPT 3

Dimly lit close-up of a wall light switch.

Announcer
(voice over):   Your business runs on ideas. Your success depends on ideas. Your survival is determined by ideas.

Silence for two beats.

Announcer
(voice over):   Ideas don't just happen. You *can* buy them—for a price. Or you can make them. *If* you know how.

Silence for a beat.

Announcer
(voice over):   *We* know how.

Hand flicks switch on. Wall and switch now in bright light.

Announcer
(voice over):   And we can show *you* how. We're Creativity Counselors, specializing in helping individuals, project teams, work groups, departments, and small businesses enhance their creative thinking. We offer a full range of seminars and creativity workshops, plus help with specific projects, providing what you need to create the conditions that build creativity, build your profits, and build your business. Join such FORTUNE 500 firms as *(list)*, who have discovered the difference Creativity Counselors makes.

     For complete information and a free consultation, call 1-800-555-0000.

Superimpose "Creativity Counselors" and phone number beneath wall switch.

Announcer
(voice over):   That's 1-800-555-0000. A step toward enhanced creativity.

SCRIPT 4

Close-up of the head of a bolt. Shot begins with the head-on view and slowly pans around to show a profile view of bolt and nut fastening two sheets of metal together. During pan, Announcer says (voice over):

Your life and the lives of your family depend on this.

Pause for a beat.

Good thing this is no ordinary nut and bolt. It's made by Custom Fasteners, and it's sold at Smith Hardware on Ronald Street in Weatherstown. They sell it because they know how important it is that the things you put together—stay together.

Pause for a beat as camera continues its slow pan.

I can tell you how much these nuts and bolts cost: *($ amount)* per *(quantity)*, compared with *(slightly lower $ amount)* per *(quantity)* for ordinary fasteners. I can tell you, too, that Custom Fasteners withstand up to *(number)* foot-pounds of torque, while ordinary fasteners give way at about *(lesser number)*.

Pause for a beat.

What that really means is that when this happens—

Stock footage of tornado. Three seconds.

—this won't—

Stock footage of twisted metal rubble left by tornado.

Custom Fasteners are just some of the more than 10,000 extraordinary products we stock at Smith Hardware, on Ronald Street, in Weatherstown. 555-0000.

Index

A

B

R